URBAN ROAD PRICING:
PUBLIC AND POLITICAL ACCEPTABILITY

Urban Road Pricing:
Public and Political Acceptability

MARTIN J. WHITTLES
University of Westminster

ASHGATE

Published by
Ashgate Publishing Limited
Gower House
Croft Road
Aldershot
Hants GU11 3HR
England

Ashgate Publishing Company
Suite 420
101 Cherry Street
Burlington, VT 05401-4405
USA

Ashgate website: http://www.ashgate.com

British Library Cataloguing in Publication Data
Whittles, Martin J.
   Urban road pricing : public and political acceptability. -
   (Transport and society)
   1. Toll roads - Social aspects - Great Britain 2. Congestion
   pricing - Social aspects - Great Britain 3. Roads - Finance
   - Social aspects - Great Britain 4. Urban transportation -
   Great Britain - Planning
   I. Title
   388.1'14

Library of Congress Control Number: 2003100753

ISBN 0 7546 3449 3

Printed and bound by Athenaeum Press, Ltd.,
Gateshead, Tyne & Wear.

Contents

List of Figures

List of Tables

Preface

Urban Road Pricing: Public and Political Acceptability

Urban road pricing has been heralded as a key option in UK central and local government transport strategies in order to solve unremitting traffic problems. Apart from the anticipated London congestion charging scheme, due to start operation in 2003, elsewhere in the UK progress towards implementation is much slower. Despite strong support for road pricing from the professional transport planning community, members of the public and politicians remain unconvinced of its potential benefits and wary of the significant changes that road pricing could pre-empt, such as shifts in congestion and environmental problems, alteration in city competitiveness and attractiveness, a revolution in the way drivers pay for road use and electoral consequences for politicians.

This book offers a method for understanding current stalemates in the planning process and suggests ways out of the quagmire, which is useful both in the UK and abroad. Based on evidence pertaining to the acceptability of a variety of forms of road pricing, from actual schemes to hypothetical scenarios, it is argued that there is divergence between professional transport planning discourse and publicly acceptable arguments, which urgently need to be resolved.

These gaps between professional planning and public discourses can be bridged using sociological techniques of discourse analysis and theory building to derive practical consensus solutions. For example, it can be seen that road pricing schemes that are being designed to ration road space and to use the revenue raised to compensate those priced off the road by providing better travel alternatives, are not providing adequate and acceptable plans for redistributing the revenue. The sociological method can be used to suggest that acceptable schemes should focus on showing how revenue raised will be used to provide services that drivers need and measures that alleviate the environmental impact that drivers cause.

There is scope to develop further scheme specific guidance, should the method of research be incorporated into individual road pricing planning processes. This method could also be applied to a range of other controversial policies both within and outside the field of transport. Consequently, it is hoped that the research method is of interest to a range of policy makers and applied sociologists.

In a special postscript to this edition, evidence from the London congestion charging plans are analysed, with respect to acceptability, and lessons are drawn for other cities and towns that might be interested in implementing the policy.

Acknowledgements

The book is based on my PhD thesis, researched and written between 1995 and 1999 at the Institute for Transport Studies, University of Leeds. The thesis is the most challenging and theoretical piece of work that I have yet produced because it establishes an alternative philosophy to transport studies. Firstly, I would like to thank the reader for showing interest in this framework of ideas and, while I fully appreciate it is time-consuming to understand new approaches and ways of thinking, I believe that it will be illuminating and of practical benefit to the study of real world problems.

I am very grateful for the support and advice that Dr Abigail Bristow, Professor Tony May and Dr Miles Tight of the Institute for Transport Studies gave to me during the research, without whose assistance it would have been impossible to realise the project. I would also like to thank the Engineering and Physical Sciences Research Council for financing my studentship at the Institute.

Very special thanks are extended to Professor Margaret Grieco at the Transport Studies Institute, Napier University for her help and advice in bringing the thesis to publication. I am also deeply indebted to my wife Dr Sofia Marçal for her support and critique during both the thesis and book writing phases.

Finally, I extend my thanks to the Transport Studies Group, University of Westminster, where I am now based, for its flexibility in allowing time for me to turn the thesis into a book.

Chapter 1

Introduction

Themes

Urban road pricing refers to a set of ideas to charge road-users to drive specifically in urban areas. Although drivers may pay fuel and vehicle taxes, it is a charge on top of these. The two main purposes for charging are to control demand, which can help improve congestion and alleviate environmental problems, and to raise revenue, to finance projects that benefit drivers and those affected by traffic. The idea of charging extra for using urban roads, though, is controversial and there is an issue of acceptability. People are unsure if pricing should be used to deter drivers and are sceptical about the need for drivers to pay more money.

This book describes a sociological study of the public and political acceptability of urban road pricing. By applying a sociological method, it has been possible to understand factors that make road pricing acceptable and to recommend how to design a road pricing scheme that optimises acceptability. Thus, there are two themes to the research: the first develops a sociological theory to understand acceptability and the second uses the theory to choose between options for road pricing in praxis.

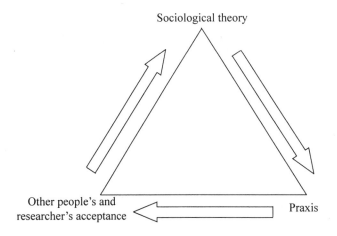

Figure 1.1   Theory and praxis

These methodological themes can be seen in Figure 1.1 by following the arrows in a clockwise direction, starting at the point of the triangle labelled 'praxis'. When presented with road pricing options – either real if a scheme is operational or hypothetical if it is a plan – people, including the researcher, will form opinions on whether the options are acceptable, labelled as 'other people's and researcher's acceptance'. Assuming these opinions can be uncovered, a sociological theory can be developed that explains and understands them – the first theme. This sociological theory can be used to choose design options that are theoretically acceptable – the second theme.

As the sociological theory has been derived from people's views about road pricing options, the theory is being applied in an area where it is relevant and thus it should be able to predict acceptable choices. However, there is a risk that the researcher's own motives can unwittingly influence the theory and its use. Firstly the researcher might base the theory on their own notion of what is acceptable and not take full account of other people's ideas – consequently the theory would not accurately reflect a full range of arguments. Secondly the researcher might develop the theory plausibly, but apply it mistakenly because of their prejudices about which options are acceptable.

To overcome these problems the research process needs to be reflexive, taking account of the researcher's influence. When data is collected the role of the interviewer must be described; theory construction must be as transparent as possible, with evidence presented for any generalisations; and when the theory is applied it must be demonstrated that the design options are being interpreted in terms of only the sociological theory.

Often sociological research is seen as too theoretical because it is difficult to give an objective understanding of a problem that necessarily fits in with the practical options. Similarly, practical planning has been accused of basing itself on theories that are not relevant to the problem. This study, if seen for nothing else, is an attempt to work to form a partnership where the sociological explanation is of use to the transport planner: transport sociology.

Research Objectives from a Praxis Perspective

Urban road pricing can be used by itself to help meet policy objectives, such as congestion reduction, environmental alleviation, accessibility improvement and economic growth, and it can be used in conjunction with other measures as part of an integrated transport policy, usually by providing revenue. The first practical research objective is to decide which policy objectives it is acceptable to use road pricing to meet and if there are any constraints that influence how it should be used as part of an integrated transport policy. In other words, the extent to which road pricing can be used to influence demand, whilst remaining acceptable, is investigated and conditions for spending the revenue to improve acceptability are found.

Given that acceptable objectives can be discovered and constraints dealt with, specific design options have to be chosen that allow the idea of urban road pricing to be implemented in practice. Decisions have to be made about who pays, because some drivers might acceptably be exempt, the extent of the charged area, the time of operation, the level of the charge, and how the charge is levied. The second practical objective then is to decide on the most acceptable design options that meet the acceptable objectives.

Methodological Objectives from a Sociological Perspective

As presented, the objectives of the research are very challenging because they go beyond a psephological approach to acceptability, where the most acceptable is the option that is most popular. The success of the research depends on understanding what makes something acceptable to everybody, finding a way that majority opinions can take on minority opinions and vice versa.

Sociology can contribute methods for studying aspects of a society. This is relevant because the idea of urban road pricing and acceptability are features of our society, and different systems of road pricing will stimulate different opinions about acceptability. The chosen sociological method aims to understand how acceptability is influenced by different urban road pricing ideas and to suggest any ideas that are universally acceptable amongst all people. This would then point to a way of implementing an acceptable road pricing scheme.

Although this vision of sociology contributing to transport planning is simple, the execution is extremely complex, because ideas about acceptability reflect the theoretical background of the decision-maker. If all people had the same theoretical perspective this would not be a problem and mutually acceptable decisions could probably be reached. However, people approach the issue of road pricing from numerous theoretical positions and it is not clear how a common denominator can be found. Thus the challenge of the research is to understand what is universally acceptable to all groups, and to be able to claim that an option is acceptable because it transcends numerous theoretical perspectives.

This synecdochical problem is common to sociology and involves making a claim that an explanation given for a phenomenon is relevant to all groups. To overcome the problem, the discipline of sociology has had rigorously to define the boundaries for which its explanations hold and to allow any explanations to be tested in future situations where the relevant parameters are the same. Thus sociology avoids accusations about drawing conclusions that are too general from a limited set of data.

The method chosen for this study is based on discourse analysis and grounded theorising and follows these delimitations. It stresses that explanations are only relevant for the issue of acceptability with respect to a bounded set of urban road pricing ideas and it is only valid for arguments from the sample of respondents that provided the data. Despite these restrictions, this research is useful because it provides new ideas that have practical purpose and allows the explanations to be tested in future research.

Research Process and Chapter Plan

The chapters are presented in the order that the research and analysis were conducted. This illustrates how the research process moved from a broad philosophical and practical research problem to a set of policy proposals for using urban road pricing. This section describes these different stages and in which chapters they are to be found.

Chapter 2: Review of Urban Road Pricing

Chapter 2 introduces the idea of urban road pricing and describes schemes and experiments that have been tried around the world. This provides an introduction to road pricing for the reader, if they are unfamiliar with it. For the research process it was important because it was the initial step to seeing if common ideas could be found in the data. While ideas that can be tested in a quantitative manner do not emerge, the literature review gives confidence that the objectives of the research are obtainable with further qualitative research.

Chapter 3: Method

Chapter 3 introduces qualitative sociology and explains the advantages of basing theory construction on the method of grounded theorising. In the research process, method development did merge in with the literature review of road pricing. However, the final methodological choices were not made until after a thorough review of the topic and therefore it is described afterwards.

The chapter concentrates on explaining the different methodological camps in sociology, such as positivism and naturalism, quantitative and qualitative research, and concludes that the most appropriate method lies at the qualitative end of the continuum because not enough information is yet available about what makes road pricing acceptable. Then the chapter describes that the method of grounded theorising is particularly appropriate because it provides a way of structuring the data while remaining practical in its orientation.

Chapter 4: Data Collection

The method is grounded in how people argue about road pricing in real life. With a lack of available arguments that cover the full range of design options that had been recorded, there was a need to interview people to provide a source of data. Chapter 4 describes how the sample and the case studies were selected. The two case studies were in Cambridge and Edinburgh, because they had transport models that could be used to assess the impact of any policy recommendations (although modelling work was not carried out in this research project). Meanwhile the samples within these case studies were selected according to the rules of theoretical sampling, as opposed to statistical sampling, because the sample is adapted as the research progresses to help test emerging theoretical ideas. This suits methods of qualitative sociology.

Then the chapter describes the design of the questionnaire. This comprises two sections. The first asks open questions that allow respondents to say what they think of road pricing. The second section is semi-structured and the respondents have to decide between the various design options for a road pricing scheme, such as who pays and the area of operation. On top of specific choices, though, the respondents are expected to explain why they find their chosen options acceptable.

Chapter 5: Development of the Concepts

In Chapter 5, the process of analysing tape recordings of the interviews to produce a grounded theory that explains the acceptability of urban road pricing is described. This draws on sociological techniques of discourse analysis. Three distinct phases are outlined, which involve discovering concepts in the data, then linking the concepts together to form a theory, and finally seeing how changes in the concepts affect acceptability. In Chapter 5 the first stage about discovering the concepts is explained.

Chapter 6: Linking the Concepts Together

Carrying on from the previous chapter, Chapter 6 describes how the concepts can be linked together to explain the acceptability of urban road pricing. This involves deriving three strategies that reflect all the arguments that people use when they are discussing the general idea and specific design options. The strategies are given names that reflect the aspect of road pricing they deal with. For example, the direct-effect strategy deals with using road pricing to affect demand, the indirect-effect strategy deals with using revenue from road pricing to fund improvements, and the contribution strategy reflects arguments dealing with the amount of money different people should contribute. Knowledge of these strategies, though, does not yet show how road pricing can be made more acceptable. To do this it is necessary to look for patterns that show how the strategies can be used in a way that is universally acceptable within the sample of arguments that was recorded. Thus the following three chapters look for these patterns and say what the consequence would be for using road pricing in practice.

Chapter 7: Finding Patterns in the Direct-effect Strategy

Chapter 7 looks at arguments that address the advantages and disadvantages of using pricing to influence directly the levels of traffic.

Chapter 8: Finding Patterns in the Indirect-effect Strategy

Chapter 8 looks at arguments about using the revenue from road pricing and how it should be spent. Combined with findings from Chapter 7, it is possible to hypothesise theoretically acceptable policy objectives for road pricing.

Chapter 9: Patterns in the Contribution Strategy

In Chapter 9, patterns in the contribution strategy are used to suggest how the burden of the charge could be acceptably distributed amongst road users. This part of the analysis tries to ensure that the interpretation of patterns in the contribution strategy is independent of the interpretation of patterns in the other strategies. Thus, even if the other patterns turn out not to be used in praxis, information in the contribution strategy could still be applied.

Chapter 10: Other Design Choices

In Chapter 10 information about acceptable strategies is combined to suggest other acceptable design options that were not dealt with in the previous chapters. This involves deciding the type of charging structure, between cordon, distance and time-based charging, the extent of the charged area, the time of operation, the scope for differential charges in different areas and at different times, and the operating technology. While definitive answers cannot be given to all these questions, because it depends on what other policies are used in conjunction with road pricing, clear guidelines do emerge.

Chapter 11: Comparisons with Other Research

In Chapter 11 the grounded theory recommendations from the previous chapters are brought together and summarised. The main arguments are then compared with other research that has focused on acceptability. It is noted that there is a difference between what the grounded theory considers an acceptable use for road pricing and what most of the other research does. While the grounded theory is grounded in a limited set of data and would need to be strengthened by further testing, it does indicate interesting ramifications, if it is proved plausible. The difference lies primarily in conceiving society in terms of rules that fit in with economic theories instead of the grounded theory rules.

Chapter 12: Conclusion

After the suggestions in the comparison chapter the research process is completed because to prove or refute any of the ideas requires further research. Chapter 12 brings the different stages of the research together and makes suggestions for further research.

Postscript

Since the main research was completed, there have been significant policy developments in the UK, and a road pricing scheme is expected to be implemented in London. A special postscript describes these latest developments and undertakes a simple analysis of evidence on acceptability from London, based on the sociological method developed in this book. This also serves to illustrate the potential and importance of further research.

Chapter 2

Review of Urban Road Pricing and its Acceptability

Introduction

The purposes of this chapter are:

1 to introduce the idea of urban road pricing by examining why it should be considered and how it could be implemented;
2 to describe the main issues surrounding the acceptability of urban road pricing by comparing past road pricing schemes and proposals;
3 to critically examine the issues of acceptability that have arisen to identify the current state of knowledge regarding how acceptably to implement a scheme.

In terms of the research process this chapter provides a starting point that indicates what types of ideas need to be discovered to meet the research objectives and improve acceptability. This then feeds into the decision about methods for the project. For example, if the literature review uncovers a clear process through which acceptability can be increased, the appropriate method might be to test that process in case studies in Britain. However, if the literature review only uncovers isolated factors that affect acceptability, the method might involve seeing if these factors can be combined to illustrate a process that can improve acceptability. As is implied in the introduction, the latter is shown to be the case.

Theory and Praxis of Urban Road Pricing

The Economic Theory of Road Pricing

Road pricing has its theoretical foundations in the neoclassical approach to microeconomics. This is also known as marginalist economics. The underlying principle is that a 'rational man' wants to maximise his utility from the consumption of commodities subject to his resources. This means that 'rational man' has a 'willingness to pay' for a commodity and this 'willingness to pay' will change according to how attractive the commodity seems. From variations in people's 'willingness to pay', a demand function can be derived, with the actual demand for the commodity dependent on the cost of it. The cost of production in turn depends on the amount being produced and from this principle a supply function can be derived.

Assuming there is fair competition in the marketplace, marginalist theory states that the economically efficient price to charge for the commodity is the amount where the cost of supply equals the 'willingness to pay' of demand. This economically efficient price is also known as the optimum price.

In the simplest case, marginalist theory allows a producer of a commodity to estimate the price at which it should be sold. Very often, as more units of a commodity are produced, the average unit production costs are lowered, and, if the demand exists for more units, it is in the interest of the supplier to produce more. This is not only economically efficient for the supplier but for the consumer as well. Occasionally the costs involved in producing more of the commodity can increase. In this case the marginal cost of producing one extra unit of the commodity will be higher than the average cost. So the optimum price for one more unit must reflect this. This was the special case argued by Marshall (1890).

The theory of marginal pricing applied to production was taken by Pigou (1920) and expanded into a general case for marginal cost pricing over the provision of goods and services. If the service was the provision of a road, marginalist theory could now be used to recommend that the optimum price for road use is where the 'willingness to pay' of demand equals the cost of supply. This is precisely what Knight (1924) did. However, Knight recognised that in congested conditions the cost of supplying one extra unit of road space increases above the average cost. This is similar to the special case in marginal economics argued by Marshall. In other words, when a driver joins other traffic in congested conditions he or she slows everyone down a little bit and the marginal cost of having this extra driver is higher than the cost before he/she arrived.

When congestion occurs, Knight argued, the cost of driving should be increased to reflect the new marginal cost. It would be an economically efficient system because people would choose to drive only if the new cost, which would be an accurate reflection of all costs including congestion, was within their 'willingness to pay'. However, if drivers do not pay for the marginal cost of congestion, inefficiencies arise, as some extra people would make a decision to drive based on inaccurate costs that do not include congestion.

In this way the economic theory of road pricing is used to argue that drivers should pay in relation to how much they use the roads, to cover the external cost of congestion for which they do not usually pay. Incidentally, the same road pricing argument could be used for the damage each extra driver causes to the environment. Here the inconvenience is not to other drivers on the road but to the community at large. The theory of pricing for road use was not given serious consideration for another 30 years until Vickrey (1955) considered the case for marginal cost pricing of transport. Then the Smeed Report (Ministry of Transport, 1964) presented an in-depth study designed to assess whether the concept had any practical relevance.

Policy Objectives: Why Consider Urban Road Pricing?

Even though there is a theoretical economic rationale for urban road pricing, it also needs to meet practical political and planning criteria in order to be considered for implementation. It would have to be expected that policy objectives, such as reducing congestion and improving the environment, would be met if a form of pricing were introduced. This section reviews typical transport-related objectives to gauge its practical impact.

Efficiency and congestion relief Road pricing can be introduced to make the cost incurred by the driver include the cost of the congestion he or she is helping to cause. In an economic sense the transport system would be more efficient and in practical terms there would be less congestion, as some people would decide not to travel or to use a different mode. Unfortunately, although traffic may be restrained in the charged area, some of this traffic may divert to another destination. This is either an advantage, as traffic is diverted onto more suitable roads, or a disadvantage, liable to cause congestion and inefficiency elsewhere.

Land use development This ability to influence demand allows road pricing to complement the aims of land use plans. However, it might not be sensible to price one area without including another because there may be substantial diversion of trips to the uncharged area. If the other area cannot be priced, though, because it is outside an authority's jurisdiction, then the transport plans would be expected to cater for the potential lack of attraction by using the revenue that has been collected to reduce the adverse effects of relocation and re-routing.

Accessibility Assuming that revenue is being distributed in a way that makes the whole transport system more efficient, accessibility to, from and in the charged area should improve. This means that for the same expenditure in time or money an individual would be able to access more destinations. However, there may be cases where accessibility improves for some and worsens for others. An example would be shorter travel times for car drivers but longer travel times for bus users if the bus service could not accommodate people who switch modes. This problem is essentially a problem of equity.

Economic growth Where accessibility does improve, there is an argument that economic growth should be stimulated as businesses have more potential customers. However, this is not taken for granted as some potential customers may be deterred by the idea of road pricing. Again, it is a problem of equity.

Environmental improvement The road pricing charge can incorporate an amount to cover the environmental damage of the vehicle. Care would have to be taken that re-routing of traffic does not shift environmental problems and improve conditions for some at the expense of others. Recent congestion pricing proposals have stressed the environmental impacts more than the congestion reduction impacts (May, 1992).

Road safety Like the environment, safety conditions could often improve with reduced congestion. However, it has been recognised that improved traffic speeds and re-routing of traffic problems onto unsuitable roads could increase accidents (May, ibid.). Meanwhile, increased walking, cycle and motorcycle use instead of driving, might lead to more accidents amongst these vulnerable groups (Roberts, 1977).

Equity Equity is both a constraint and a potential objective of urban road pricing. If the benefits of road pricing are not distributed fairly some people are likely to be disadvantaged. But it is also fair to argue that those that contribute more to congestion and environmental damage should pay a share of the inconvenience that they cause to others.

Revenue generation Each road pricing scheme will collect revenue. Maintaining favourable land use patterns and not re-routing traffic problems, by providing alternatives for those people priced off the road, ultimately depends on redistributing this revenue to increase the overall benefits of a scheme (Small, 1992). However, instead of merely mitigating adverse effects of road pricing, the revenue generating possibilities can also be used as an objective in themselves in order to finance transport and non-transport related projects.

Practicability If urban road pricing is used as a measure to achieve some or all of the above objectives then it must also be practical. This means that the scheme must be easy to administer, understandable, enforceable and cost-effective. With the redistribution of revenue inextricably linked to the fortunes of the scheme, it would be detrimental to waste a large proportion of the revenue on operating costs.

Acceptability The final policy objective that is often included in practical assessment is the subject of this book. It is reviewed in the subsequent sections of this chapter and to a large degree reflects opinion about the appropriateness of road pricing to meet the above objectives.

Designing Road Pricing Schemes

The design of an urban road pricing scheme depends upon the policy objectives of the operating authority. If the objectives were associated with economic efficiency and congestion relief, the amount of the charge and the hours of operations would most likely vary throughout the day dependent upon the level of traffic. However, if the objective were connected with merely raising revenue then there would be less need to vary the charge. The other predominant concern for design is practicability, which may mean that the ideal charging structure cannot be implemented due to technological or human limits. For example, a charge that exactly mirrors the social marginal costs could not be implemented as these costs continually vary and could not be known in advance for a driver to make a rational decision. However, schemes that come close can be implemented.

The only schemes that have been used are based on vehicles paying to cross cordons or boundary points located on the edge of cities and area licensing, where drivers must purchase a supplementary licence to be within a restricted area of a city. Depending upon the objectives, the charges to cross cordons or purchase area licences vary; if the objective is to reduce congestion the charge would typically be higher than if it was to raise revenue but not deter people from driving. Likewise, the extent of the scheme, by size of restricted area and length of operating time, differs according to objectives; if the objective was to reduce congestion the scheme might operate in only the city centre for the peak commuting hours, where and when congestion is usually worst. However, if the objective was to raise revenue then the scheme might encompass the whole city and for longer hours to increase the amount of revenue collected. The technology of operation can also alter from electronic schemes which automatically bill drivers or deduct money from pre-purchased smart cards, to simpler schemes where drivers display vignettes in their windscreens which are checked by teams of police or traffic wardens.

It is possible, however, for the charging structure to be based on time of travel and distance travelled. In the former case the charging structure would reflect the time spent in congestion and thus be appropriate if the objective is to reduce congestion. In the latter case, charging by distance might be suited to a stretch of road where there is no congestion and distance travelled could reflect the amount of use. In urban situations these charging structures have not been used or developed in any great detail. Thus, most of the work on acceptability focuses on cordon and area licence schemes.

Past Urban Road Pricing Schemes and Proposals

Past urban road pricing schemes and proposals can be divided into five groups:

1   Singapore Area Licence Scheme and Hong Kong electronic road pricing experiments;
2   Bergen, Oslo and Trondheim toll rings;
3   Randstad and Stockholm proposals;
4   Greater London Council, London Planning Advisory Committee and Department of Transport research programmes;
5   Cambridge, Edinburgh, Bristol and Leicester investigations.

This section compares how urban road pricing was either implemented or considered for use in the first four of these groups by reviewing the policy objectives that road pricing was assigned, how it was integrated with other transport policies and the design options. The fifth group does not form part of the comparison, though, because in Bristol and Leicester the studies were ongoing at the time of this research and in Edinburgh an in-depth study looking specifically at road pricing had only reached an inception stage. However, their findings have been compared with the findings of this book in Chapter 11.

Policy Objectives and Complementary Policies

Singapore and Hong Kong Although Singapore introduced road pricing in 1975 and Hong Kong rejected its road pricing proposal in 1985, in both cases road pricing was targeted at reducing congestion in their central business districts. In Singapore it was argued that road pricing would improve the efficiency of the whole transport system by freeing road space to allow public transport to be more frequent and faster. This improved public transport service would enhance accessibility, which in turn was seen as sustaining economic growth. The policy measures chosen to complement road pricing had the same rationale: increasing parking charges, increasing additional car registration fees, improving bus-based public transport and introducing park and ride alternatives. More information on the objectives in Singapore can be found in Holland and Watson (1978).

The Hong Kong road pricing proposal was an idea to improve upon the already high car ownership tax because it was more equitable (Dawson and Brown, 1985). The resulting reduction in congestion would, as in Singapore, improve the efficiency of the network, free road space for public transport and improve accessibility and help sustain economic growth (ibid.). In the Hong Kong proposal it was assumed that the pricing scheme would be implemented in conjunction with the existing transport policies. These were new road and rail construction, traffic management, parking charges and physical restrictions. As in Singapore, the complementary policies taken together have the same objectives as the urban road pricing measure itself, which is in contrast to the Norwegian toll rings that are used to finance measures with different objectives.

The Norwegian toll rings The Norwegian toll rings all have the common objective of raising revenue without causing traffic reduction or changes in mode and departure time. This revenue is then used to fund other measures – and this is where the schemes differ – in the objectives of their complementary policies. This is the opposite of Singapore and Hong Kong, where road pricing was seen primarily as a congestion reduction measure and less emphasis was placed on uses of the revenue.

The first Norwegian urban road pricing scheme to be introduced was in Bergen in 1986. It was argued that road pricing was needed to fund a satisfactory road system because in recent years the funds provided by central government had not kept pace with traffic growth. The second city to introduce road pricing was the capital Oslo in 1990, in order to fund the Oslo Package, which was aimed at environmental improvement. Although 80 per cent of the revenue was spent on road improvements, most of this money funded the construction of a tunnel taking traffic under the city centre, for environmental reasons, while the remaining 20 per cent of the revenue was available to spend on public transport. The last toll ring to open in Norway was in Trondheim in 1991. Again the objective was to raise revenue and this time the money was available to spend on a wider range of transport improvements than in Oslo: the Trondheim Package. This includes bypasses, cycle routes, pedestrian routes, bus lanes and accident remedial measures.

Randstad and Stockholm In both the Randstad in Holland and Stockholm in Sweden there are proposals for road pricing schemes. Unlike their Asian and Norwegian counterparts they are in comparatively early stages of development and there are no concrete proposals. However, the planning process has produced some insight into issues of acceptability.

In Stockholm urban road pricing has been driven by the goals of environmental protection, congestion relief and improving accessibility. Urban road pricing was seen as a measure to achieve these objectives by financing new road construction, public transport improvement, environmental enhancement and accident remedial measures, and restraining traffic, providing it was practical and acceptable (Gomez-Ibanez and Small, 1994). It was also suggested that the commencement of road pricing could coincide with the completion of the city's Western bypass, which would have a separate toll on it, and inner ring road improvements.

In the Randstad – which is the region that comprises the cities of Rotterdam, Amsterdam, The Hague, and Utrecht – proposals for road pricing have been driven by three separate sets of objectives. Under the 1988 Rekening Rijden (road pricing) proposal, the objectives were to reduce congestion – so improving the efficiency of the road network – to improve the environment and to improve accessibility. By 1990 it was apparent that support for the proposals was waning because of the practicality of implementing the proposal and unease about using pricing to restrain traffic directly. Thus the proposal was renamed Project Tollheffing in 1991 with the objective of raising revenue from a simple toll ring, as in the Norwegian examples. Road tolls would be used to cover the costs of road improvements and maintenance and then the government's road funds could be used to invest in public transport. However, within a year plans for road pricing had changed again, not only because there was not enough spare land for toll booths, but also because of worries over local traffic diversions (Gomez-Ibanez and Small, 1994) and pressure from the freight lobby groups to reduce non-essential traffic during peak times (Lewis, 1993). In 1992 the title and brief of the project team was once again changed to reflect this, this time to Project Spitsbydrage (peak contribution), whereby the idea of simple vignettes to travel at peak times was to be examined. Here the objectives of the scheme returned to the original set, of congestion reduction and environment and accessibility improvements, but with more emphasis on encouraging economic growth and being practical and acceptable. Since Project Spitsbydrage was set up, though, enthusiasm for road pricing has diminished further.

The London Research In 1974 the GLC study was briefed to investigate a supplementary licence scheme (similar to the Singapore Area Licence Scheme) as a means of traffic restraint. The study looked at which alternatives were appropriate, the effects, if it would be practical and acceptable, and how soon it could be introduced (May, 1975). Tests predicted that several options would meet the transport policy objectives of congestion reduction and improved traffic efficiency, economic growth and environmental improvement. The study did not directly consider using the road pricing options in conjunction with other transport measures.

In view of the largely negative public reaction, the idea was carried no further. Then, in 1987 the LPAC commissioned a series of scenario-testing exercises. The objectives were fostering economic growth, improving the efficiency across all modes, promoting choice and accessibility, improving safety and personal security, improving and conserving the environment and minimising future costs of the transport network (May and Gardner, 1991). In contrast to the GLC study, the LPAC options for road pricing directly considered the integration of the policy with other transport measures and it recommended using road pricing as part of a transport strategy to include new rail systems, traffic management, improved bus services and no increase in road capacity in Central and Inner London (Gomez-Ibanez and Small, 1994).

The Department of Transport commissioned its own study in 1991 following the LPAC recommendations. The London Congestion Charging Research Programme (The MVA Consultancy, 1995) investigated feasible options for congestion charging and what the impacts would be on London, its people and its economy. It was shown that road pricing could meet objectives shown in the previous studies and also help finance other transport-related measures.

Design and Implementation

Singapore and Hong Kong In Singapore, the restricted zone was designated as the central business and shopping areas. To enter the zone motorists had to display a valid pass during the morning peak hours unless they stayed on the inner ring road, which was excluded because it was a bypass route for motorists whose destination was beyond the city centre (Holland and Watson, 1978). Exemptions were given to commercial vehicles, motorcycles, cars with at least three passengers, buses and emergency vehicles. Then in 1989 substantial revisions were made to tackle congestion outside the morning peak and to reduce the numbers of commercial vehicles in the restricted zone. The times of operation were extended to include the afternoon peak and exemptions were lifted on all vehicles except buses and emergency vehicles (Gomez-Ibanez and Small, 1994). This situation remained until 1994, when further revisions were prompted by increased traffic in-between the peaks. The time of operation was extended to 07:30 to 18:30 on Monday to Friday and introduced on Saturday from 07:30 to 15:00. Two types of licences were available: one for the whole day and the other a part-day licence for the inter-peak period (ibid.). In 1998 an electronic system of operation was introduced where vehicles are now charged when they cross a cordon, similar to the Hong Kong proposal.

The design in Hong Kong was based around drivers being charged to cross cordons via an electronic system that recognised an in-vehicle tag (Catling and Harbord, 1985). This was thought to offer the most flexibility and be best suited to the geography. The options that were tested had different charge structures and cordon densities (Gomez-Ibanez and Small, 1994). Initially the only groups planned to be charged were private and company car owners. Every other vehicle would be exempt. Also, no discounts were planned (Dawson and Brown, 1985).

Broadly speaking the road pricing policy packages achieved or were predicted to achieve their objectives. In Singapore, economic growth has been maintained and has grown at a faster than expected rate after the introduction of the 1989 reforms, although how much road pricing contributed to this is not known (Gomez-Ibanez and Small, 1994). Congestion relief has been achieved in the restricted area, but some re-routing of the problems has been recorded (Holland and Watson, 1978) and small improvements were noted in overall ease of travel and the quality of the environment McGlynn and Roberts (1977). However, Wilson (1988) argues that not all commuters benefited and in particular there was a decrease in utility for bus users, as the increase in the number of passengers raised boarding times and this offset the advantage of higher speeds between the stops. Similar impacts were predicted in the Hong Kong trial, although the reduction in the peak traffic would not be so pronounced (Gomez-Ibanez and Small, 1994).

The Norwegian toll rings Bergen, Oslo and Trondheim all adopted toll rings, which are like single cordons used to form one cell. The Bergen toll ring charges inbound traffic to enter the central business district from 0600 hrs to 2200 hrs from Monday to Friday. Exemptions from payment were given only to scheduled buses, motorcycles under 50cc and emergency vehicles (Larsen, 1988). Initially the Oslo toll ring operated on a low technology system of toll collection and pass verification as found in Bergen, but after a few months an in-vehicle read-only electronic system was introduced that deducts the charge from car drivers' accounts without them having to stop. However, Oslo has still kept staffed tollbooths at each of the gates and some also have automatic coin lanes. The toll ring is in operation 24 hours a day everyday, but as in Bergen, only inbound traffic is charged. Exemptions have been given to buses, motorcycles, disabled drivers and emergency vehicles (Lewis, 1993; Gomez-Ibanez and Small, 1994). In Trondheim operation is based on the electronic system, as found in Oslo. Tolls are collected from 0600 hrs to 1700 hrs from Monday to Friday from inbound traffic only. Exemptions from payment have been given to disabled drivers, public transport and motorcycles. Also, for every driver there is a limit to the amount they have to pay, equivalent to one trip per hour or 75 trips per month (Meland, 1995).

The Bergen toll ring more or less achieved its objectives. Traffic did decline after the introduction of the toll ring but this figure is distorted by economic conditions. The scheme has proved practical although, at 16 per cent of total revenue, the running costs are high. Also, the toll ring generated the required amount of revenue for reinvestment. The Oslo toll ring achieved its objectives, although, as in Bergen, there was a decline of about 8 per cent in the amount of traffic entering the city (Lewis, 1993). However, Lewis does point out that the toll was introduced at a time of recession and that fuel price increases might be the main cause for trip reductions. Trip rates returned to the pre-toll levels within the first year (Gomez-Ibanez and Small, 1994). The Trondheim toll ring has achieved its objectives but there is evidence that it has reduced trips crossing the cordon by 21.5 per cent (Polak and Meland, 1994).

Stockholm and the Ranstad In Stockholm the intention was to have a cordon surrounding the entire city just inside the outer ring road, with either a variable charge between peak time and off-peak time or a flat rate charge. Using the flat rate tariff appeared to give the best results measured against the Stockholm objectives (Lewis, 1993). The suggested operating system was to be based on electronic read-write tags which can deduct the charge from smart cards inserted in the in-vehicle meter, although provision would be made for purchase of passes on a manual system (ibid.). Other details such as exemptions and discounts had not been decided upon.

Project Rekening Rijden in the Randstad proposed a system of multiple cordons across the whole Randstad area (Gomez-Ibanez and Small, 1994). No information on plans for differential charges for vehicle type, exemptions or discounts has been found. The next project in the Netherlands, Project Tollheffing, considered placing toll stations on the inter-urban road network. The system was to use conventional manual means of toll collection. However, Project Tollheffing also considered a supplementary licence scheme, the idea of which was developed further in the next Project Spitsbydrage (peak pricing). This project proposed that vehicles should display a supplementary licence to travel on the inter-urban road network, between the cities in the Ranstad, at peak times.

The London research programmes   The GLC, LPAC and DoT research programmes have experimented with a wide variety of designs and the feasible options that have been suggested range from simple area licences to complex systems of cordons extending out to the North and South Circulars.

The GLC study was restricted to looking at area licence schemes for London because the technology had not yet been developed to make more complex cordon systems feasible. The study recommended that passes could be purchased from existing shops or vending machines and should be valid per day or per month. Exemptions should be given to motorcycles, buses and emergency vehicles, but no discounts given to monthly pass holders. In all options commercial vehicles were to be charged at between two and three times the car rate (May, 1975).

Twelve years later the LPAC series of studies tested a small number of road pricing scenarios. As mentioned before these studies did not give a great deal of attention to the practicalities of road pricing but were more interested in a broad brush analysis to decide upon a strategy. Within these tests, though, there are two clear sets of options. The first set was the scenarios based on area licence schemes similar to the GLC alternatives. The second set was electronically operated cordon schemes.

The DoT congestion charging research programme then developed options for road pricing that refined the cordon charging system and filled details omitted by the LPAC strategic studies. Although the DoT programme did consider other road pricing options, all the recommendations were based around cordons and using an electronic operating system. There were seven favourable options that varied according to size and charging structure. All options included a cordon surrounding Central London. Options 4 to 6 had an additional cordon around Inner London. Option 7 had three cordons: one around Central London, one at a radius comparable with the South Circular and the final one at a radius comparable with the North Circular. Options 4 to 7 also used a small number of screenlines to form cells within the areas bounded by the cordons and thus limit orbital diversions. In all options the charge was levied at peak times and all day, from 0700 to 1900 hrs, on working weekdays and was set at low, medium and high levels, ranging from 50p to £8 to enter Central London. In the tests, exemptions were given to motorcycles only and all the other vehicles were charged at the same rate. The programme recommended exemptions should be considered for those disabled drivers who are exempt from vehicle excise duty, regular buses and emergency vehicles. Qualifying drivers could either be given credits entitling them to a certain amount of free travel in a specified time period or have an account where only a limited number of trips in a designated time period would be charged for. The system of caps is similar to that found in Trondheim (The MVA Consultancy, 1995).

In all the studies, congestion reduction and environmental improvements were predicted. However, equity, practicality and land use issues have been major constraints, with all research recognising that some groups would lose. The DoT programme found that non car-users would benefit, high income car-users would lose, low income car-users who continue to drive would lose and the effect on the middle classes would be variable. In addition, the programme highlighted the negative benefits for residents living on the boundaries of the cordons. The LPAC, though, countered this potential negative effect by arguing that the equity impact of introducing road pricing is an improvement on any of the other scenarios without road pricing (May and Gardner, 1991).

In the DoT programme, the effect on the economy was considered in depth. It was estimated that businesses in London would contribute an absolute maximum in charges of £400 million, whereas the gross domestic product of London in 1991 was £70,000 million. Thus the economic effect of road pricing will be small. However, businesses in Central London would gain and businesses in Inner London might suffer a slight negative effect in the options that included Inner London in the charged area (The MVA Consultancy, 1995).

Acceptability of Past Urban Road Pricing Schemes and Proposals

Evidence

Overall, in Singapore in 1975 the area licence scheme was received favourably. McGlynn and Roberts (1977) found the supporters of the scheme to be government, the city, bus companies, pedestrians, residents, bus passengers and car pools. Company car users were neutral. The opposition comprised taxi drivers and users, middle income motorists, residents living outside the restricted area and upper income motorists. The dissatisfaction of the taxi drivers was remedied by changes to the scheme. In Singapore, though, the main opposition is against the high car ownership taxes and the Certificates of Entitlement (Gomez-Ibanez and Small, 1994).

Despite the favourable predictions in Hong Kong the idea was rejected. Lewis (1993) suggests the following reasons:

1   private car owners felt that road pricing was a punitive measure;
2   electronic road pricing was seen as an invasion of privacy;
3   public scepticism that a reduction in tax would follow;
4   reservations as to whether there would be a reduction in traffic congestion;
5   public transport was due to be improved anyway;
6   there had been a decline in income after a stock market crash;
7   political uncertainty before the Sino-British declaration.

Borins (1988) also suggests that it was a question of bad timing and poor presentation. In the run up to the transfer of Hong Kong to China it was decided to strengthen the democracy of the Legislative Council by consulting more closely with district boards. This change occurred in September 1985 and the first issue the district boards were able to exercise their greater power on was the question of road pricing. As they had been poorly consulted in the past there was strong evidence that there was an element of resentment in their opposition, as well as genuine worries.

Broadly speaking the Bergen scheme has proved acceptable. The city council drew up an agreement with the central government that guaranteed a special grant for road construction that would match the net revenue from the toll rings, effectively doubling the money available. Combined with the lack of other solutions to the funding problem and the fact that no major political party wanted to make an issue of the proposal, the council voted it through with a comfortable majority.

However, amongst individuals opinion of the scheme before introduction was, on balance, negative. This improved dramatically, though, after the introduction of the toll ring (Larsen, 1988). The reason given for this is that immediate road improvements were seen because the introduction of the toll ring coincided with the completion of a new tunnel (Lewis, 1993). During the planning stage of the toll ring there had been public meetings, thus the reasons for the scheme were well known. Also, fears that the tollbooths would cause congestion were unfounded.

As in Bergen, the Oslo toll ring achieved its objectives without causing major changes to trip patterns. However, whereas in Bergen public opinion changed in favour of the scheme after its introduction, polls suggest this has not been repeated in Oslo. In 1989, 29 per cent of people were in favour of the plan and 65 per cent of people were opposed. By 1992, 39 per cent of people were in favour of the toll ring but a large number, 56 per cent, were still opposed (Gomez-Ibanez and Small, 1994). One reason for poor opinions of the scheme is that Oslo motorists feel aggrieved that they pay a lot more in motoring taxes than is spent on roads in the city. During the consultation period road organisations vigorously argued that the tolls were unfair because Oslo motorists contribute NOK 2.5 billion in taxes and only NOK 300 million is spent on roads (Lewis, 1993). The response of the planners was to counter this opposition with an intensive marketing campaign and persuade the motorists to subscribe to the scheme in advance by giving them 20 per cent discount. Some groups, particularly businesses, still feel unfairly treated though; 60 per cent of subscriptions are paid by employers as opposed to their employees (Gomez-Ibanez and Small, 1994). As in Bergen there was no major political movement against the scheme. Also, a similar financing deal was made where central government promised to contribute a certain amount on top of the toll revenue. Forty-five per cent of the Oslo package was to be financed by the government and the remaining 55 per cent from toll revenue (Lewis 1993).

Opinions of the toll ring as a method of financing the Trondheim package are negative. Before the toll ring opened 7 per cent were in support, 72 per cent opposed and 21 per cent unsure. Two months after the opening 20 per cent were in support, 48 per cent opposed and 32 per cent unsure. However, when asked about the Trondheim package, about 30 per cent were in support and 25 per cent opposed. A large number of people, 45 per cent, were unsure though (Gomez-Ibanez and Small, 1994). The poll was conducted very soon after the toll ring had opened and before the Trondheim package had been implemented. This could explain why a large number of people were still opposed and the large number of reservations. In Bergen, where opinion did change dramatically, the poll was conducted one year after opening and improvements were noticed immediately with the opening of a new tunnel. Prior to the introduction in Tronheim, planners used a public information campaign that focused on the environmental advantages of the package, but also included arguments about improving the efficiency of the transport system and maintaining economic growth. Also, the campaign was used to allay fears by stressing its simplicity. As in Oslo, discounted rates were offered to motorists who subscribed to the scheme in advance and, as its operation was electronic, the in-vehicle tags were issued free of charge.

The people of Trolla, on a peninsula to the west of Trondheim, argued against the toll as it was particularly unfair to them because they already paid a fee to use a ferry. Their argument was considered valid by the planners, as the cost of the ferry meant they had already paid a toll of sorts. Thus the toll ring does not operate on the western approach from Trolla. As in Bergen and Oslo, no major political party opposed the toll.

In Stockholm road pricing was part of the transport strategy that had been agreed upon by the major political parties and was linked to the improvement of roads. Thus drivers would see where money had been spent. Meanwhile in the Randstad road pricing proposals have not achieved consensus. This is in part due to the size of the area involved. What has been seen is gradual watering down of the proposals from an electronically operated multi-cordon scheme to a paper based supplementary licence that has in turn been put on hold. However, as in Stockholm, planners have tried to increase acceptability by associating the rationale for road pricing with the objective of raising revenue to fund the road system. This point is recognised by Grieco and Jones (1994) and the importance of it is discussed in Chapter 11.

Issues about the acceptability of road pricing schemes were not given much consideration in the GLC and LPAC studies, although acceptability was recognised as the largest potential obstruction to implementation. In an application to the DoT by The MVA Consultancy for the award of the London congestion charging research programme, they said that 'transcending all technical issues, however, is that of public and political acceptability' (The MVA Consultancy, 1995).

The programme did commission some research into acceptability issues. They found that worsening congestion conditions had encouraged several large groups to come out in favour of some form of road pricing; notably the Chartered Institute for Transport, the Confederation of British Industry and the Institute for Public Policy Research. This support, though, is countered by the worries of small business and London residents in particular.

The acceptability problems identified (The MVA Consultancy, 1995) were:

1 the need for such a radical alternative;
2 there were more acceptable alternatives;
3 personal privacy;
4 the charge being seen as another tax;
5 whether congestion charging would have the intended effect;
6 the effectiveness of high technology systems;
7 cash losses to commercial road users;
8 the positioning of the cordon boundaries;
9 fairness.

These problems are similar to those mentioned in the other road pricing schemes from overseas. However, the programme suggested that 'attitudes to congestion charging might be affected by early decision on measures designed to alleviate its secondary impacts' and 'a carefully-designed programme of information and consultation could contribute to the development of procedures to protect those sectors of the community which would be particularly adversely affected, including the less well-off who are car-dependent' (Richards and Gilliam, 1996, p. 440).

The beneficial effects of complementary policies on public acceptance of road pricing were described in research for the National Economic Development Office (Harris Research Centre, 1991). A sample of Londoners was asked for their preliminary views on the acceptability of road use charging. Only 43 per cent of the respondents found road pricing acceptable. Then the respondents were asked what they would like the revenue spent on if there was road pricing. Next they were asked about their attitude to road pricing if the revenues were spent as they wanted. The number finding road pricing acceptable rose to 62 per cent. Within this response group, people from the social class AB were much more likely to find the idea acceptable than the middle class C2 respondents. Also, young and middle-aged women were more likely to be opposed to the idea. However, the potential acceptability of road pricing, if used to fund other measures, is not as promising when the respondents were asked how they felt other people would react: 83 per cent thought that there would be a lot of opposition (ibid.). The most popular choices to spend the revenue on were public transport and new roads in the London area.

Similarly, research by Jones (1991) finds 'that support for road pricing virtually doubles when it is presented as the cornerstone of a package of measures that improves alternative modes and provides a safer and more pleasant environment' (ibid., p. 195). As a stand-alone policy, 57 per cent of respondents opposed and 30 per cent supported road pricing in heavily congested urban areas. When road pricing was combined with a package of measures, only 34 per cent of respondents opposed it and 57 per cent were in support.

As the most effective complementary policies that were tested in the London congestion charging research programme were based on provision of public transport alternatives, the programme concludes that 'it should be possible to design schemes which, together with complementary public transport improvements provide net benefit to most broad groups of traveller' (Richards and Gilliam, 1996, p. 440). Although problems of acceptance will remain, Richards and Gilliam (ibid., p. 441) infer that road pricing might be the best method in comparison to other possibilities, including doing nothing.

The findings from the programme were considered in a Parliamentary Select Committee. The government decision was to encourage debate on the subject and keep it under consideration for the longer term, but not implement it in London in the short term (Department of Transport, 1995). However, the government said that it would consider making arrangements for a local authority outside London to implement congestion charging.

Analysis

At the start of this chapter it was noted that the point of the literature review was to identify factors that affect acceptability, but also to see if there was a common view about how acceptability could be improved. If there was, then the implication for the research would be to test this common theme, but if one did not emerge, then the research would need to discover one. The contention is that this literature review has identified common factors about acceptability, such as belief in the effects of the proposals, equity and privacy issues, but a common theme about how these problems can be overcome has not been identified because the actions or proposals to achieve acceptability in each of the comparison groups have been different.

The Singapore Area Licence Scheme went ahead with few concessions to fairness concerns and, while disadvantages for some commuters were identified, the scheme met its policy objectives by contributing to congestion reduction and helping sustain economic growth. In terms of lessons for acceptability of the policy in general, the Singapore experience indicates that road pricing is a feasible method of achieving typical urban transport objectives. Meanwhile, in the Hong Kong electronic road pricing experiment it was argued that the proposed scheme would be fairer than the existing methods of vehicle taxation, while still achieving the city's policy objectives. This different approach to justifying the proposal was not successful, though, in part due to failure to guarantee that car ownership taxes would be reduced following the introduction of road pricing and to answer criticism that the policy was excessively punitive.

In Norway, where demand management was not a salient objective and the money was largely spent on roads for motorists, three toll rings have been introduced. In these revenue raising schemes fairness has been a key concern and the design adapted to improve the fairness. For example, the central government arranged to contribute money to improvements on top of the toll revenue, to answer criticisms that motorists already paid too much in taxation. However, while highlighting the importance of fairness issues and how to tackle them, Norwegian experience is not directly transferable to Hong Kong as the scheme objectives are different.

If the Norwegian model for road pricing is followed then the contribution to congestion reduction and environmental relief has to be watered down. This is illustrated in the Ranstad where the original idea for using road pricing was changed into a system of tolls for road infrastructure. When the original congestion reduction and economic growth objectives were re-introduced at a subsequent stage, the proposal had by that time been changed into an additional road fund licence for travel on inter-urban motorways. Meanwhile, in Stockholm, although the traffic restraint advantages of road pricing were retained in the plans, the policy was promoted by aligning it with funding road improvements.

In contrast, in the London research programmes, while the road pricing debate did not fully enter the political arena because no political party supported it in practice, the research on acceptability found popularity could be enhanced by funding public transport improvements. Financing such complementary policies would also maximise the overall congestion and environmental benefits and help minimise disadvantages by providing alternatives for people priced out of driving.

Several other issues have been raised about the acceptability of road pricing, such as possible problems a scheme may have in meeting the intended objectives and worries about protection of privacy. Different scheme designs will cause different groups to be concerned with different issues. The groups whose acceptance is important are likely to be national and local politicians, organisations directly affected, such as the transport operators and businesses, and individuals who need to travel, such as residents, commuters and the disabled.

While there are common factors relating to acceptability in the comparison groups there is no clear strategy for overcoming the problems. Jones (1991, p. 196) says that research into public acceptance needs to identify:

1   which measures should form part of the local policy package (e.g. is there a role for local new road construction);
2   how should the balance be struck between the level of charge, the intended degree of vehicle restraint, and the amount of investment in environmental improvements and transport alternatives that could be supported;
3   in what form should road user charging be introduced, bearing in mind perceived public sensitivities regarding privacy, equity, etc.?

The different approaches to dealing with acceptability that have been described do not provide a common view for any of the above three questions. Complementary policies that have been associated with road pricing differ, as does the balance between using road pricing to meet financing and traffic restraint objectives. Also, the design of the schemes and proposals vary in their extent and use of differential charges. To a certain degree, it is expected that schemes will differ because each area has unique geographical and economic characteristics; however, there may be answers to Jones' questions on acceptability that are transferable between proposals. This research, aimed at developing a theory of acceptability, will help discover the extent to which a common theme about acceptability between proposals and schemes can be derived.

Other research on acceptability does not counter the supposition that only common factors about how attitudes to road pricing are known and that there is no common theme about how the problems can be overcome. On commenting on the prospects for winning political approval for congestion pricing, Gomez-Ibanez and Small (1994) raise a number of issues of acceptability:

1   concern over the protection of privacy: If more direct charging is used then the technology might be able to track individual vehicles. Some drivers would be wary of supporting such a system that could be open to abuse;
2   the burden of tolls on low income motorists: While richer motorists may be able to afford to pay the charge, low income motorists may feel they still need to drive yet cannot afford to pay more. Thus there is a fairness issue;

3   damage to businesses in the area: some people believe that the charge
     would deter people from visiting an area and this would have consequences
     on the competitiveness of some businesses;
4   failure to redistribute the revenue: the success of road pricing to overcome
     some of the problems depends on redistributing the revenue to ensure that
     low income motorists have a viable alternative to driving;
5   opposition because it represents drastic change: there will be a failure to
     understand the rationale, distrust in the motives of the planners and the
     technology and scepticism that there will be no unanticipated side-effects.

While the issues concur with points that have been raised in the comparison,
they do not point to a common strategy for overcoming unacceptability. Jones
and Hervik (1992) raise similar issues about invasion of privacy, equity, the
charge not being seen as another tax and behavioural aspects. They argue
that privacy can be protected using technology that protects the anonymity of
the driver and data collected to predict how drivers will react to the charge.
However, they say that 'the taxation issue is a particular problem in countries
such as the United Kingdom, where governments do not hypothecate revenue
for particular expenditure' and equity is 'a matter of viewpoint' (ibid., p. 139).
Their suggestion to reduce these types of problems is to ensure revenue is
used, as already mentioned, to finance packages of transport and environmental
measures. They do not, though, provide a suggestion on reaching an acceptable
balance between amount of restraint and investment.

Seale (1993) also supports the notion of linking road pricing to a package of
transport measures and recognises the role that exemptions and discounts could
play in improving acceptance. He attributes unease that remains about road
pricing to a 'lack of any particular scheme against which to test attitudes' (ibid.,
p. 124) and thus resolve problems. However, controversy about acceptable
scheme design and the award of exemptions 'reveals different interpretations
of the function of road pricing' (ibid., p. 127). The question that arises from this
research is, as above, how to identify an acceptable function for road pricing.
Sheldon et al. (1993) agree with the aforementioned acceptability issues and
stress the need to keep the design simple and understandable, which is an
important message again, but one that does not answer the questions posed
by Jones (1991) above.

The only research to date that has taken a more theoretical turn in defining
how an acceptable road pricing scheme can be designed and implemented is by
Sager (1994) and Langmyhr (1995, 1997). They take the idea of Forester (1989)
that planners should be comprehensible, sincere, legitimate and true, and if

this is the case conflicts that arise in implementing a plan can be managed. Sager and Langmyhr illustrate this process with data from public and political consultations about the Norwegian toll rings. In the later work by Langmyhr, he then focuses on translating this theoretical idea to practical issues about fairness of road pricing in general. Although the work has implications for acceptability, it is limited to studying proposals in Norway. Also, it is not proven that the theoretical model actually could help to decide what are general rules about acceptability, because concepts such as legitimacy are very broad in definition and difficult to use to pinpoint a fair scheme design, while other concepts, such as sincerity, are without doubt important but add little to the debate about how to insist that planners are open in their motives. For these reasons Sager's and Langmyhr's work did not provide enough theoretical grounding to offer a reliable method that could improve acceptability. However, their ideas about acceptability and fairness are used later as ideas in the development of the sociological theory of acceptability in Chapter 5.

Conclusion

The research progresses from the understanding that a common theory about what would make an urban road pricing scheme acceptable does not exist. Therefore the emphasis on the method should be to discover a sociological theory that can explain the full range of views regarding the acceptability of road pricing and be capable of suggesting design options that are theoretically acceptable.

This literature review has identified factors that affect public and political acceptance of road pricing by describing theoretical and practical reasons for using the policy and comparing past schemes and proposals. For example, road pricing can be associated with economic efficiency or with achieving practical transport policy objectives such as congestion reduction, environmental relief and raising funding for transport and environmental measures. Analysis of schemes and proposals indicate that road pricing can be used to achieve combinations of these objectives, however, each region has compiled a different balance of objectives, in part to enhance acceptability. Regardless of scheme objectives, though, there are common acceptability concerns such as equity and the protection of privacy amongst the schemes and proposals. These, as well as being addressed through the choice of policy objectives, can be tackled in scheme design such as through the use of exemptions or technology that protects anonymity.

None of the research that has been reviewed points either to a method of deciding which policy objectives road pricing could acceptably be used to meet, or to suggestions for acceptable ways of designing the scheme by, for example, providing discounts and exemptions to some users and deciding on charging technology. However, the research is thoroughly explores acceptability issues that arise from these design options. Consequently, subsequent chapters in this book work towards developing a theory of acceptability that can help choose policy objectives for which road pricing could be used and suggesting criteria for acceptable designs. The issues of acceptability that this literature review has identified can be used to check that any theory has incorporated a full range of arguments.

Chapter 3

The Sociological Method

Introduction

In Chapter 2 the idea of urban road pricing was introduced from theoretical and practical perspectives and past urban road pricing schemes and proposals were described. In Chapter 3 this piecemeal knowledge about the acceptability of urban road pricing is used to decide on a method that can meet the research objective. Firstly, different approaches to methodology in social science are described. This divides methods into two broad divisions: positivism, which is best for testing theories, and naturalism, which is best for discovering theoretical explanations. Next, the relevance of this is applied to the problem of the acceptability of urban road pricing; because there is no plausible theory to be tested, the best method should come from the naturalist school. Then an appropriate method to guide the derivation of a theory about acceptability which can contribute to a practical design of an urban road pricing scheme is found. The method is called grounded theorising and among its advantages are that it provides a framework to develop theories grounded in real situations and that it places emphasis on allowing the theory to be tested in future research. To conclude, the method of grounded theorising is described in broad terms. This gives an overview of the type of data that needs to be collected and the type of analysis that is done. More specific methodological details, such as sampling, questionnaire design and the process of analysis, are given in Chapters 4 and 5.

Methodology in Social Science

Options for Classifying Methodology

Methodology can be classified by the techniques that it involves or by the reasons that it is used. In the first case, methodology is usually split between quantitative and qualitative research methods, where quantitative methods use statistical techniques and qualitative methods use interpretative techniques. In the second case, methodology is often classified as being influenced by positivism or naturalism (Hammersley and Atkinson, 1995). These terms are described in detail below, but in short they refer to the type of philosophy that a researcher might assume in order to study the world.

In carrying out research projects combinations of techniques might make up the research methodology. For example, in order to quantify a phenomenon a qualitative decision has to be made about which of its aspects count. Similarly, qualitative research methods do not exclude quantifying aspects of a phenomenon in order to make the qualitative interpretations more plausible. Therefore thinking about methodology in terms of quantitative and qualitative methods does not offer a way of classifying methodology in a holistic way, which reflects the needs of a whole research project.

The superior classification is based on the philosophical dichotomy, positivism and naturalism, which reflects how the researcher wants to see the world. The decision about how to see the world is not arbitrary, though, and is governed by research objectives. Depending on the research objectives the appropriate methodological camp can be found, which reflects the reasons for doing the research, and then the best combination of qualitative and quantitative methods can be decided at a later stage. This is the approach to choosing the methodology that this research has taken, and so the first step is to define the philosophical terms.

Positivism

The philosophical definition of positivism comprises a number of rules. The following is Kalakowski's interpretation (from Hammersley, 1993). First, there is the rule of phenomenalism that states that positivists accept as knowledge only what is visible or manifest. The second is the rule of nominalism that states that ideal types, which do not exist in reality, can be used to allow the positivist to model phenomena. The third is the rule that refuses to call value judgements and normative statements knowledge. The fourth is the rule about the unity of the scientific method. This means that a scientific approach to any problem involves following the above rules.

The positivists and the logical positivists had eminent followers in both the natural and social sciences (e.g. Comte and Durkheim): however, it is now accepted that it provides neither an adequate description of what science does nor a blueprint of what science should do. But positivism has had such a great influence on social science that the largest methodological camp can still be analysed in positivist terms. While accepting that no study is strictly positivist, the term 'positivism' now refers to those methods influenced by positivism (Gartrell and Gartrell, 1996).

In their review of sociological methods, Gartrell and Gartrell (ibid.) note characteristics that indicate which methods come from a positivist tradition. These features likely to indicate the influence of positivism are:

1   concepts being related in law like statements;
2   nominal definitions of concepts;
3   operational definition of concepts to allow empirical measurement;
4   derivation of hypotheses for testing;
5   a formal language to express ideas;
6   variables being related together empirically;
7   the use of statistical/quantitative methods.

Positivist influenced methodologies often use quantitative techniques. Other philosophical terms have been used to describe this type of methodology, such as realism and retroduction (Blaikie, 1993).

Naturalism

Naturalism takes a different stance to positivism. Although naturalism covers a range of methods, the defining element of all the methodological strategies for investigating social phenomena are that they are describing the insider's point of view and not imposing an outsider's view: 'It is to the process of moving from lay descriptions of social life to technical descriptions of that social life that the notion of naturalism is applied' (Blaikie, 1993, p. 177).

Further to this descriptive element, naturalism is concerned with uncovering the meanings, intentions and rules that provide orientation for our actions. These meanings are largely unarticulated and are constantly being modified, produced and reproduced in our everyday lives. Thus, contrary to positivism, which is concerned with only what is manifest, naturalism is concerned with what is hidden and as a consequence naturalist methods are sometimes referred to as interpretivism. Where the positivist will look for indicators of nominalist concepts in the data, the naturalist prefers to use ideas collected in the data (not imposing an outsider's view on the data). As a consequence of this emphasis on uncovering hidden connections, naturalist methods often use qualitative techniques.

Examples of the Methodologies

A good example of positivist-influenced method in transport studies is stated preference, where:

> the term 'stated preference' methods refers to a family of techniques which use individual respondents' statements about their preferences in a set of transport options to estimate utility functions (Kroes and Sheldon, 1988, p. 11).

In these methods the researcher will present a respondent with a choice of travel alternatives (i.e., to complete a specified journey by bus or by car) that are pre-specified in terms of levels of different attributes (such as cost and travel time). Then respondents state their preferred behaviour, which in some circumstances can be confirmed with revealed behaviour. By using statistical techniques the researcher can then say that people's behaviour depends on certain attributes and build up a model of behaviour (called a utility function). According to the Gartrells' list of features, this method is influenced by positivism because the presentation of the travel alternatives in terms of attributes that can later be used in a utility function represents the linking of concepts in lawlike statements (such as 'behaviour depends on a combination of cost and travel time'). Furthermore, the attributes are chosen to allow empirical measurement and correlation is made using statistical techniques.

Examples of naturalist methods in transport studies are harder to find. However, a list might include work by Sager (1994) which analyses the transport planning process, including planning for road pricing, in terms of the hidden concepts based on Habermas' communicative theory (1984). This involves taking some of the ideas from Habermas, for example, that communication is often distorted with ensuing problems. Sager looks for these distortions, including lack of comprehension and dishonesty, and argues that where they existed there were problems in implementing plans, and where they did not exist the plans were implemented smoothly. This can be described as naturalist because the ideas about comprehension and honesty are not manifest, in that to discover them in the data the analyst must read between the lines. Also, these concepts are normative, in that they can depend on value judgements to define what is comprehensible and honest. Furthermore, the concepts are difficult to measure and the analysis involves qualitative techniques.

When Each Method is Appropriate

For a simple research problem, such as choosing between travel alternatives, stated preference techniques might quite accurately reflect the factors that influence people's travel choices. There would be little need to turn to naturalist methods because there is no doubt that the factors that are used in the utility function are correct. Thus there would be no need to look beneath the surface for new concepts and connections that explain how people reach their decisions. Also, stated preference is appropriate for the type of problem that transport studies often have to answer, namely predicting changes in travel behaviour given changes in transport service levels. It can be argued that other models might more accurately represent how people change behaviour, but simple utility function models are better at forecasting. Talvitie (1997) argues that simple utility function models, as used in stated preference, do not accurately describe how people behave and there are more accurate models, some from psychology. Thus, Talvitie argues that positivist models could be replaced with better models that perhaps have been derived from naturalist techniques. However, Bell (1997) responds by saying that the best explanatory equation (used for making predictions) does not have to be the best theory of understanding. Thus if the research objective is prediction, the method does not have to have the most realistic model.

There are other research topics where the best theory of understanding is needed. In the area of decision-making, social science models should reflect as closely as possible what is legitimate in order to make decisions that are acceptable. If this is not the case, the decision-maker might suggest an option that is unacceptable. For example, Banister (1994) says that 'priority must be given to the principles and legitimation of change rather than confidence in the objectivity' of the analysis' (p. 222). This can be understood as meaning that transport planning needs some naturalist methods to define the principles.

An Appropriate Methodology for the Study of Acceptability

The main objective of the research is to learn how to improve the acceptability of urban road pricing. In Chapter 2 past road pricing schemes and proposals were analysed in terms of acceptability, to see if there was a technique to improve the acceptability of road pricing. Beyond the work of Sager and Langmyhr, which argues that plans need to be comprehensible and honest, there was no approach for implementing road pricing that could be found acceptable. If there had been a pre-existing theory, the most appropriate methodology to study acceptability might derive from the positivist tradition. This could involve using the information from past proposals to derive an hypothesis about what is acceptable, then testing this scenario in case studies in Britain. The contribution of the research would then be to test if the common knowledge about what makes an acceptable road pricing scheme was applicable in Britain. However, this is not possible because the literature review showed that there was no common view about what is acceptable from past experience. In fact there were numerous opinions about the best course of action for implementing road pricing. In terms of the link between different people's opinions and a sociological theory, it could be said that a theory of acceptability does not exist. It is not known what is acceptable to others.

Given this lack of knowledge, the appropriate method should come from the naturalist school. This is because naturalism would focus on how all the different views about acceptability can be understood under a common theoretical framework. If this was tried from a positivist method it would be difficult, given that a positivist approach would involve deriving a model and then testing it. This is problematic because the model would either come from the researcher's own or others' ideas about what is acceptable. Thus whether the model would be appropriate or not would be hit and miss. The naturalist methodology, on the other hand, would reflect on the different opinions about acceptability, the researcher's and others', go beneath the surface and derive what is shared between the opinions. This might or might not solve the problem about what is acceptable, but it does work towards the goal in a scientific manner.

Choosing the Method of Grounded Theorising

The main techniques in naturalist methods are described in this section and it is shown how they can help meet the conditions of the research project. The following distinction – between descriptive and interpretive techniques in the naturalist school – is the author's own classification.[1]

Descriptive Techniques

Both naturalist and positivist methods are extremely rigorous in their recommendations for describing phenomena that are being researched. They are aware that the researcher's own opinions can surreptitiously taint how data are recorded, and the researcher's presence at interviews and social settings can influence the phenomena under investigation. In turn, these influences can affect the plausibility of the analysis. However, whereas positivist methods recommend a standardisation of research procedures, to normalise the influence of the researcher across data collection, traditional naturalist methods have recommended that researchers immerse themselves in each social setting to understand how a lay person thinks about the research topic, or becomes a fly-on-the-wall observer to minimise their influence (Hammersley and Atkinson, 1995, p. 16).

More contemporary naturalist researchers think such approaches are flawed because the methods assume that a researcher can remain neutral, and ignore the fact that all data collection involves theoretical presuppositions (ibid.). Therefore they recommend that the research should include a specification of how the researcher influences the data collection. To do this effectively the data collection should all be recorded (e.g., with tape recorders), so the influence of the researcher can be reviewed and is accessible for criticism.

One of these more contemporary approaches is ethnomethodology, which can be grouped with naturalist methods because it supposes that order in society is unstable (referring to order in social interaction) and has to be constantly created and recreated through shared meaning of participants. Specifically ethnomethodology is concerned with describing how people create order – such as enough order to carry out a conversation. However, instead of only focusing on the shared meanings of people who are being studied, ethnomethodologists put equal effort into studying the social researcher as well. Thus the researchers themselves become an area of inquiry. When this is done it can be seen how researchers create order in data collection through their own hidden sets of meanings, or theoretical assumptions (Benson and Hughes, 1983; more recently, Button, 1991).

In terms of a sociological study of the acceptability of urban road pricing, ethnomethodology and its recommendation to tape interviews and study the role of the interviewer as well as the interviewee is useful and will be followed up in the next section and Chapter 5. However, ethnomethodology is not a method that is entirely appropriate for this study because it is anti-theoretical and the research objective is to develop a proposition about acceptability. Ethnomethodology stays at the level of uncovering shared meanings and reflexivity; it does not then turn these findings into theoretical claims and generalisations, because to do so would involve analysing the motives of the researcher – and it is the interest of ethnomethodology to put the analysis of the researcher ahead of any wider research goal. Consequently, ethnomethodology also remains outside traditional sociology, which is usually concerned with theory and generalisations, and it would be wrong to say it could be used to develop a theory.

Interpretative Techniques

Within the naturalist school there is set of methods adjacent to ethnomethodology which take a larger leap in defining groups of concepts and hidden connections. These methods are still focused on reflexive influence of the researcher in imposing meanings on data, and still insist that the meanings should be illustrated by examples in the data. However, they are more easily reconciled with theoretical goals. Examples of these methods are symbolic interactionism (Blumer, 1969) and phenomenology (Schutz, 1972). In symbolic interactionism the assumption is that human beings act towards things on the basis of meanings and these meanings are created and modified with social interaction. Thus the role of the researcher is to uncover these meanings or symbols. The criticism of this approach is that its meanings and theoretical formulations can be quite vague as there are no controls over how the researcher can derive them. In phenomenology, the assumptions are the same as in symbolic interactionism, in that they believe that people create meanings through social interaction. However, phenomenology is more structured in its ideas about how the researcher can uncover these meanings. It argues that a person puts phenomena in a meaning context; this is called a first order typification. Then the researcher observes the initial subject and interprets their actions and puts them in another meaning context. This is a second order typification.

In terms of the topic of the acceptability of urban road pricing, these methods are interesting because they suggest how meanings are constructed, but they do not offer a method that can increase confidence that a theory which explains the meaning of acceptability can then help choose between practical design options. Thus the approach of phenomenology is kept in mind because it offers a reflexive method of deriving meanings. However, other techniques are needed to help keep the theory relevant to the practical problems.

Combinations of Descriptive and Interpretative Techniques

Some sociologists use combinations of descriptive and interpretative techniques to meet their own agendas. In doing so they suggest methods that can be used to study the social world and theories that explain aspects of the society. Examples are Gidden's structuration theory and Habermas' communicative theory.

In both cases the writers draw on ethnomethodology and phenomenology. This shows that they recommend reflexive observation and concentration on how meanings are created. For this reason they both fall into the naturalist school. In viewing the world this way Giddens (1984) develops a theory that social systems are structures that are created through social interaction and the researcher can uncover their structuring properties. Meanwhile Habermas (1984), also viewing social systems as created by social interaction, develops a theory that problems in social systems can be explained by distortions in the social interaction.

While this type of work can comment on the nature of acceptability at an abstract level, it is unlikely that it can suggest recommendations that are any less abstract. Although these theories can help to give an explanation for the acceptability of road pricing, the explanation would probably not offer a way of chosing between specific urban road pricing design options. For example, Forester (1989) analyses planning in terms of Habermas' communicative theory and has been criticised for leaving the practitioner no closer to overcoming problems (Useem, 1990, p. 565). The work of Sager (1994) and Langmyhr (1995, 1997) is open to the same criticism because they also try to apply Habermas' ideas.

Other qualitative sociologists, though, use some of the guidelines of ethnomethodology and phenomenology to develop theories that are not as abstract and are developed for an empirical area of inquiry, as opposed to the work of Giddens and Habermas, which can be considered more conceptual. The abstract theories have been called formal theories and the empirical theories have been termed substantive theories (Glaser and Strauss, 1967, p. 32).

If substantive theories are developed they stand a greater chance than formal theories to offer practical suggestions that can be used in the empirical area of study. For example Dunn and Swierczek (1977) study the theories about planned changes in organisations and conclude that substantive (also known as grounded theories) offer the most practical relevance:

> The most important cognitive resource available to applied behavioural scientists is theory itself, provided that theory has maximum informational value with respect to the problem domain of planned change. Here we have argued [in their article] that such informational value will be enhanced as we move further toward grounded theories of planned change, whose application promises to contribute to improvements in the degree to which findings are internally and externally valid, conceptually reflexive, and translatable among change agents, sponsors, and targets (ibid., p. 154).

In a more generic sense Turner (1981) talks about the practical benefits of grounded or substantive theories as promoting:

the development of theoretical accounts and explanations which conform closely to the situations being observed, so that the theory is likely to be intelligible to, and usable by, those in the situations studied, and is open to comment and correction by them (ibid., pp. 226–7).

These grounded theories still use the methodological techniques of naturalism that can promote reflexive description and interpretation, but they remain grounded in actual observations more than the formal theories do, to help suggest practical options. While formal theories can be abstract and lose touch with the situation under investigation from the perspective of a non-sociologist, grounded theories have a requirement not to be too abstract and not to become incomprehensible to a person wishing to make a practical decision. Although formal theories can be used to formulate practical guidelines, there is a greater possibility that grounded theories can be used to do so, and with respect to the study of acceptability of urban road pricing, grounded theorising comes the closest to achieving a theory that both explains acceptability and can offer practical guidelines.

Method of Research

The Method of Grounded Theorising

The development of a theory that can be described as grounded or substantive presupposes the method is based on the work of Glaser and Strauss (1967), who coined the phrase 'grounded theory' and developed guidelines to help sociologists generate these theories. In their seminal work they explain that they were concerned with the problem that many sociological theories at the time could not be verified because they used nominal concepts. Thus qualitative research could be seen as providing ideas that quantitative research could not refute. This position, they argued, was untenable and contributed to a split between quantitative and qualitative methods, with the result that the importance of the role of social theory was being lost. Quantitative and qualitative research schools could concentrate on describing the world using their own techniques, yet, they argued, it was debatable that the goal of sociology to understand the world was being met.

Glaser and Strauss argued that sociology needed theory to understand the world, however, and because sociology was a type of science the theories should be refutable. This is in direct opposition to quantitative techniques that concentrated on only finding statistical links and qualitative methods that were more concerned with description. Thus instead of arguing that sociology needed less theory, Glaser and Strauss argued that it actually needed more, as long as it could be tested. In this way they mediated between quantitative and qualitative methods, and set an agenda for sociologists to generate more theory.

They also describe in their seminal work (ibid.) how they think grounded theory can be generated. They do not offer a blueprint because to do so would be to constrain the creativity of the researcher to look for links in the world in an unbiased manner. However, they offer guidelines that cover data collection and analysis, so the researcher knows how much and what type of data to collect, what a theory looks like and how to gauge if it is plausible. In the case of data collection they introduce the idea of theoretical sampling and for the purpose of analysis they describe the method of constant comparisons.

Glaser and Strauss suggest that a grounded theory can use data from most sources in its development. For example, strict qualitative participant observation can be used as well as data from statistical surveys; similarly findings from structured interviews can prove as useful as those from open questions. In short, the development of a grounded theory should not exclude data *a priori* and the development of a plausible grounded theory will probably involve using data from more than one source. As analysis on data progresses, researchers will develop theoretical ideas and, to ensure that they are plausible, Glaser and Strauss recommend that researchers carry out more data collection to explore the viability of the original ideas. Thus there is a duality between the process of analysis and data collection that is not found in quantitative studies. This approach to data collection is called theoretical sampling.

The process of analysis is necessarily concerned with the development of a grounded theory. Glaser and Strauss describe how a grounded theory will be made of concepts that have indicators in the actual data and, importantly, these indicators will have dimensions that can be measured. In this way a theory can be tested and the relative importance of the factors gauged by quantitative techniques. To discover concepts – the building blocks of the theory – researchers need to categorise the data. They then need to look at another set of data and check if the same concepts are used. If they are found, the concepts gain in plausibility, but if the concepts are not found the researcher has to consider changing the method of categorisation, or perhaps adding in a new concept. After this process the researcher needs to look at a new set of data and then see if the same concepts are used. This process is called the method of constant comparative analysis.

The first grounded theories were developed by Glaser and Strauss (1967) within medical sociology. Since then the idea has been used in other substantive areas of research, such as divorce, home-building negotiations and domestic violence (Riley, 1996, p. 23), religious studies (Vela, 1996), social work (Holland and Kilpatrick, 1991) and management studies (Connell and Lowe, 1996, p. 226). In other disciplines the usefulness of the method of grounded theory has been considered, although specific grounded theories might not have been developed. An example of this is in tourism studies (Riley, 1996).

Locke (1996) describes how the method of grounded theorising has proved very influential with qualitative studies within management. She describes how 16 out of 19 qualitative studies that were published in a major journal in the last 20 years cited their method as being influenced by grounded theory. However, only nine out of these 16 explained how they used the idea of constant comparison, and only seven out of 16 used the idea of theoretical sampling (ibid., p. 243). Locke concludes two things from this observation: firstly, that people adapt grounded theory to fit their own research agendas; secondly, researchers show a tendency to cite grounded theorising to add legitimacy to their studies (ibid., p. 244). On the first point Locke thinks it is fair to adapt the method; however, in the second case, citing its authority undermines its value and the contribution it has made to social research.

Since the original work on grounded theory, the procedures in the method of grounded theorising have been adapted. Glaser and Strauss consider this appropriate because they do not wish 'to see an orthodoxy of approach imposed upon those using grounded theory' (Turner, 1981, p. 226). Glaser (1978, 1992) has added to the method, Strauss (1987) and Strauss and Corbin (1990) made alternative suggestions and Turner (1981) has also contributed. Others have shown how grounded theory techniques can contribute to an improved qualitative research in sociology, without advocating the development of grounded theory (Hammersley and Atkinson, 1995, p. 205).

Stern (1994) says that two methodological schools have developed within grounded theory, the Glaserian and the Straussian. The difference can be understood in terms of the background of the two researchers, Glaser having trained in quantitative methods and Strauss in qualitative methods (Locke, 1996, p. 239). Thus, the Glaserian method stresses that the researcher must let concepts emerge from the data by looking only at what is on the surface. Meanwhile the Straussian approach suggests ways the researcher can look beneath the surface descriptions and be more inventive in constructing concepts. Glaserians might criticise the other approach because it is forcing concepts (Connell and Lowe, 1996, p. 228), whereas the Straussians would defend their method by arguing it is within the tradition of qualitative research. The difference can also be understood in terms of the distinction between positivist-influenced and naturalist research methods. The Glaserian approach focuses on concepts that are manifest, while the Straussian approach looks under the surface for hidden connections.

In the case of the study of the acceptability of road pricing, the previous discussion has rejected the positivist-influenced methods. As a reminder, this is because the positivist methods would only show surface factors, not the underlying principles about what makes arguments acceptable. The naturalist methods, on the other, hand focus on uncovering underlying structures in action and interaction. In order to have an idea about what could improve the acceptability of road pricing, it is essential to understand the underlying principles. Therefore the school of grounded theorising that this research chose to follow is Straussian, of which the main text is Strauss and Corbin (1990).

This decision is justifiable as long as the use of the grounded theory method is understood in the wider context of the goals of naturalistic research. These are to make sure that data collection and analysis are done in a reflexive manner, taking care that it is apparent how the researcher influences the findings. Thus in the development of the specific method that this thesis adopts, the grounded theory ideas are explained and used alongside other qualitative research techniques.

How Grounded Theorising is Applied

Data collection and description As urban road pricing is an idea that has not yet been applied in Britain, it adds a new twist to data collection in the method of grounded theorising because people have no shared experience of it. Unlike some research topics, the researcher will not be able to make sense of some responses because they do not share the same idea as the respondent about the form road pricing might take. Therefore any data collection about acceptability involves establishing the type of road pricing scheme on which respondents are basing their opinions or arguments. Otherwise the context of the responses would be lost in the analysis.

Data from a range of sources can be used to develop a grounded theory. This might be new data, collected specifically for the research in interviews, or second-hand, from surveys and other research projects. But as the prime analysis technique involves comparing responses, it is advantageous to have batches of data that are based on similar conceptions of road pricing. It is less likely that enough secondary data could be collected which could be subdivided into meaningful groups that cover a full spread of design options for road pricing, than could be obtained through trying to collect new data. Therefore, in this project, data collection concentrated on collecting data in interviews, where respondents had to give their opinion about a range of road pricing scenarios. Secondary data was not completely excluded from the development of the grounded theory though and where it has been used, this is indicated. However, the bulk of the data comes from interviews. Specific details, such as case study selection, choice of respondents and interview design, are described in Chapter 4.

Data collection in grounded theory building is guided by the principles of theoretical sampling. However, to ensure that the study meets the goals of naturalistic research and is reflexive, these guidelines can be bolstered by other techniques such as ethnomethodology – Lester and Hadden (1980) argue that grounded theorising and ethnomethodology can be used together. Accordingly, the data collection process could be recorded to illustrate how the interviewee might have led the respondent. By looking at transcripts of the data a reader can then judge if the theoretical ideas are plausible. However, the influence of the researcher cannot be avoided, only specified. Hammersley and Atkinson (1995, p. 19) recommend that instead of trying to eliminate or standardise the influence of the researcher, any effect is used to the advantage of the research. By the researcher asking questions that vary between respondents and by behaving differently, the validity and robustness of the research findings can be established. In other words, Hammersley and Atkinson recommend that, because social order is unstable and in need of being constantly reconstructed by the respondents using shared meanings, behaving non-uniformly can provide a check that the shared meanings the research is uncovering are used in different situations.

> Once we abandon the idea that the social character of research can be standardised out or avoided by becoming a 'fly on the wall' or a 'full participant', the role of the researcher as active participant in the research process becomes clear. He or she is the research instrument par excellence. The fact that behaviour and attitudes are often not stable across contexts and that the researcher may influence the context becomes central to the analysis. Indeed, it can be exploited for all it is worth. Data should not be taken at face value, but treated as a field of inferences in which hypothetical patterns can be identified and their validity tested (ibid., p. 19).

Hammersley and Atkinson go on to say that one of the approaches where this technique has been used in part is grounded theorising. Therefore, augmenting grounded theorising with these ideas is compatible. Data collection in this thesis can be understood as testing developing ideas for a grounded theory during the interviews, as recommended by grounded theorising, yet doing this in a way that allows the influence of the interviewer to be seen in the analysis, as suggested by Hammersley and Atkinson. This does not make it close to an ethnomethodology study of reflexivity; rather, to assess the influence of the researcher it is necessary at times to look at the research from an ethnomethodology point of view. This is similar to the account of doing social research, occasionally looking at research problems from an ethnomethodology perspective, sketched out by Fox (1990, p. 21).

Analysis and interpretation Specific details about the method of analysis are described in Chapter 5. This subsection explains the philosophy behind the decisions by showing how the grounded theory idea of constant comparisons is combined with phenomenology. While interviews could collect data about acceptability, the analysis needed a framework in which acceptability could be analysed. The method of constant comparisons was not enough by itself because it does not offer a way of understanding how people make interpretations and subsequently how the researcher interprets what these people say. If the research is to be naturalistic these problems of reflexivity have to be addressed. The approach taken was to adapt ideas from phenomenology, underlying which is the principle that people interpret the world by putting it in a meaning context. This process is known as typification. The role of the sociologist is to undercover these meaning contexts. But in order to do this the sociologist also needs to put the world in a meaning context. This is another process of typification, called second order typification. The questions in the interview represent a phenomenon of the world that the respondent places in a meaning context. This process of typification will involve many concepts. By asking questions, the respondents verbalise how they establish meaning about acceptability. Then the analysis puts these responses in another meaning context, a second order typification. It was important in the analysis to understand that this is what the analysis was aiming at. In doing so, the emphasis was placed on making sure that the concepts reflected, as closely as possible, the first order processes of typification used by the respondent. The grounded theory ideas were then used on top of this phenomenological idea to help make sure the concepts were plausible.

Conclusion

This chapter has described how the method of studying the acceptability of road pricing is strongly influenced by grounded theorising. This involved describing the two main methodological camps in social science as positivist-influenced and naturalistic. It was argued that naturalistic studies were the most appropriate for the study of acceptability because they are reflexive and could focus on underlying principles of acceptability. Once the naturalistic methodology was chosen, the discussion showed how the method of grounded theorising was relevant to transport planning concerns. This is because it is a method suited to substantive areas of study and likely to produce a theory that has practical relevance. More specific methodological details, such as sample selection, interview design and theory construction, are given in Chapters 4 and 5.

Note

1   The distinction between descriptive and interpretative techniques in the naturalist school was chosen because it seemed a simple, if slightly crude, way of leading a lay person through a number of different methods that all draw on each other. While no method is entirely descriptive or interpretative – indeed some might argue all description is interpretation – it seemed that the methods did lie on one side or the other, depending on the extent to which they were prepared to make explanations.

Chapter 4

Data Collection:
Sampling and Interview Design

Introduction

In Chapter 1, Figure 1.1 illustrated a process of using sociological theory to mediate between practical design options and people's views about acceptability. In Chapter 2 it was shown that no theory existed that seemed to explain acceptability and so, in Chapter 3, a methodology to develop a theory was derived. This is based on the method of grounded theorising and involves comparing a range of responses about the acceptability of road pricing to develop a theory that is grounded both in people's actual opinions and in the topic of road pricing – preventing the theory from becoming too remote from the subject and enabling it to be used to suggest practical design options. Grounded theorising involves two inter-related processes called theoretical sampling and constant comparative analysis. The former refers to the data collection stage of the research and encourages the researcher to adapt the sample and the questions asked to test the robustness of the theoretical ideas as they emerge from the analysis. The latter guides the analysis by recommending that the researcher is always looking for exceptions to emerging theoretical ideas by constantly comparing them with other parts of the data set. By following these rules a plausible theory should be created.

Chapter 5 shows how the data collection stage of the research was derived from the above methodological guidelines. First though, in this chapter, the philosophy of sampling for grounded theorising is expanded on, and the case study and sample selection are described. Also, the interview protocol is shown, which enabled respondents to express their opinions on road pricing scenarios.

Sampling and Selecting

More Theoretical Sampling

Mason (1996) expands on the theoretical sampling ideas of Glaser and Strauss (1967) introduced in Chapter 3 (p. 42) by describing how qualitative research approaches sampling. She highlights three key questions that researchers must answer in order to select plausible samples: firstly, what is the wider universe or population from which a sample is needed; secondly, what are the relevant 'sampleable' units within the wider population; thirdly, what relationship should be established, or assumed to exist, between the sample and the wider population.

To answer the first question, and identify a section of the wider universe that the study will be interested in, it is necessary, according to Mason, to approach the topic from both an empirical viewpoint and a theoretical perspective. Empirical answers will help identify people, groups, policies and activities that are relevant to a research project. For example, if the project is concerned with transport policy in contemporary Europe, the wider universe is likely to include the population of Europe and European transport legislation since 1945 (example adapted from Mason, ibid., p. 84). Meanwhile, a theoretical perspective related to how a research project is going to try to interpret the social world will help narrow down which aspects of the empirical wider universe are relevant. Mason illustrates this point with an example of a study aimed at interpreting gender relations (ibid., p. 85). She argues that there is unlikely to be an empirical set of gender relations from which one can 'simply draw a smaller sample' and similarly gender relations are not going to be 'straightforwardly embodied, or personified by, women and men, in a way that would make it meaningful simply to draw a representative sample of people by gender'. However, researchers are able to use their theoretical ideas to help investigate how gender relations might be constructed. Therefore theoretical ideas such as 'discourse which construct subjects of gender relations' and 'structures of power between men and women' can help define the wider universe by identifying aspects of the empirical population that are most relevant to the study.

The answer to the second question, on choice of 'sampleable' units that are relevant to the study flows out of the approach to the first question: the units will be dependent upon the theoretical aspects of the empirical universe. In many studies the chosen units will be discrete people who have certain characteristics such as age, gender, ethnicity, race and income level, where these characteristics have a theoretical purpose for the research project. Other studies might use documents or video images as discrete units. However, according to Mason, in qualitative research it is often experiences that are not exclusive to one person which is more interesting, and basing classifications on discrete people or documentation might not be appropriate. In the gender study example above, experiences of power relations, if that is the theoretical perspective of the study, are likely to be more apt units than discrete social characteristics. But in choosing the units, be they social characteristics or experiences, there is a danger that these concepts become the variables that dictate the results of the study *a priori*. Therefore the research must also show that the choice of units will not bias the findings. Once the units are decided, one also needs to put them in temporal, spatial and organisational settings. For example, the units (particularly if they are based on experience) may alter at different times, in different settings and vary within organisational structures.

In answering the third question about establishing the relationship between the sample and the wider population, Mason identifies four relationships used in social research. The first is 'representative' and is based on choosing a sample that has a spread of units similar to the wider population. If this is done, generalisations between the sample and wider population can be made because the make-up is similar. This type of sampling is also known as statistical sampling and is the least used in qualitative research because it does not support naturalist research methods, which often involve defining new units as the study progresses. The second relationship is *ad hoc* or 'unspecifiable' and involves no logical pattern to the sample collection, which proceeds in a random manner. According the Mason, this is often perceived as the alternative to representative sampling but is not to be followed because it fails to define the relationship between sample and wider population. The third relationship provides a 'meticulous view of particular units' and would be used where one wants to describe a social process in a specific context. For example, in a study about social interaction between people on buses, relevant units would be different experiences of social interaction and one of these experiences, such as aggressive behaviour might be examined in depth. The fourth relationship links the sample to the wider population by encapsulating a 'relevant range' of units known to exist in the wider population; however, it does not try to be statistically representative. For example, in the bus study illustration, all the types of social interaction, from physical assistance of fellow passengers to talk about the weather, might be examined. However, just because the assistance of elderly passengers might be a more common occurrence than aggression does not mean that more instances of assistance should be sampled. The third and fourth relationships are widely used in qualitative research methods.

In grounded theorising, too, both the third and fourth relationships are used. Any theory is concerned with the operation of social processes (Craib, 1992, p. 22) and as such theory construction must involve inspecting how social processes work, invoking the third relationship. These social processes can be researched by looking at one or more units in detail. Grounded theorising also makes use of the fourth relationship by seeking a relevant range of units to add a new perspective to the theoretical ideas. In other words, while the third relationship aids the detailing of a social process, the fourth relationship helps make the theoretical ideas more robust by looking at similar instances of that social process.

The choice of sample for theory construction, Mason (1996) says, is intertwined with the process of analysis, concurring with Glaser and Strauss (1967), and cannot be decided upon before the outset of research. Thus there is no predefined rule to calculate a sample size. The usual approach in grounded theorising is to stop collecting more data when 'theoretical saturation' occurs. This means that when the analysis, which involves comparing different cases, is turning up nothing new that is not already explained by the theory, the data collection may stop. At this stage the theory may be said to be plausible, although it is still possible, and desirable, to test its robustness in subsequent studies.

Applying the Sampling Guidelines to the Study of Acceptability

From the above discussion, the first step to deciding on a sample is to identify the aspect of a wider population in which this thesis on the acceptability of urban road pricing is interested. Empirically, acceptability issues will be exhibited by people and organisations that are in some way affected by road pricing, but also in transport policies and in studies on road pricing. However, this wide empirical universe can be narrowed down by defining the theoretical perspective of the thesis. This, as described in Chapter 1, is to develop a sociological theory that can explain differing opinions about the acceptability of road pricing and that can be used to decide on a universally acceptable strategy to implementing road pricing with respect to the sample. This theoretical purpose implies that within the wider empirical universe of people, policies and studies, it is the opinions and arguments, for and against road pricing, that should be the central aspect of the study.

The 'sampleable' units are derivable from the aspects of the wider universe that the study is interested in and can be based on characteristics of discrete people or documents or on some type of experience. In this study, the appropriate unit is not the opinion of an individual person or policy document, however; it is the argument for or against acceptability, which can be shared amongst several people. Therefore the 'sampleable' units should be understood as the arguments about road pricing, and not as opinions from individual people.

By selecting arguments as units, the criticism that the sample will bias the theory is avoided. This is because the theory aims to explain different opinions about road pricing and basing the sample on these opinions cannot be understood as affecting the outcome. However, if the sample had been based on types of people then there would be more chance that some types of arguments might have been missed and the finding might consequently be skewed.

Arguments will vary across time, in different locations and in different organisations. Therefore, the relevant set of units (arguments) will take this into account. Spatial variations have been reflected in the study by the choice of case studies, and organisational variations by picking organisations that were likely to have different concerns and hence arguments about road pricing. Meanwhile temporal variations will affect arguments in two ways: firstly, acceptability might depend on the time of operation of the scheme; secondly, acceptability might change over time. In the first case the interview, described later in this chapter, includes options that alter the time of operation. However, the second case is more problematic due to the fact that the study is conducted over a relatively short space of time. By checking that arguments that are recorded in the sample are similar to others recorded in the previous studies, as outlined in Chapter 2, the possibility that temporal variations might lead to the omission of some arguments can be minimised.

After deciding on the 'sampleable' units the relationship between the sample and the wider universe of arguments about road pricing has to be established. When developing a theory the research is not concerned with ensuring that the sample of arguments is quantitatively representative of the number of arguments given by a random sample of people. This is because the study objective is to develop a theory that explains all arguments and having a statistically representative sample of arguments does not aid this goal. Therefore the first 'representative' relationship is rejected as inappropriate. At a later stage, once a theory is developed and needs testing, it is more appropriate to look for a statistical spread of the concepts of the theory in a random sample; however, that is a different type of study.

The second *ad hoc* relationship between sample and universe is rejected *a priori*. The third and fourth relationships do fit the study aims, though, to provide a 'meticulous view of particular units' and to make sure that all 'relevant units' are covered. In developing a theory it is important that the theory describes the social process involved in respondents presenting their arguments. If the grounded theory is not a valid interpretation then it cannot be used to then suggest a theoretically acceptable road pricing policy. Therefore by providing a 'meticulous view of particular units' it will be seen in detail how acceptability arguments are constructed. The fourth relationship is used to ensure that a full range of units – i.e. arguments – is analysed. Thus the sample can be extended to include an argument that might not have been covered. The full range of arguments cannot be determined in advance of data collection and will alter as new arguments and approaches to road pricing are uncovered.

Case studies: Cambridge and Edinburgh

Deciding on the Case Studies

The need to introduce spatial variation into the data collection to increase the chance that more arguments about road pricing would be uncovered suggested that more than one case study should be investigated. Furthermore, to ensure that the case studies were relevant to urban road pricing policy, they should be cities or towns where road pricing could realistically be introduced.

These sampling guidelines, of course, do not help narrow down the choices very much. Therefore other criteria were used, based on other goals of the research project. It was thought that if distinct options for improving the acceptance could be suggested, then a further stage could be to model the effect of road pricing schemes based on these options. As it was not known if the suggestions to be derived would be specific to the cities in which the interviews were conducted, the choice of case studies was influenced by the need to have a model available. In the end, the suggestions, to be described in subsequent chapters, are not specific to the case studies and no modelling of road pricing scenarios was conducted.

At the start of the research project a number of towns in Britain had computer models that could predict the impacts of road pricing. Avon County Council was undertaking the Avon Traffic Restraint Study, which involved testing road pricing scenarios in Bristol. Cambridgeshire County Council had considered some form of urban road pricing and several investigations had been conducted. Lothian Regional Council had tested a limited range of road pricing options in the Joint Authorities Transportation and Environmental Study. Meanwhile, in London a strategic model had been developed, along with a detailed network model of West Inner London and a model called MEPLAN to assess economic impacts. Other cities in the UK had considered versions of road pricing and had models available that could be adapted to test the policy, for example, Leeds and York. However, the research wanted to avoid commitment to using models that had not yet been adapted to test road pricing. Also case studies that had already tested several scenarios could be advantageous if some of the scenarios overlapped with the acceptable options.

In London the models were considered too complicated for their use to be learnt in a short space of time, should the need arise. Therefore this option was ruled out. Meanwhile in Bristol, the County Council was uncomfortable with the idea of someone else approaching interest groups and overlapping with their own study that was being done at the same time. Therefore this was also ruled out as an option for interviews, leaving only Cambridge and Edinburgh – where there were no objections.

Cambridge

Cambridge is a free-standing city in southeast England, approximately 100 km north of London. It is bounded by the M11 motorway to the west and the A14 trunk road to the north, covers about 40km^2 and in 1996 the population estimate was 109,000. The economy is prosperous and diverse: there are many computer manufacturers located in the business park to north of the city, there is the university and the city centre is a major tourist attraction. Between 1980 and 1990 traffic grew by 47 per cent and was set to grow a further 40 per cent by 2000.

There is two-tier local government in Cambridge comprising the City Council and Cambridgeshire County Council. It is the latter that has responsibility for long-term transport policy, is able to bid for money from central government for transport projects and can raise taxation locally via community charges. Consequently, it is the County Council that explored the idea of road pricing as a way of controlling demand for car travel, improving access and funding public transport improvements.

A plan was floated in 1990 for time-based congestion charging, known as congestion metering. An on-board meter would use a combination of speed and distance travelled to calculate how long a vehicle had been in congestion, and charge the driver accordingly. For example, if a driver's average speed fell below a threshold, about 10kmph, a charge would be levied. The interest of the scheme is that it mirrors the marginal social cost of driving better than other charging structures. However, there will be times where delay might not be caused by congestion. The technology for congestion metering was successfully demonstrated in 1993 (Clark et al., 1994).

At about the same time, modelling work on the impact of road pricing was conducted. Although the exact proposal of congestion metering could not be modelled, a similar scenario was, along with other variations of road pricing. Smith et al. (1994) assessed road pricing in Cambridge using network models. They compared the effects of cordon charging, distance pricing, time-based pricing and delay-based charging, which is the closest to congestion metering. While all the models met the objective of reducing traffic, delay based charging achieved the best effects at the lowest charges. Smith et al. ranked the options, according to effectiveness as: delay-based, time-based, distance-based followed by cordon pricing. The boundaries that were used in these models were those that were adopted in the options shown to the respondents (described later).

No form of road pricing was pursued in Cambridge though because it was considered unpopular and a political risk. Ison (1996) describes the Cambridge proposals from an acceptability perspective. In particular, he mentions the complicated operation of congestion metering, in comparison to cordon pricing, as being instrumental in its rejection.

Edinburgh

The city of Edinburgh is located in southeast Scotland, covers an area of 262km^2 and has a population of about 410,000. The densest settlements are within the A720 ring road, although the administrative district of the city stretches further south. The M8 motorway from Glasgow, the A90 trunk road from the Forth Road Bridge and the A1 coming from the south all meet the ring road, which does not fully encompass the city because the Firth of Forth bounds the city to the north. Edinburgh, like Cambridge, is prosperous and is home to a diverse set of industries: government, tourism, further education and manufacturing. Between 1990–2010 its traffic growth was predicted to be 31.3 per cent.

Until 1996 there was two-tier local government in Edinburgh, which was administered by Edinburgh District Council and Lothian Regional Council. The latter had responsibility for long-term transport policy, similar to Cambridgeshire County Council. In 1996 local government reorganisation saw the City of Edinburgh Council established to take on unitary control for Edinburgh, so now there is only one tier of local government. This was the situation when the interviews were conducted. In 1999 a Scottish parliament was established in Edinburgh, which changed the political map once again, as it takes over certain powers from central government.

However, it was the original Regional Council that first developed road pricing plans for Edinburgh in the Joint Authorities Transportation and Environmental Study, conducted by The MVA Consultancy (1991). Many transport scenarios were tested, including several involving cordon pricing options. These road pricing strategies performed favourably in comparison to scenarios without road pricing, which prompted work into the potential for road pricing in Edinburgh. However, this work only got to an 'inception' stage, in 1993, and a full project was never pursued. Thus in Edinburgh the proposals that were given serious consideration only used cordons.

Edinburgh contrasts with Cambridge because it did not explore more complex road pricing options and did not bring the issue to greater public attention by conducting field trials of the technology, but it did look at road pricing in the context of an integrated transport strategy. However, numerous press reports have brought road pricing to the attention of the public, so it is not a completely unheard-of option.

Samples within the Case Studies

The objective from the case studies was to get a full range of opinions about road pricing. The samples, as described earlier, are best understood as comprising these arguments opposed to the people that give the arguments in the data collection. It is also important to remember that the sample of arguments is not intended to be representative in a statistical sense. The number of different types of argument in a sample is not related to the actual amount of different types of argument that would be recorded from a random sample of individuals. Instead, the aim of sampling is to provide data that can be analysed to show how an acceptability argument is constructed and to provide a range of acceptability arguments to make the theory development more robust. The fact that the arguments might not be representative of the views of the general public makes no difference to the theoretical aim of the thesis; it is important to get an example of each argument.

Nevertheless, in order to record and discover arguments, it is necessary to interview individuals and people that represent organisations, even though these people are not the sample *per se*. Also, a full sample of arguments cannot be predetermined and needs to be discovered as the interviews progress. Thus ideas about who to obtain new arguments from can be developed as the interviews progress – a snowball effect of asking interviewees who might offer a different view.

Urban road pricing has the potential to affect many aspects of people's lives because all drivers in a city might be subject to paying the charge and both drivers and non-drivers could be recipients of benefits from road pricing, whether indirectly from traffic reduction or directly as a result of projects funded by revenue. Consequently, the empirical population, to choose the sample of arguments from, is quite large. In the research it was decided to interview interest groups which represent the views of major groups of people likely to be affected by road pricing. Further interviews were conducted with individuals unaffiliated with interest groups as well, in order to check that their arguments were congruent with the arguments from interest groups and to provide an opportunity for other arguments and opinions to emerge. To a large extent the sample of arguments was predicted in advance, simply because previous research had already identified groups that would be affected in different ways by road pricing. While the research process involved seeing if these people would suggest others who might have different opinions, it was found that most arguments had already been given by the groups identified in advance.

By mode of transport, motorists, public transport users, cyclists and pedestrians were considered the prominent groups to be affected by road pricing. Although motorists would be the only group to pay, the others might receive benefits such as improved travel times and a more pleasant environment because of less traffic, and investment in public transport and environmental enhancements. Due to these benefits, these groups might offer different arguments about road pricing and so interest groups that represented these users were interviewed. In the case of individuals that were interviewed they all drove, but also used other modes. This possibly better reflected the fact that few people travel exclusively by a single mode and overcame a weakness of only interviewing interest groups, who tended to look at the problem from a single mode perspective. By trip purpose, commuting, shopping, recreation, tourism and at-work trips were considered the main trips that people make that would be affected by road pricing. While few interest groups would exclusively represent the needs of people making these trips, the categories do overlap with the briefs of many groups. For example, no group represents the interests of people making at work trips exclusively, but business and freight lobby groups would cover them. Meanwhile, individuals were selected to have experience of all the trip purposes and not be tied to describing urban road pricing from a single perspective. Finally, a selection of special interests was also included. These included the interests of environmental groups, disabled people and civil liberty organisations. In the event no civil liberties organisation agreed to be interviewed, but as other interviewees had raised civil liberty arguments it was not considered a serious gap in data collection.

In a small number of interviews more than two participants were questioned at the same time. This arose when interest groups presented more than one representative or when couples of individuals were interviewed. In all cases the joint interviewees did not give the same opinions and the presence of other people stimulated more debate. In a couple of cases more than one interest group member agreed to be interviewed, but on separate occasions. In one case, an interest group wished to participate by giving written answers, which was accepted.

In Edinburgh, 20 interest group members were interviewed, some from the same organisation. In Cambridge, 15 interest group members were interviewed, again some from the same organisation. In four of these interviews there were joint participants. In Edinburgh, addresses of interest groups were obtained from a list provided by the local authority and via the Voluntary Organisation Directory and the Directory of British Associations. In Cambridge, addresses were obtained from the above directories and from an Internet site of local groups. In both case studies, interviews covered groups representing the interests of small and medium-sized businesses, road haulage, bus and rail operators, taxi drivers, civic trusts, environmentalists, disabled people, cyclists and motorcyclists.

In both case studies the groups were approached by way of a letter explaining that a research project was being undertaken on road pricing and asking if one of their members would be willing to be interviewed. It was stressed that their chosen respondent need not know anything about road pricing and it was not expected that their organisation would have an established policy towards it. A promise of confidentiality was also made. Included in the letter was a stamped addressed envelope and a form on which a member's name and the best method of contact could be written. The option of not participating was also given on the returnable form.

In Edinburgh 10 individuals were interviewed. These people were met through an acquaintance and at a pre-general election conference on transport policy. In Cambridge a further 15 individuals were interviewed, met through acquaintances. The method of selecting the individuals to interview was based on the 'snowball' effect described at the start of this section. While interest groups are easy to identify in advance and are likely to want to put their case forward, individuals are more reticent to participate in an interview on a specialised topic. Therefore it was a case of asking people to suggest who would be willing to answer the questions and put forward a different view. In four cases, participants were interviewed in couples.

The interviews in Edinburgh were conducted between November 1996 and March 1997. The interviews in Cambridge were conducted between May and August 1997. As mentioned, the sample should exhibit a range of opinions about road pricing and also a full spread of arguments. Table 4.2 shows the number of respondents in favour, unsure and against road pricing. Table 6.2 in Chapter 6 shows the spread of arguments for and against road pricing that were used in each case study city. Combined with the range of interest groups interviewed, these tables indicate that the sample reflects a full range of arguments. Also, these tables not only provide information about the types of respondents and their responses, but also allow the researcher and reader to assess if the theory construction is influenced by the preponderance of a particular class of argument.

Table 4.1   Acceptance of the general idea of urban road pricing (in number of respondents)

Group	Acceptable	Unsure	Unacceptable
Edinburgh (interest groups)	11	3	6
Edinburgh (general public)	5	1	4
Cambridge (interest groups)	7	3	5
Cambridge (general public)	9	4	2

It is recognised that the views of interest groups and individuals might exclude political concerns that are of primary importance to institutions such as central government, local government or large businesses. Consequently, a complete range of arguments regarding road pricing might not be obtained without exploring institutional perspectives. For example, these types of institutions might have particular constraints or a history of approaching pricing questions in certain ways that will influence the type of road pricing scheme that they could find acceptable.

In order to explore alternative perspectives on road pricing, which might not be used by interest groups and members of the public, there is a research need to uncover the approach of institutions. However, Strauss and Corbin (1990, p. 174) suggest that a grounded theory is developed in one situational context first and is then extended to wider types of situations at a later stage, such as during further testing to enhance theoretical plausibility. Thus a grounded theory can first be developed at the level of interest groups and individuals, and then applied to institutions, to see if it still has relevance or to explore how it can be adapted. The research project has not investigated institutional arguments regarding road pricing, preferring to leave this to further research. The omission of a study of institutions can also be justified because the methodological approach is largely experimental; to a large degree it is being seen if it is possible to develop a grounded theory of acceptability and to do this only arguments in one situation have to be recorded. In addition, the views of institutions towards road pricing were under development at the time of the research and it would have been difficult to obtain information. To a certain degree, the postscript to this book addresses some of the institutional arguments that are now emerging.

Interview Design

Objectives of the Interviews

The interview must present the respondents with a description of road pricing on which to base their opinions, and must involve asking questions, to get respondents to verbalise their opinions. This is because the methodological approach, shown in Figure 1.1 in Chapter 1, involves getting opinions about road pricing options, developing a theory about what is universally acceptable within the sample, then using this theory to decide between the options that the respondents formed their opinions about.

The presentation of road pricing was kept as similar between respondents as possible – allowing for the fact that some features would be different in the two case studies – and was done in two sections. In the first section a typical urban road pricing scheme was shown, based on an inner cordon covering the city centre. In the second section, a series of design choices about the type of charging system, area and time of charge, and who to charge were given. Although the presentation could have been changed, if the developing grounded theory needed to focus on one particular option, it was found that the respondents clearly understood the logic of the way road pricing was presented and were prepared to discuss all aspects of the design – and as no aspect was being ignored by respondents it was not necessary to change the presentation.

As design options for road pricing were presented the respondents were asked about their acceptance. For the typical road pricing scheme they were asked if they would find the scheme acceptable and what the advantages and disadvantages were. If the respondents had focused, perhaps, on the advantages in their opinions about acceptability, it might only be necessary to add a question about the disadvantages – showing that the questioning can be adapted. Similarly, in later interviews, once all the reasons for finding road pricing acceptable or unacceptable had emerged, it was possible to ask more specific questions to see how the respondents reacted to statements that might contradict their opinion. In this first section the respondents were also asked how they thought the revenue from road pricing could be used.

In the second section of the interview the respondents were asked to choose the most acceptable design option among the choices or to suggest an alternative. Then they were asked to explain why their choice was the most acceptable. Again, it was possible to challenge the respondent's choice to see how they defended it.

Section One: Typical Urban Road Pricing Scheme

Figure 4.1 shows the typical urban road pricing scheme that was shown to the respondents. The decision to present this style of scheme was made after an informal meeting with two local authorities – left unnamed on purpose – where they thought the most useful typical road pricing scheme to examine would be an inner cordon scheme because it was likely to be the most feasible to introduce as a trial, and therefore the opinions of that style of scheme would be most useful. While it would be quite feasible to introduce other schemes, it was decided to stick with the informal local authority opinion, for the reasons given and because it was a simple scheme that could be easily explained and could be used to build in more complex design options in the second section of the interview.

The decision to break down the description of the typical scheme into seven dimensions (type of charging structure, area, time, amount, who pays, how the charge is levied and how the revenue is used) was derived from Jones (1995) and Sheldon et al. (1993), who describe key elements of scheme design in terms of the above dimensions. Describing the typical scheme in this way had the added advantage of establishing a pattern of description that could be added to in the second section of the interview by giving more options.

Type
Cordon Road Pricing Scheme
(vehicles are charged when they cross cordons)

Area
One inner cordon encircling the city centre. See map overleaf.

When
Drivers are charged when they cross the cordon in an inbound direction
between 8 a.m. and 6 p.m. on weekdays.

How much
Drivers are charged £1.50 per crossing.

Who pays
Emergency vehicles and scheduled buses will have exemption. Everyone else
will pay.

How
All vehicles will be installed with a meter. Drivers can buy credits before or
after making their journey.

The revenue the scheme will raise will be invested in public transport
improvements.

Figure 4.1   A typical urban road pricing proposal

The typical charging basis (type) was chosen as cordon because it is
considered practical yet different enough from, say, a simple area licence
scheme to require some new type of technology. Therefore it seemed a
suggestion that could be seen as controversial, yet also one that could not be
discarded as completely impossible to implement. The area the scheme covered
was the city centre, for reasons described above, and again because it seemed
a practical first step to implementation, rather than having cordons throughout
the entire city that would require more detection equipment to be installed.
On the reverse of the laminated sheet on which the scheme description was
presented, a map showing the cordon boundary was shown. Figures 4.2 and
4.3 show the cordon boundaries for Edinburgh and Cambridge.

The scheme was described as operating all day, between 0800 hrs and 1800
hrs on weekdays because it is simple to understand. Other options included
charging at peak hours, around the clock (24 hrs per day) and over weekends.

Figure 4.2   Position of inner cordon in Edinburgh

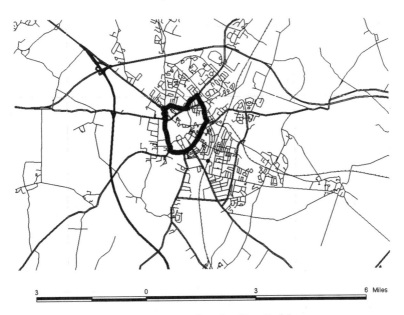

Figure 4.3   Position of inner cordon in Cambridge

Under this section it was also explained that drivers would be expected to pay when they drove into the city, but not when crossing the cordon in the other direction. The charge level was set at £1.50 per crossing because this amount had been covered in tests of road pricing previously undertaken in Edinburgh (The MVA Consultancy, 1991) and London (The MVA Consultancy, 1995) and was not the lowest figure, and yet was far from the highest.

Under the section about who pays, it is possible to enter many options. However, simplicity was considered paramount and exemptions were only given to emergency vehicles and scheduled buses – emergency vehicles because they are often regarded as deserving exemption and scheduled buses because it seemed contradictory to suggest that revenue could be spent on public transport, only to take some of it away by charging. Then the operating technology was described as based on a meter system.

This implies that vehicles would have electronic meters installed in their cars and credits would be deducted from accounts when they passed through the cordon. Finally, a short statement at the end suggesting that the revenue could be spent on public transport improvements. While the revenue can be used in many ways, spending on public transport is considered popular.

Once the respondents looked at the scheme a number of questions were asked to elicit the respondents' opinions. These questions were adapted in each interview and throughout the course of the whole interview process. Initially the general questions asked were:

1   Would you find the typical road pricing scheme acceptable? Give your reasons;
2   An urban road pricing scheme would raise considerable revenue. How would you recommend it was spent?;
3   If road pricing was spent this way would urban road pricing be more acceptable to you?;
4   Do you think urban road pricing should be used to reduce congestion in Edinburgh/Cambridge? What are better ways of doing this?;
5   How do you think transport and environmental improvements should be financed?

The most important question in terms of the goal of the research is the first one, which allowed the respondents to verbalise what they thought about the acceptability of the typical urban road pricing scheme. The respondents were allowed free rein to develop their arguments about why they found the idea acceptable, unacceptable or could not decide. The role of the interviewer was to encourage the respondent to talk. In the first interviews, this encouragement would be cagey and involve asking the respondents to clarify certain points and getting them to talk about disadvantages if they happened to have concentrated on the advantages, or vice versa. In the later interviews, it was possible to challenge the respondents' opinions with arguments that other people had used.

The next most important question was about how the revenue should be spent. By the time the respondents had given their opinions about the typical idea of road pricing they were eager to consider how the revenue should be spent, which indicated that it was a productive combination of questions. Also, nowhere else in the interview was the question about how the revenue was to be spent directly considered. The role of the interviewer was primarily to get the respondent to explain the reasons why revenue should be spent on the options that they favoured and different respondents needed varying amounts of encouragement.

The third question was asked because Jones (1991) finds that acceptability of road pricing increases if the revenue is spent how the respondent would like. This question aimed to see how far spending the revenue could overcome problems that the respondents identified in the first question. However, it was soon discovered that respondents did not want to take back the points they had made, yet they could also not find a solution to the suggestion that spending revenue how they wanted would not increase acceptability. Because of these reasons this question was dropped as it disrupted the flow of talk in the interview without encouraging the interviewee to add anything new. This decision occurred after 20 interviews had been conducted.

The fourth and fifth questions were aimed at getting the respondent to specify transport policy objectives for which road pricing should be used – namely reducing congestion or providing finance – and asking the respondent if they preferred other policy measures to achieve these objectives. In the interviews it became clear that the interviewees did not feel comfortable discussing which other measures might be more acceptable. This is probably because it was an extremely broad question and after being quizzed about the acceptability of road pricing the respondents did not also wish to reflect on the acceptability of other measures in the same level of detail. Therefore after 40 interviews had been conducted, the question about alternative policy measures was dropped. Meanwhile, the parts of the questions about policy objectives for road pricing were proving partially useful in the ongoing analysis. This is because the analysis was pointing to acceptable objectives for which to use road pricing and it was useful to see how the respondents reacted to specific options.

Thus questions 4 and 5 were altered and changed into one new question that reflected the way the previous respondents had been comfortable discussing road pricing and that gave extra information about objectives for which to use road pricing:

> Which broad policy option for using urban road pricing would you favour?
> a) As part of a carrot and stick policy:
>   – to restrain traffic and to provide revenue to improve the transport system;
>   – this would involve a charge of about £2–3 to cross the cordon.
> b) As part of a carrot policy:
>   – to provide revenue to improve the transport system;
>   – this would involve a charge of less than £1 to cross the cordon.

As it transpired this question did not encourage the respondents to add new arguments, but it did serve as a way of summarising their opinions.

Section 2: Design Options

After the respondents had commented on the typical road pricing scheme they were given the opportunity to adapt the typical scheme to a form they would find more acceptable. This involved making decisions about each of the aspects of scheme design and as the respondents progressed through the choices the interviewer encouraged them to explain why they found their chosen option more acceptable. As in the first section, in the first interviews the interviewer merely listened and reminded the interviewee to give reasons. However, in the later interviews it was possible to challenge the respondent's reasons with those that had emerged in the previous interviews.

Type Figure 4.4 shows the first set of options that the respondents had to decide between, regarding the type of charging structure.

The only option of charging for road pricing that was not included was area licensing, where drivers are required to show a permit to be in an area at a specified time, because it was thought that the simplest form of cordon charging, with paper permits to display in windscreens to be able to cross into a restricted area, was very similar. If the respondents had indicated that they preferred an area licence scheme in the discussions then it would have been added to the list of options. However, this need did not arise.

Type

Time-based congestion pricing
Drivers are charged for the length of time they spend in congestion in a restricted area.

Time-based pricing
Drivers are charged according to how much time their journey takes.

Distance pricing
Drivers are charged according to how far they travel within a restricted area.

Cordon pricing
Drivers are charged only when they cross cordons.

Figure 4.4   Choices for a charging basis for road pricing

After they picked a charging basis for road pricing they turned to different sections in the interview, which worded the other options in a way suited to the charging basis they chose. However, all the respondents were asked a similar set of questions.

Area The area options are shown in Figures 4.5 and 4.6, which also illustrate how the wording and intent of the questions differ to suit the charging basis. Associated with these options were maps which illustrated the boundaries that were being suggested. For Edinburgh the boundaries are shown in Figure 4.7 and for Cambridge in Figure 4.8.

| In city centre | See map |
| Throughout the whole city | See map |

Figure 4.5   Area options for congestion time-based, time-based and distance pricing

Inner and outer cordons with screenlines	See map
Inner and outer cordons	See map
Outer cordon only	See map
Inner cordon only	See map

Figure 4.6   Area options for cordon road pricing

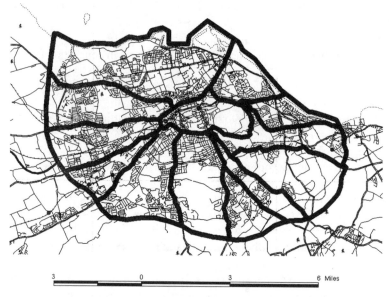

Figure 4.7   Position of inner and outer cordons and cordon screenlines in Edinburgh

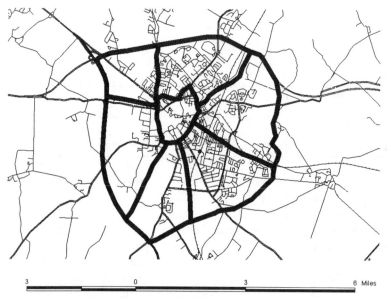

Figure 4.8   Position of inner and outer cordons and cordon screenlines in Cambridge

* Reproduced by kind permission of Ordnance Survey © Crown Copyright NC/03/10696.

When The options for when to charge cover the range of choices and are shown in Figure 4.9. Respondents that chose cordon pricing were also asked the direction of travel in which the charge should be levied, shown in Figure 4.10.

Hours
Morning peak (8 a.m. to 10 a.m.)
Morning and evening peaks (8–10 a.m. and 4–6 p.m.)
All day (8 a.m. to 6 p.m.)

Days
Working weekdays (Monday–Friday)
Working weekdays and Saturdays
Everyday

Figure 4.9   Options for time of charging for all charging bases

---

Crossing the cordon in an inbound direction only
Crossing the cordon in either inbound or outbound directions

Figure 4.10   Additional question asked to respondents who chose cordon pricing

Who Different groups can be charged at different rates and some groups can even be given exemption. In the next set of options the respondents were asked to indicate which groups they thought should pay the full price, which groups should be eligible for a discount or exemption and if any should pay more. To help them they were shown a grid (Figure 4.11) which divides road users into groups, on which they could make a decision. The same grid was shown to all respondents, independent of which charge basis was preferred.

Level of charge The respondents were also asked how much would be an acceptable charge and to help with their decision brief information was included about the effects, approximated from the Edinburgh Council study into road pricing (The MVA Consultancy, 1991) and Smith et al. (1994), who modelled road pricing scenarios in Cambridge. As the respondents had chosen different scheme designs at this stage, it must be stressed that the impacts are very approximate and new work is being done all the time that alters the predictions. Also the respondents had chosen different areas, so they were told to expect the changes only within their preferred boundary. Figures 4.12,

	Pay	Discount	Exempt	Pay more
Emergency vehicles				
Utility vehicles (e.g. gas)				
Scheduled buses				
Coaches				
Taxis				
Light goods vehicles				
Heavy goods vehicles				
Motorcycles				
Drivers living within area				
Drivers living on the boundary				
All drivers resident in the city				
Visitors/tourists				
Disabled drivers				
Other				

Figure 4.11   Grid to help respondents decide on charge privileges

4.13 and 4.14 show how the presentation of the charge level options altered according to which charging basis the respondents had chosen earlier in the interview.

With charging for the length of time the charge will vary day to day. Which price range would you prefer to implement for a 5 mile journey in the morning peak?

50 pence–£1
(Not much traffic restrained. Minor improvements in accessibility and environment.)

£1–£3
(10% reduction in traffic in charged area Noticeable improvements in accessibility and environment.)

£2–£4
(25% reduction of traffic in charged area. Very noticeable improvement in accessibility and environment.)

Figure 4.12   Options about charge level presented to respondents who chose time-based charging bases

> *What do you think the charge to make a 5 mile journey should be?*
>
> *£1*
> (Not much traffic restrained. Minor improvements in accessibility and environment.)
>
> *£2*
> (10% reduction in traffic. Noticeable improvements in accessibility and environment.)
>
> *£3*
> (25% reduction in traffic. Very noticeable improvement in accessibility and environment.)

Figure 4.13   Options about charge level presented to respondents who chose distance pricing

> *What do you think the total cost should be to cross the cordon/cordons to reach the city centre?*
>
> *£1*
> (Not much traffic restrained. Minor improvements in accessibility and environment.)
>
> *£2*
> (10% reduction in traffic in charged area. Noticeable improvements in accessibility and environment.)
>
> *£3*
> (25% reduction in traffic in charged area. Very noticeable improvement in accessibility and environment.)

Figure 4.14   Options about charge level presented to respondents who chose cordon pricing

The respondents who chose cordon or distance pricing were also asked if the charge should be altered throughout the course of the day. This question was not asked of respondents who chose congestion time-based or time-based pricing because it was thought that these respondents would realise that time-based options would alter throughout the course of the day if there was more congestion. This question is shown in Figure 4.15.

> If this fee was levied all day would you prefer a differential pricing structure? This means that drivers who travel in the peak hours pay more than drivers who travel in-between the peaks.

Figure 4.15   Option for differential pricing by time

Operating technology   The final design option covered the operating technology and the respondents were asked to chose between low technology paper-based options and high technology electronic operation. The choices are shown in Figure 4.16.

> Low technology (with vehicles having to display paper badges in their windscreens)
>
> High technology (with vehicles being issued with electronic boxes to enable detection by road-side beacons)

Figure 4.16   Options for operating technology

While the time-based and distance pricing options would be infeasible without electronic operation, it was still thought useful to present all respondents with the options in case they wished to go back on their initial choice of charging basis.

Conclusion

This chapter can be understood as bringing together the methodological strands that have been described in previous chapters in order to establish the book's practical research method. The theoretical sampling ideas were expanded by describing how a qualitative research sample aims to provide a meticulous view of a particular unit and cover a range of relevant units. In the study of acceptability, the units of interest are the arguments for and against road pricing – therefore the sample and interview itself sought to provide a meticulous view of these arguments. Of course, opinions will vary across time, space and organisation; thus the sample also needed to cover a range of different arguments.

Case studies were selected to provide opportunities for the construction of arguments to be meticulously inspected. While the guidelines on sampling pointed to conducting more than one case study for comparative purposes, and picking case studies where road pricing is a relevant policy option, this did not narrow down the choice enough. Therefore the availability of transport models, which could be used to test road pricing scenarios, became the deciding factor. Accordingly Cambridge and Edinburgh were chosen as the case studies.

On the choice of interviewees, the guidelines on sampling were more applicable. In order to provide a meticulous view of arguments, participants were sought who were prepared to discuss road pricing in detail. Interest group members whose interests overlapped with transport were a productive source of help as was the network of individuals that was built up through a 'snowball' effect. To ensure that a relevant range of opinions was recorded, a selection of interest groups representing the main modes of transport and the main trip purposes that would be affected by road pricing was approached. In the case of the individuals, they were asked to recommend an acquaintance who might present a different argument.

Finally in this chapter, the interview protocol was described. This aims to provide the interviewee with a full selection of road pricing options on which to form opinions and to encourage the respondents to verbalise these opinions. Thus the analysis can establish which options are likely to be more acceptable from a theory about how acceptable opinions are constructed. In the first section of the interview a simple inner-cordon road pricing scheme was presented. Respondents were then free to talk about the advantages and disadvantages of this proposal and the general idea of road pricing. They were also asked to specify how they would recommend revenue was spent and give reasons. In the second section of the interview, once respondents had established their principles and philosophy towards road pricing, they were shown a series of options in order to design a road pricing scheme that they thought was more acceptable than the one presented in the first section. This involved deciding on the charging basis (cordon, distance, time-based or congestion time-based), charged area or position of cordons, time of operation, whom to charge, charge level and operating technology. As in Section 1 of the interview, the respondents had to give reasons for their opinions to provide data from which to derive how acceptable arguments are constructed. These data are illustrated and analysed in the next chapter.

Chapter 5

Description of a Grounded Theory and the Open Coding Stage of the Analysis

Introduction

Chapters 5 and 6 describe how the grounded theory of the acceptability of urban road pricing was derived through the method of constant comparisons. By way of background, the process of analysis is outlined, building on the description of grounded theorising found in Chapter 3. Then in the subsequent sections the first stage of the analysis, called open coding, develops the basic concepts in the grounded theory. However, after this coding the concepts are only at a preliminary stage of development and further adaptation needs to be done in order that they can link together to form a theory. This linking is called axial coding and is described in Chapter 6.

Review of the Method of Grounded Theorising

The Different Parts of a Grounded Theory

Grounded theorising methodology (as expounded by Strauss and Corbin, 1990) uses a paradigm model to help practitioners visualise what a theory looks like and what it is trying to achieve. This is shown in Figure 5.1. The causal conditions represent the input that respondents think about and act upon. In this research this input was the hypothetical proposal for an urban road pricing scheme that the respondents discussed. The phenomenon is the key concept that the theory wishes to explain. In this case it is 'acceptability'. Then the context is the set of concepts that explain the key concept. As will be mentioned these are ideas about utilitarianism, fairness and sincerity.

In a grounded theory there is a strict hierarchy between the concepts, and this is mentioned now to avoid confusion later on. As the word 'concept' means 'idea' and theorising is full of ideas, grounded theorising adopts different terminology. The key concept, in this case 'acceptability', is known as the core category. Then the concepts that explain the core category and place it in some type of context are known simply as categories, in this case utilitarianism, fairness and sincerity. Then the concepts that explain the categories are known as subcategories, and these are introduced in Chapter 6. This hierarchy is shown in Figure 5.2.

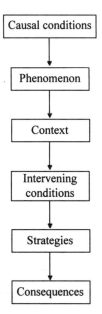

Figure 5.1   Paradigm model of grounded theorising

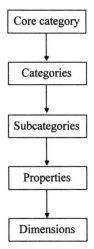

Figure 5.2   Hierarchy of concepts in grounded theorising

It is also possible to have subcategories of the subcategories but, as one of the purposes of a theory is to be concise, this is rare. It is important that all the categories have indicators that allow for measurement and observation. This is reflected by the use of properties and dimensions, also shown in Figure 5.2. While the core category, categories and subcategories can have a generalised meaning, it is important for the properties to be directly related to aspects of the phenomenon that is being observed. This is what keeps the theory grounded.

Returning to Figure 5.1, the second half of the figure (intervening conditions, strategies and consequences) is used to add plausibility to the theory. First, intervening conditions are used to alter the causal conditions. This is important because an effective theory must not only be able to explain a 'snapshot' of a phenomenon, but must be flexible enough to explain the phenomenon in other circumstances. This was achieved by having two sections to each interview: a general section and a specific section, where respondents had to answer more detailed questions. If the categories are to be useful they must be able to explain both the general reactions to road pricing, in the first section of the interview, and the detailed arguments that are found in the second section of the interviews.

Secondly, the strategies refer to how the categories are linked together to form arguments. If the theory merely describes the concepts that are used in conversations about road pricing it does not explain the full process; a theory must not only have concepts, but must show how the concepts link together in real conversations. For example, in a conversation about road pricing a respondent might talk about acceptability, the fairness of charging for road space and the sincerity of the planners in wanting to use a road pricing policy. While the first half of the paradigm model identifies the concepts of acceptability, fairness and sincerity it does not show how they link together in real conversations; this is done in the identification of strategies. Thus strategies are a reflection of real arguments in terms of the concepts of the grounded theory. The difficulty and skill of grounded theorising is to discover concepts that are found in all the real arguments and to discover strategies that reflect the real arguments.

Thirdly, consequences, at the end of Figure 5.1, are there to make sure that the theory also explains the consequences of any strategies. Certain strategies are likely to affect the phenomenon and possible patterns might emerge. In the case of this research, consequences show which strategies increase the acceptability of urban road pricing. These patterns meet the objectives of the research to improve the acceptability of urban road pricing. On one level the grounded theory is complete without a full investigation of consequences. Therefore, in this research consequences are explored after Chapter 6.

The Coding Stages in Developing a Grounded Theory

The process of developing a complete grounded theory can be broken down into three stages: open, axial and selective coding. Open coding is the process of breaking down, examining, comparing, conceptualising and categorising data and 'through this process one's own and others' assumptions about phenomena are questioned or explored, leading to new discoveries' (Strauss and Corbin, 1990, pp. 61–2). In other words, this stage is about proposing the categories and assigning properties and dimensions. At this stage there is no need to link the categories together. This is done in axial coding, which is:

> A set of procedures whereby data are put back together in new ways after open coding, by making connections between categories. This is done by utilising a coding paradigm involving conditions, context, action/interactional strategies and consequences (ibid., p. 96).

After axial coding the process of developing the theory is nearly complete. All that needs to be done is selective coding: 'The process of selecting the core-category, systematically relating it to other categories, validating those relationships, and filling in categories that need further refinement' (ibid., p. 116).

These stages are not separate and overlap with each other considerably. For example, while open coding may uncover several options for categorising the data, not all of the options will work for axial coding and be able to link together to form strategies. Therefore during axial coding there may be a need to revert to open coding. Similarly, during selective coding, problems may emerge with the way the categories have been linked together, and this creates the need to revert to axial coding. This research adopts the tripartite division of open, axial and selective coding to describe the process of analysis.

Open Coding: Deriving Ideas for the Concepts

What is Acceptability?

Before even looking at data from interviews, the first step in the analysis involved thinking about the meaning of acceptability and the type of categories acceptability might have. The starting point was the dictionary definition (taken from the *Shorter Oxford Dictionary*, 1993).

Acceptability	(c.1630–69)	The quality of being acceptable.
Acceptable	(c.1630–69)	Worth accepting; likely to be accepted; pleasing; welcome; tolerable.
Accept	1 (c.1350–1469)	Take or receive with consenting mind; receive with favour or approval.
	2 (c.1350–1469)	Receive as adequate or valid; admit; believe; tolerate; submit to.
	3 (c.1500–29)	Undertake (an office), take upon oneself as a responsibility.
	4 (c.1630–69)	Acknowledge the receipt of and agree to pay (a bill or draft).
	5 (c.1900–29)	Of an inanimate object: physically receive or accommodate, absorb (another object, energy, data, etc.).

In the first recorded uses in the English language the verb 'accept' has two meanings. Firstly, it is used to refer to a range of feelings about receiving something, from favour to toleration. Secondly, it is used to refer to whether something is received as valid or true. A little later on, a third meaning comes into useand comes to mean 'to undertake a responsibility'. As time progressed the term was used less to refer to something that is pleasing and more along the lines of something tolerated, seen as valid or undertaken. This development has been aided by the use of the verb in commercial terminology. Here 'accept' means to acknowledge and agree to pay. This subsumes definitions 2 and 3 above. At the same time the noun 'acceptability' came into use. The latest development in the verb sees it refer to a scientific mechanism. This esoteric definition was considered of no relevance to this study.

From these semantic explorations three concepts of acceptability emerged. Firstly it is an opinion or preference. Secondly, it is whether something is valid or true. Thirdly, it is a responsibility or involvement. These concepts were then tailored to suit the requirements of planning. To do this a framework of what planning involves was needed. As there are many different models and theories of how the planning process operates care was needed at this point. Luckily, as there have been many disagreements and competing theories on the planning process, a number of models have emerged that take this diversity into account. Multi-rationality planning is an apt metaphor (Langmyhr, 1995) and an approach of this nature is found in Forester (1989). He divides models of planning into five types, each of which has a different rationality. This covers the breadth of views:

1 comprehensive unbounded rationality (seeing people as rational actors);
2 cognitive bounded rationality (seeing people as fallible actors);
3 socially differentiated rationality (seeing people as actors with different views);
4 pluralist rationality (seeing people as actors in competing interest groups);
5 structurally distorted/political economic rationality (seeing people as actors in political economic structures of inequality).

This idea is similar to ideas found in rational and incremental planning (Lindblom, 1959; Simon, 1967, pp. 196–206). Forester argues that, at the stage of implementing a plan, the planner should be operating under the rationale that he or she is in a structurally distorted and political economic environment. In other words the planner can no longer afford to assume that the lower level models, such as comprehensive and cognitive rationality models, are valid. Forester goes on to mention the dangers that occur if planners do not realise this. They range from worsening conditions to perpetuating inequalities.

As no model exists to reflect the diversity of rationality on the highest level, Forester argues that the response of the planner must be communicative. The planner must interact with the rest of the world. For simplicity, the rest of the world for planners can be divided into individuals, organisations and the political economic structure. For Forester this interaction should be comprehensible, sincere, legitimate and true. Forester also believes that the most successful communication is two way, so, as well as giving opinions, Forester wants to see participation.

How These Ideas Led to Concepts of Acceptability

The overlaps between the dictionary definition of acceptability and Forester's planning argument are plain. Acceptability, as developed above, refers to opinion, validity and responsibility. Planning for implementation for Forester involves these, but also the caveats of comprehensibility, sincerity and legitimacy. Thus a logical starting point to developing concepts for acceptability as used in transport planning was a combination of the two sets of ideas.

The concept of legitimacy was broadened somewhat to be interpreted as meaning fairness. This makes sense as the law and legal institutions are supposed to safeguard justice and fair play. Also, the idea of responsibility was merged with participation because both imply taking part. So possible concepts of acceptability in planning are opinion, validity, participation, comprehensibility, sincerity and fairness. These concepts should apply to the individual, the organisation and the political economic structure. The next step was to take these ideas for concepts and use them as a starting point for open coding on actual data. As an aid, summaries of the concepts are given below, along with examples of relevance to arguments about road pricing.

Opinion Politicians, organisations and individuals are likely to oppose and support a radical alternative such as road pricing. The reasons for their positive or negative opinions may fall into one of the other concepts.

Sincerity Some people are opposed to the idea of road pricing because they consider some methods of charging an invasion of privacy, creating potential for abuse by the state. Other people are afraid the politicians will not redistribute the revenue from the road pricing scheme in a way that compensates losers. These people think the government will see the revenue as a source of general taxation to use according to their own political agenda.

Validity Whether a road pricing scheme will meet its objectives is often challenged. It is also argued that there will be diversions causing a loss of trade and a rerouting of traffic onto less suitable roads, which merges into fairness issues if the ability of other areas or groups of people to meet their objectives is affected.

Comprehension Both the reasons for implementing urban road pricing and the operation of the actual scheme need to be clear and simple. This creates less risk of confusion and involuntary violations.

Fairness In the general discussion about the objectives of road pricing in Chapter 2 the problem of equity came up several times. Although there may be an overall gain in utility, some groups may lose.

Participation If people do not participate in the planning process, wrong decisions can be made and the scheme may not be acceptable when put into practice. One obvious result would be people not obeying the rules of the scheme and so not participating properly. A large number of violations could ruin the credibility of the scheme and hamper its progress in meeting the objectives.

Grounding the Concepts

In order for the above ideas to form categories in the grounded theory they needed to be assigned properties and dimensions. Properties keep the categories (which can be quite abstract) linked in with the real data, and dimensions show how the properties can be gauged. The process by which this was done is shown below. It must be remembered that the point of showing this is to illustrate the development of the theory and some of the connections that were made did in fact prove to be wrong or unworkable once more data was collected. The reader is following the path of the researcher, and sometimes this led to dead ends! The most notable category in which this happened was for 'comprehension'.

Two earlier ideas for categories – participation and opinion – are omitted because no data could support their use without overlapping with other categories, and the order of the presentation of the remaining categories has been changed to reflect a level of importance that was emerging. Also, the examples of the properties and dimensions that are shown do not cover a full range of arguments about road pricing because at this stage of the data collection and analysis procedures, not all the interviews and analysis had been conducted.

Comprehension Road pricing is a large and complex issue, but it was noted that respondents focused on specific features of the proposal or tried to consider the general idea behind the proposal. This phenomenon prompted the first property of the comprehension category to be called 'typification', i.e., the respondents typify what they are interested in.

At the same time the respondents seemed to assign characteristics to the part of the proposal they were focusing on. These characteristics were essentially the effect that they believed the scheme would have. The characteristics they chose to assign to the scheme seemed to reflect the proposal's policy objectives, what the respondent saw as the problems facing transport in the case study city and their own values. However, there was not enough evidence from the transcripts to call policy objectives, perceived problems and values properties of the comprehension category. So the second property of the comprehension category was simply called 'meaning context'. This phrase seemed to cover the range of characteristics.

Category: Comprehension

Properties: Typification   *Dimensions*: Specific scheme details
               The general idea

               Meaning context   Congestion
                                                            Economy – business
                                                            Economy – shopping
                                                            Public transport
                                                            Practicability

Typification and meaning context are concepts that were borrowed from phenomenological sociology and their relevance to the analysis stage is described in Chapter 3. In the final version of the grounded theory this complex way of looking at comprehension was sidelined. It is included here to illustrate that respondents have different ways of thinking about road pricing and in the development of the grounded theory these needed to be addressed.

For this comprehension category the dimensions did not have different levels, rather a selection of options. This is because what people think about these proposals' characteristics is reflected in the subsequent categories.

Validity The category of validity was used to refer to the respondents' decisions about whether the scheme (or the aspect of the scheme the respondent had typified) would be a successful approach to achieving a chosen characteristic (selected from the meaning context above), or if the approach was considered to be flawed.

Thus the properties of the category were the advantages and disadvantages of that proposal. These were closely related to the dimensions of the meaning context. Also, because respondents have different views, the dimensions of the properties of validity reflect this by showing different levels of agreement.

Category: Validity

Properties: Too complex   *Dimensions*: Agree/disagree
               Too expensive an investment
               City centre trade damaged
               Congestion alleviated/rerouted
               Public transport more efficient

As more data was collected there was much refining of the arguments that form the properties. The above are very rough and ready, taken directly from the data, and are only included to illustrate the line of thought that the process of analysis took. In terms of a retrospective of the process that was used, the way the concept of validity was being used was showing problems with the concept of comprehension. For example, under 'meaning context' the dimensions were related to transport policy objectives and were not measurable; yet under 'validity' the properties were related to transport policy objectives and the dimensions became measurable. This indicates that the process of analysis was getting confused and diverting from the rules of grounded theorising (in terms of the strict hierarchy between categories, properties and dimensions). Of course, the process of analysis had a learning curve and it was not taken for granted that the method of grounded theorising was infallible.

Sincerity The category sincerity refers to whether the person believed the intentions of the plan. This appeared to be very important to those people opposed to the proposal. As in the validity category the dimensions of the properties are reasons for or against the proposal. Thus:

Category: Sincerity

Properties: Another tax   *Dimensions*: Agree/disagree
            Does not believe money will
            be ring-fenced

Fairness This category referred to whether or not the respondent thought the scheme was fair. Thus the properties were of the same style as found under validity and sincerity, i.e. reasons for or against the scheme, and they refer to groups of people who might be unduly affected by the scheme. As the analysis progressed this rather simplistic treatment of fairness was changed considerably; while fairness was evidently important to arguments about road pricing it is a complicated concept that needed careful handling to encapsulate the different ways it can be used.

Category: Fairness

Properties: Not fair to pay for   *Dimensions*: Agree/disagree
            something that was free
            Disadvantage traders
            Unfair to people living
            inside cordon

Acceptability Even though acceptability was the main concept in the research, the process of open coding still had to check that acceptability could be used as a category by making sure it had properties and dimensions. Then a decision had to be made about whether the other categories could explain this category. Because the property was called 'opinion', which was very general it was felt that the other categories could be used to explain the meaning of this 'opinion'.

Category: Acceptability

Properties: Opinion   *Dimensions*: Acceptable

                                                 Not acceptable

                                                 Acceptable with conditions

Checking Ideas for Categories with Discourse Analysis

Notation used in Transcripts

Once ideas for the categories emerged they needed to be checked against data. The technique that was used is called discourse analysis. This involves looking for indication of the grounded theory in actual excerpts of taped data. Thus the tapes of the interviews had to be transcribed and then checked to see if the transcripts could be interpreted in terms of the categories of the grounded theory. The purpose of using tape recordings is fully described in Chapter 3.

When making transcripts for discourse analysis, a decision has to be made about how closely the transcript should reflect the actual recording of the discussion. For example, the transcripts can indicate overlapping speech, intonations, pauses and even gestures. If they are not included the rhythm of the conversation will be open to different interpretations and this could alter the meanings. Garfinkel and Sacks did experiments that showed how these subtleties of speech are very important in establishing meaning.[1] However, if every stutter and movement is transcribed there is a danger that the transcript might be too detailed.

Balancing the need to reflect the contextual meaning and the time constraints of the research, a decision was made not to use the entire transcription notation. The ones that were omitted were to do with sound reproduction and indicate words whose pronunciation might be elongated. It was felt that to apply such detail to every word was not necessary in this research, where the emphasis was on the actual arguments, not the social structure of conversation. However, stresses on words and overlaps in speech have been included. This helps confirm the main points of argument and how the other person in a conversation might have influenced the speech by interrupting. Also, to help the reader follow the pace of the conversation, times of gaps are given. The convention has been taken from Sharrock and Anderson (1986):

⌈   A single bracket indicates the point at which   A   Do you
⌊   one utterance is overlapped by another.   ⌈ agree
                                                                 B   ⌊ yeah

=   The equal signs indicate no interval between   A   Do you
      the end of one piece of talk and the start of   ⌈ agree=
      a next. This convention is used as between   B   ⌊ yeah
      one speaker's talk and another's and as   A   =with me
      between parts of a same speaker's talk.

(0.0)   Numbers in parentheses indicate elapsed   B   I'm (0.5) not
       time, measured in seconds to the nearest   sure.
       tenth of a second.

(.)   The dot in parenthesis indicates a very brief   B   I'm (0.5) not (.)
      silence, say, 1/10 second or less.   sure.

?   The question mark is not used as a   A   Do you agree
      grammatical marker but to indicate   with me.
      intonation. So, for example, a question may   B   I'm not (.) sure?
      be transcribed with a comma or a period
      while question-marks may be used for
      utterances that are not questions.

( )   Single parentheses indicate that transcribers   A   I'm going to
      are not sure about the words contained   (go)
      therein. Empty parentheses indicate that   B   Oh I need ( )
      nothing could be made of the sounds.

(( ))   The double parentheses surround   B   Can you stay
       descriptions of the talk, such as 'clipped',   and help
       or stand in place of an attempt to transcribe   A   If I must
       some utterance, such as 'laughs'.   ((clipped))
                                                                   B   You'll enjoy it
                                                                    ((laugh))

Analysing the Transcripts

The following three examples show how initial ideas for the grounded theory described above were read into transcripts of the data. These three excerpts are also shown in the next chapter (pp. 117–20) when they are interpreted using the completed grounded theory. The interested reader is able to see how the preliminary ideas differ from the final idea.

Example 5.1

IV   Are you saying that every car is going to have to have a meter in it? But
M   In that proposal yes
IV   In that proposal well (0.5) certainly with that one we'd argue with
     ⌈but
M   ⌊O.K
IV   but that's a huge investment and someone has got to pay for that hmm. Our line on road pricing would be that its an interesting idea which has many pros and some cons and that we would very much like to see a detailed road pricing experiment we'd be very interested to see what happens to the ones happening down south we'd like to see one in Scotland and Edinburgh seems like a good case but because it is only an experiment and it must be something that doesn't involve a huge amount of capital to set up and a meter in each vehicle certainly seems like a problem in that case. But the idea of a cordon (0.2) something like the map that's shown here (0.2) err (0.2) these timings (0.2) this idea of a single central zone I think we'd be quite happy with as the basis for an experiment.
M   What do you think some of the pros and some of the cons would actually be?
IV   Well the cons really are just the complexity of it and (0.2) the cons that the public will see other than simply having to pay for something they didn't pay for before are that certainly the traders will say that they are going to be suffering economic disadvantage particularly if there is a price as high as one pound fifty to go into the city centre. They say whether its right or wrong that their trade will suffer because people won't come into the city centre they will go to the out of town shopping centres ...

This paragraph refers to the first five lines in Example 5.1. IV (the respondent) focuses on an aspect of the proposal, the fact each car has a meter to enable the charge to be levied. This is the typification. Then IV states his disapproval of such a method of toll collection. This refers to acceptability. IV goes on to say the reason – because it is a large investment that someone has got to pay for it. Thus IV assigns the characteristic of investment to the meter aspect of the scheme – in other words he sets the meaning context – and then

IV gives the problem he sees which is that someone has got to pay for it – a reason that falls into the fairness category.

In the second part of Example 5.1, IV goes on to say that road pricing is an interesting idea and he would like to see a detailed road pricing experiment. Here IV focuses on the general idea, as he sees it – this is the typification. Then he states his view – acceptable with the condition it is an experiment. Then M (the interviewer) has to prompt for the reasons. In the final section of IV's dialogue he mentions three problems – complexity, paying for something that was free and traders suffering economic disadvantage. So the meaning contexts have been set as practicality, cost and trade. He then gives an opinion on each of these that fall into the validity and fairness categories. In the subsequent part of the interview, which is not shown, IV discusses the advantages of the proposal and clarifies his position further.

Example 5.2

M   Ermm. Would you find such a scheme acceptable?

III   Well, obviously I'll be a bit selfish here I'd find anything acceptable that controlled the use of cars in city centres.

M   OK

III   But being realistic and I've I've listened to some of the arguments in you know various (0.5) areas. I mean no where do you mention how you cater for people that actually live there. You know ((softly)). Are they going to be disadvantaged that they have to live inside who live there and maybe commute the opposite way.

M   Yeah

III   Are you going to disadvantage these. They're not really contributing to congestion because there's nothing opposite at all. Are you going to let these have a resident's (0.25)
⌈whatever

M   ⌊hmm hmm

III   resident's permit or whatever I don't know

M   Yeah

III   The other drawback is that erm and what I've heard said is that is if these screens are set up it really is national situation

M   ⌈hmm hmm

III   ⌊one of the arguments they'll put up is that everyone will go and shop at Falkirk or Stirling or Glasgow. Certainly in some other towns generally Manchester or Yorkshire they're even more attractive because there are a lot of towns close by and they all tend to (0.25)

M   Yeah

III   The other thing is and I maybe going off at a tangent here is that the (0.2) the (0.2) one of the points that people raise is that if they can then reinvest the revenue from that into public transport maybe train whatever one or the other. But that's a Catch 22. If you're successful in banning cars you're going to reduce your revenue.

Example 5.2 begins with M (the interviewer) prompting with a question. Then in the next two lines III (the contributor) does several things. He states his position – acceptability. He says what aspect of the scheme he is interested in, the general idea, indicated by the word 'anything' – typification. He assigns the characteristic that interests him, the control of cars – meaning context. He also gives the reason as being selfish. To understand this, though, one needs to know that the respondent is from a public transport interest group, but it can be subsumed under the category validity (i.e., he agrees that traffic should be restrained in the city centre). It is also important to note that III is being slightly sardonic here: however, the storyline still holds.

III goes on to give a more realistic opinion. Between lines 5 and 8 he focuses on people living within the cordon – typification. He assigns the characteristic of commuting to these people – his meaning context. Then he says he thinks they may be disadvantaged because they do not contribute to congestion – fairness. Then III makes a suggestion of a resident's permit. In a later question, not shown in the example, M follows this up and discovers that III assigns the characteristic of practicality and sees a problem in the validity category. Back in the example, III goes on to focus on the general idea, of setting up cordons/screens – typification. He assigns the characteristic of maintaining retail trade – meaning context – and then poses a validity problem. In the final part of III's dialogue he assigns the characteristics of revenue and reducing car traffic. Then he sees a problem that reducing car traffic will reduce the revenue – validity.

Example 5.3

II   Err, I don't think frankly that the determination to spend the money all on public transport would come about. I I just don't believe it. Err, its suggested something like £200,000 a day would be gained as a take in Edinburgh.

This third example has been included to show the category of sincerity. The interviewee II focuses on the revenue – typification. Then he assigns the characteristic of investing revenue in public transport – meaning context. Then he says that he does not believe the will is there – sincerity.

Conclusion

Comparison of the ideas for concepts shown in this chapter, and those that were finally used, presented in the following chapter, shows that they are very different. However, this preliminary stage of the analysis is needed to get to a more coherent set of theoretical concepts and to demonstrate why certain options were ruled out in favour of the final selection. This chapter also serves to introduce the practical analysis that was done, thus building on the theoretical and philosophical aspects of grounded theorising that were described in Chapter 3.

Note

1   Garfinkel (1984, pp. 47–9) reports how he asked his students to act like boarders in their homes. The students reported how their family members 'vigorously sought to make the strange actions intelligible and to restore the situation to normal appearance'. The lectures of Sacks (1964–72), collected in Jefferson (1992), illustrated how there are many taken-for-granted rules of speech. If a speaker diverts from these rules then meaning and the conversation often breakdown.

Chapter 6

Axial Coding in the Development of the Grounded Theory of the Acceptability of Urban Road Pricing

Introduction

In the previous chapter some problems with the categories were noted; namely in the use of the comprehension category and with the simplicity of the fairness category. While there was evidence for their use in the early transcripts, as more data was collected it became evident that they would have to be changed. In this chapter the final decision that was made about the choice of concepts is described. These concepts are illustrated with excerpts from the taped interviews and the next analytical stage of axial coding is described, which involves showing how the concepts are linked together to reflect actual arguments about road pricing that the respondents use. These links are called strategies and are illustrated with more examples from the interview data. The chapter concludes with reference to selective coding, which primarily in this study involves discovering when a specific use of a strategy is found acceptable amongst all respondents. These patterns can then help meet the thesis research objective of deciding between road pricing options on the basis of a theory about what people find acceptable.

Deciding on the Concepts

Layering the Concepts

The final selection of concepts was based on the grounded theorising hierarchy of concepts (shown in Figure 5.2) and the theoretical requirement that concepts should be layered 'like the skins on onions'. If a concept is too general it can be broken down further, and if the concepts are still too general they can be disaggregated even more. It was realised that the analysis described in Chapter 5 had been too constrained, and to fully explain the arguments more use of the potential of layering concepts needed to be made. Only two layers of categories had been used (the core category and the categories). It was necessary to add another layer of categories (so there would be a core category, categories and subcategories). Once this conceptual change had been grasped the grounded theory fell into place, because this extra layer of categories allowed the analysis to reflect precisely all the arguments.

An overview of the final concepts that were used in the grounded theory of acceptability is shown in Figure 6.1. The categories and subcategories have been portrayed as overlapping sets to illustrate that when the respondents consider whether a road pricing option is acceptable the strategy can involve a combination of arguments. Later on this notation was useful because it let the analyst imagine how the concepts could be used together to form strategies that reflect real arguments.

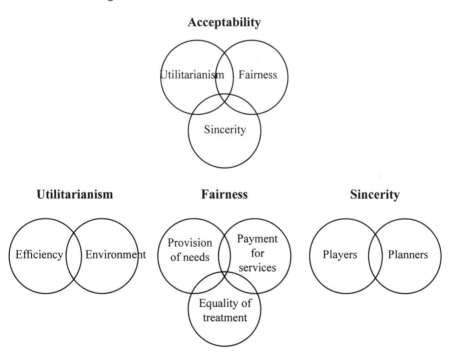

Figure 6.1   The concepts of the grounded theory of acceptability

Utilitarianism 'The doctrine that actions are right if they are useful or for the benefit of a majority; spec. in Philos., the doctrine that the greatest good of the greatest number should be the guiding principle of conduct' (*Shorter Oxford Dictionary*, 1988). This was chosen because most respondents seemed to use arguments that weighed the ability of road pricing to meet a broad set of transport policy objectives, rather than specify an exact transport policy objective and then consider the appropriateness of road pricing. This combination of assessing the utility of a road pricing scheme and aggregating the effect over a wide area suited the concept of utilitarianism. The other advantages of utilitarianism are that it neatly opposes the category of fairness, which assesses the utility of road pricing for an individual or group (i.e., in a disaggregated way), and that it alludes to the link between policy acceptance and political system.

The category of utilitarianism was divided into two subcategories: efficiency and environmental concerns. These subcategories do overlap each other, but all the strategies that were identified as utilitarian can be classified as belonging to efficiency, environmental or the combined efficiency and environmental subcategories.

Fairness The problem of 'fairness' being too generic was overcome by assigning subcategories that cover its different uses. Fairness is concerned with whether the needs of an individual, or group, are being met; if an individual or group is paying a proper amount for a service; and if there is equality of treatment. Thus the subcategories are provision of needs, payment for services and equality of treatment.

While philosophical works on fairness might be able to claim a more logically rigorous definition of fairness, the concern of the research was to find a workable definition that allowed classification of the collected data. The chosen subcategories do this, possibly because it is unlikely that the respondents would be using a more sophisticated meaning of fairness. The decision to use this category and these subcategories can be further justified by the research of Willman (1982), who adopted a similar practical classification to investigate fairness in wage agreements between trade unions and employers. He argued that fairness should be categorised according to how it is used in the situation under investigation.

Sincerity The final category of acceptability is sincerity. This may be concern over the role of people in a planning or operating capacity, or about the honesty of the drivers to obey the rules of the scheme. Thus the subcategories are trust of planners and trust of players. Again, problems about the generic meaning of sincerity were overcome by using subcategories to reflect its different uses.

Properties and Dimensions

In grounded theorising, the broad conceptual ideas of subcategories are exemplified by properties, which are real life illustrations of the subcategories. In this research the properties of the subcategories are closely connected to the set of transport policy objectives that have been associated with road pricing and that have been documented (see Chapter 2): transport efficiency, raising revenue, promoting desired land use, accessibility, economic growth, environmental improvement or alleviation, safety and practicality. Different subcategories can share the same property, although they will be concerned with different aspects of the property. For example, taking the property of raising revenue: the utilitarian subcategories are concerned with whether using the revenue will improve the efficiency or the environment of the system; the fairness subcategory of payment for services is concerned with whether an individual or group gets a return for the contribution made to the revenue; and the sincerity subcategory of trust of planners is concerned with whether the operator will abuse its authority and use the system to raise money for other ends. How the different properties have been associated with the different subcategories is shown in Table 6.1 and the discussion in the next section elucidates the connections.

In grounded theorising it is also important to discover possible dimensions to the properties that would allow for their measurement. This is done by recording more than one respondent's opinion of examples of the properties and deriving the most appropriate scale. For the topic of acceptability the dimensions are logically quite obvious, and tend to be a simple agreement or disagreement with whether the transport objective, worded in terms of the meaning of the subcategories, would be met. Examples of the dimensions are given in the next section. Meanwhile, Table 6.2 shows the population of arguments surrounding the concept of road pricing, which the respondents used in the first section of the interview, when they were discussing its acceptability. These arguments correspond closely to the properties of the grounded theory, and the split between acceptable and unacceptable arguments reflect the different dimensions that respondents can assign to the same properties. Table 6.2 can also be used to gauge if dominance of one style of argument has prejudiced the theory construction.

In Table 6.2 only one type argument from each respondent has been noted where respondents repeated arguments. For example, where a respondent repeated that road pricing was acceptable because it might improve the environment several times throughout the course of the interview, only

Table 6.1   Which properties are linked with which subcategories

Categories	Subcategories	Properties
Utilitarianism	Efficiency	Transport efficiency
		Using revenue
		Accessibility
		Practicality
	Environment	Environmental
		Safety
		Using revenue
Fairness	Provision of needs	Transport efficiency
		Land use changes
		Accessibility
		Economic growth
		Environmental
	Payment for services	Transport efficiency
		Using revenue
		Environmental
	Equality of treatment	Land use changes
Sincerity	Players	Practicality
	Planners	Using revenue
		Privacy

one entry under overall environmental improvement has been made. This classification decision was made because it provides a truer picture of the spread of the types of arguments that the respondents used; otherwise an argument that was only found in one interview could seem more common simply because that respondent repeated it several times.

Also in Table 6.2, although a respondent might recognise that an issue is an acceptability concern, it is the issue that decides his/her opinion in that section of the interview that is included. For example, when arguing that road pricing is acceptable because it improves congestion overall, a respondent might make the interviewer aware that there could be a relocation of congestion problems in some areas. In this case, an entry would only be made under the improvement of overall congestion, because it is the improvement of overall congestion that dictates acceptability. In another example, it might be the relocation of congestion problems that outweighs any concern with the overall improvements, in which case an entry would be made under congestion relocation. This classification decision was made to keep a table of the spread of arguments simple and to make sure that all the arguments recorded had some link with a locution about acceptability.

Table 6.2   Spread of road pricing acceptability arguments amongst respondents

Description of argument:	No. of respondents using argument in:		Frequency of argument as % of total in:	
	Edin.	Camb.	Edin.	Camb.
Road pricing would be acceptable because it could:				
Alleviate congestion overall	24	15	17	10
Improve environment overall	12	21	9	14
Improve safety overall	0	0	0	0
Improve accessibility overall	4	3	3	2
Promote economic growth overall	1	0	1	0
Provide revenue to solve problems	21	12	15	8
Be fair and efficient way to pay	12	12	9	8
Road pricing would be unacceptable because it could:				
Worsen congestion overall	2	0	1	0
Relocate congestion problems	5	7	4	5
Worsen environment overall	3	3	2	2
Relocate environmental problems	3	6	2	4
Worsen safety overall	0	0	0	0
Present safety hazards	3	3	2	2
Worsen accessibility overall	3	1	2	1
Worsen accessibility for some	9	11	7	7
Hinder economic growth overall	6	3	4	2
Hinder economic growth for some	12	18	9	12
Be an unfair additional tax	12	24	9	16
Be impractical to operate	3	1	2	1
Be open to charge evasion	2	4	1	3
Fail to protect individual privacy	1	3	1	2
Total arguments in favour	74	63	54	43
Total arguments against	64	84	46	57
Total of all arguments	138	147	100	100

Illustrating the Hierarchy of Categories

Utilitarianism

The properties associated with the efficiency subcategory of utilitarianism are transport efficiency, raising revenue, accessibility and practicability. These are illustrated in Excerpts 6.1 to 6.4. In Excerpt 6.1 the respondent argues a case for an economic efficiency in road use, and as a consequence he might find road pricing acceptable. There are many other examples where respondents did not base their notion of transport efficiency in economic theory, but simply on the practical concern of reducing congestion. This practical argument merges in with the property of accessibility, but accessibility specifically addresses the arrival at a location, rather than how congested the journey was. This is shown in Excerpt 6.2, where the respondent realises that the efficacy of the journey can be improved by reducing congestion, but places his acceptability of the policy option in question on the interference the policy may have on the ability of people to arrive at their destinations.

Excerpt 6.1 (on transport efficiency)

M　So would you actually support that proposal?
A　Yes I would I suppose I would
M　On what principle?
A　I think on the principle that (0.5) road space in congested city centres is a is a free good in inverted commas in economic terms
M　Yes OK
A　And if you're only only going to try and deal with the problem of congestion from the supply side i.e. from the provision of road space
M　⌈Yes
A　⌊you've got to try and attack it from the demand side
M　⌈Right
A　⌊and in a free society it's vital.

Excerpt 6.2 (on accessibility)

C　Yes we've got to do something to try to reduce the traffic congestion within the city centre err but not to the detriment of people you know for people to be able to get to their location.

The problem of how the transport system can be made more efficient is addressed under the property of raising revenue to spend on improvements and how the respondents recommend the money is spent will depend on their needs. In the analysis all the reasons for how to invest the money could be divided between efficiency and environmental needs. Therefore the property of raising revenue is shared between the efficiency and environmental subcategories, and examples do occur in the data where it is not clear how to classify a strategy; this supports the use of overlapping sets to visualise the theory. In Excerpt 6.3 the respondent focuses the use of revenue on improving efficiency needs, though.

Excerpt 6.3 (on raising revenue)

B   So, in each region you will find there are specific major road schemes that should be pursued, because we're not talking necessarily about the whole length of the road but there some instances where there are those black-spots which if they were actually addressed the whole thing would move much more smoothly.

The final property of efficiency is practicality, because if the scheme is not practical it cannot be useful (refer to the definition of utilitarianism). This is illustrated in Excerpt 6.4, where the respondent ponders the difference between the physical restriction of traffic entering a city and a road pricing scheme with the objective of reducing congestion.

Excerpt 6.4 (on practicality)

D   You could have a combination of either a high price and freedom of access, err
M   Yes=
D   =should you wish it or you could have some means of err physical restraint, that obviously that in itself would be more costly anyway and would probably require the higher price as well to pay for it.
M   Yes
D   Err (.). You wouldn't probably get, the cost of providing physical restraint would not be met from say a pound, you would spend all your pound providing the physical restraint, so I think you you in itself it would be a costly exercise err I mean if you were going to just put a ring around it and make it a err an offence to cross the ring.

Under the subcategory of environmental concerns the properties are using revenue, environmental needs and safety. Any strategy to do with the environment or safety tended to be easily classifiable under the environmental subcategory. These are illustrated in Excerpts 6.5 and 6.6. However, arguments dealing with how to spend the revenue that is raised overlap with the efficiency subcategory. Excerpt 6.7 shows one such example where it is unclear whether the respondent wants the revenue spent on public transport to improve the efficiency and/or environment. In these cases classification can only be made with reference to other comments in the data that can clarify the context.

Excerpt 6.5 (on the environment)

E   What I think would be more to the benefit is hmm environmentally stop cars coming in a bit hmm yes. I think I would go along with it.

Excerpt 6.6 (on safety)

F   If road pricing is introduced care must be taken that it is not at the expense of road safety. Specifically, charging by the length of time that a journey takes or by the length of time that a vehicle spends in a jam are potentially dangerous. Drivers will respond by speeding when they are unable to, overtaking unsafely, jumping queues, and 'rat-running'. This will be dangerous for all vulnerable road users: pedestrians, cyclists and motorcyclists.

(Excerpt 6.6 is from correspondence, not taped interviews).

Excerpt 6.7 (on raising revenue)

G   Obviously I think the first advantage is obviously the revenue that is generated by such a scheme. Any revenue that then goes back into the area that ( ) can then be used to improve the public transport system in Edinburgh.

Fairness

Under the subcategory of the provision of needs the properties are transport efficiency, rerouting, accessibility, economic growth and environmental impacts; in other words, all the needs that the respondents felt able to talk about in an interview on transport. These are shown in Excerpts 6.8 to 6.12. In Excerpt 6.8 the respondent describes why buses might be given exemption, because they are an efficient way to transport people, and tries to equate the same logic to goods vehicles. In Excerpt 6.9, the respondent is concerned with road pricing affecting taxis being able to access places. Incidentally in both these quotes there is a possibility that they could be classified under the subcategory of equality of treatment, because both respondents compare their group needs to those of public transport.

Excerpt 6.8 (on efficiency)

H   Looking at it from the point of view of freight movement
M   Yeah
H   Hmm and I note in particular on on in in the err err the
⌈example

M ⌊example
H given that err there is an exemption there for buses.
M Yes, but but not provision for heavy goods vehicles.
H No, obviously the reason there's for buses is because the object of the exercise is is the maximisation of err err maximum utilisation if you like of means of transport. Obviously if you've got a full bus fine you're going to accept that is maximising the the movement of people.
M Yeah
H Err and therefore will be beneficial. You've got one bus full of 50 people instead of 50 cars with one person.
M ⌈Yes
H ⌊So definite benefit (.) The very extension of the fact that it's felt necessary to to exempt buses means they're treated as essential users, they are an essential user of that road. Now if we're looking at it from a freight movement point of view err (.) looking at it in very simplistic terms err nobody with a lorry runs in and out of Cambridge for the sheer hell of it. You know?
M Yes
H And nobody in their right mind would go to Cambridge with anything. Its as simple as that.

Excerpt 6.9 (on accessibility)

I But being part of the public transport network we've got to have free access.
M OK
I I don't necessarily mean cost free but free access to get into these places you know.

Although the properties of transport efficiency and accessibility are intricately linked with economic growth some respondents argue for or against road pricing on their perceived business needs. This is shown in Excerpt 6.10, and while it would be possible to read into the quote accessibility concerns the most pertinent property is about business needs. As the property must directly represent real arguments, economic growth should be a property.

Excerpt 6.10 (on economic growth)

J Having said that you've also got to bear in mind the types of business that would be involved and with the growth in small businesses think of the number of times that they would be crossing this cordon. It could be in and out in and out. If it was just a question of coming in the morning and leaving in the evening fair enough but you've got a number of businesses delivery area couriers that would be crossing this cordon on a continuous basis throughout the course of the day and that would be a cost that they would either have to absorb or pay on (.) This could be a problem for them.

M   Yeah

J   Now the problem could then be that they have a one a day delivery or whatever which means reducing services or losing business whatever. I could see a downside a downside on the service.

In Excerpt 6.11 the respondent considers the pros and cons of environmental improvements for disabled travellers. The fact that he focuses environmental needs on a specific group puts this in the provision of needs subcategory. In the last line of this excerpt the respondent mentions that the requirements of the disabled do not mean they should be exempted from paying, rather they can make a contribution. Thus the respondent is linking in the provision of need with the fairness of paying for a service.

Excerpt 6.11 (on environment)

K   Basically I don't think there is going to be a significant environmental gain from B. Err (0.3) I have very severe doubts that we will see in the medium term medium term improvements to the transport system that will really help disabled people errm but traffic restraint obviously does help disabled people provided it meets their needs properly because of this of this improved environment, lower pollution err and yes disabled people do actually suffer from increased noise and increased bustle, they do actually like to be able to cross the street at a good, for example, a good pedestrian safe pedestrian environment is very attractive to disabled people. The problems are when they don't ideally meet the needs of disabled people properly. Hmm and that doesn't necessarily mean total exemption which is what we sometimes see.

In Excerpt 6.12 the issues of land use and re-routing effects are broached. These are categorised as a fairness in the provision of needs argument because the respondents have to disaggregate between benefits and disbenefits in different areas, as opposed to the aggregated assessment used in the utilitarian strategies.

Excerpt 6.12 (on land use)

L   And whilst (0.2) no one wants to suggest that road pricing would create the donut effect I think people will go somewhere else. I guess we all know pedestrianisation is good for business and so on and so forth but at the end of the day people vote with their wheels.

M   Yeah

L   That's why you have places like the Gyle here and and all these huge shopping centres in the Midlands that have wrecked Dudley and so on and so forth. People do actually like to shop with their cars, and the city centre shopping I think will become a different experience from going for weekly groceries, that will be done by car and city centre shopping will be a leisure activity.

M   Yeah

L   As far as the commuter is concerned people who have to work in the city centre and so on, well if you take our case here we've moved out.

M   Yeah

L   And I've just said to you six of us drove into the city centre, now there are hundreds of us that use cars (0.2) to come to a business park.

The subcategory of 'payment for services' refers specifically to the idea of paying a charge and getting something in return. Although a more esoteric subcategory than the broad provision for needs, it arises several times in the data. The properties that have been associated with it are transport efficiency, environmental improvements and raising and using revenue. Examples are shown in Excerpts 6.13 to 6.15. In Excerpt 6.13 the respondent addresses the operation of roads and, from the context of the interview, by this he bothered about efficiency. In the excerpt he argues that people have to understand that they have to pay for roads that work. In Excerpt 6.14 the respondent says he does not mind paying more for environmental improvement but wonders if he already pays enough to the treasury. A similar argument is found in Excerpt 6.15 where the respondent does not know if it is fair to raise more revenue from motorists.

Excerpt 6.13 (transport efficiency)

N   And this is all to do with the fact we haven't addressed how we're operating our roads and pricing is one of those things. It's a very difficult thing to actually operate and we need to have that discussion and the debate hasn't really been held as it should be held to educate people to understand yes if we do things now it won't be as difficult for us in the future and they're just putting off the evil day.

Excerpt 6.14 (environmental)

O   And so the same would apply. It's the same principle isn't it. All right I'm willing to pay for that to go into that town because it it will be to benefit to the local economy. It will will go towards making the local economy better or the local environment better but by the same vein err I would expect there to be a reduction in the figure that I pay notionally to the exchequer which is not used to any benefit of that local environment, it just goes into the general exchequer, its not ring fenced or …

Excerpt 6.15 (raising and using revenue)

P   I think if you're talking about raising capital that car drivers pay more than enough already as far as hmm taxes and road tax and tax and petrol taxes err, but how I think it should be spent err is probably improving other forms of transport.

The final subcategory of fairness has been called 'equality of treatment'. It is possibly the most central idea that people might have of what fairness entails (Willman, 1982), but in the data it does not occur very often. However, its omission or combination with the other subcategories proved impossible. The example given in Excerpt 6.16 focuses on the land use property, where the respondent identifies a relocation of trade problem and solves it by saying she expects equality of treatment, between Edinburgh and other towns. In later sections of the interview the concept is used more when respondents consider the amount that they should pay in relation to others. This is covered in greater detail in Chapter 9.

Excerpt 6.16 (on land use)

Q   It's going to (1.0) I was going to say it would make things unequal from one town to another but it's unequal anyway (laugh).
M   Don't you think that's a problem that if people knew they had to pay to go into Edinburgh they would maybe do their shopping in Glasgow perhaps.
Q   I would hope if there was a scheme like this it would be a universal scheme.

Sincerity

Concern about the sincerity of planners is illustrated by the properties of raising and using revenue, and privacy. This is illustrated in Excerpts 6.17 and 6.18. In Excerpt 6.17 the respondent says he is cynical about raising money from motorists, which implies a lack of faith in human nature, or sincerity. Then the respondent goes on to say, with respect to motorways, that he had paid enough, which illustrates the close connection of sincerity in raising revenue with the fairness in the payment for services. In Excerpt 6.18 the respondent ponders the option of charging by distance, then dismisses it on the grounds that the technology used would be an infringement on civil liberties.

Excerpt 6.17 (about raising revenue)

P   I'm a cynic about all that, they get a lot of money from motor vehicles in England don't they or Great Britain into the national exchequer we don't spend it on the roads of course we spend a fraction of it.

M   Yes

P   And now they're proposing to toll motorways as well which an awful lot of people think that they've paid for once in their taxes and in their road licensing and they find that they've got to pay again. I mean its a good old horse that you can flog to death I suppose.

Excerpt 6.18 (on privacy)

Q   … How far they travel? Well again that means you've got some sort of tachometer, you've got to be recording. Again infringement of civil liberty and all sorts of things.

The subcategory about concern over the sincerity of players focuses on the behaviour of the drivers in the scheme and whether they will be able to flout the rules. The argument is illustrated in Excerpt 6.19, where the respondent thinks the scheme will not work because drivers will interfere with their on-board meters to avoid paying the charge. Thus he is saying he does not trust the sincerity of other drivers.

Excerpt 6.19 (on practicality)

R   You know if you've got meters people will dock the meter how many people clock their gas meter and electricity meters OK.

M   Yeah

R   How many people are caught and how many people you know get away with it?

M   Right

R   Many many people I should think get away with it. You know you put the magnet on there and it will slow it down yeah take it off once every two days or whatever. I think if you're telling people they've got to have a meter in the car apart from the obvious cost of it I think you'd have to. OK electricity meters are you know sealed and you can't get into them apparently you can buy seals for them and the same will (happen) they'll just bring up technology to get around it.

Summary

The above quotations have illustrated how the concepts of the grounded theory can be read into the arguments people used to argue for and against road pricing. However, as some of the examples showed, there are cases where more than one concept is being used to form the argument. This can cause some confusion about how best to categorise the data. These problems are addressed in the next stage, which specifically looks at the strategies through which the concepts are used together. Once these strategies are known it helps put the arguments in a context and confusion is reduced.

Linking the Concepts Together

Definition of Strategies

The second major stage in axial coding is the creation of strategies that reflect actual arguments and use the categories that have been described. As mentioned in Chapter 5, strategies are an essential part of completing a theory. A theory has to describe how categories fit together to create a structure that explains the phenomenon under investigation. In this case the phenomenon is the acceptability of urban road pricing proposals and the building blocks are the categories and subcategories. It is not sufficient to say that acceptability seems to be dependent on the categories of utilitarianism, fairness and sincerity; this does not explain how the concepts fit together in real arguments. Rather, it is necessary to take real arguments and describe the ways in which the concepts are used together. Once these are identified, groups of strategies can be formed. Then when an argument about road pricing is analysed it is possible to understand it in terms of the grounded theory of acceptability. This section describes the process of deriving the strategies, and as in the previous sections on analysis, failed attempts are given as well as the final version. This illustrates the learning curve to theory development.

Rejecting the Option of Strategies Reflecting the Respondents' Opinions

The first option that was considered was grouping the strategies according to whether or not the respondents found the scheme acceptable, unacceptable or were unsure. As the objective of the study is to discover how road pricing can be made more acceptable this was a logically attractive option. If it was possible it would then be easy to say that in order to be acceptable road pricing should be presented according to the 'acceptable' strategy. However, no such 'easy option' emerged as feasible.

The respondents could talk about the same aspects of the scheme, yet have different opinions. For example, on the environment it is possible to argue that there would be both an improvement from less traffic in the charged area and an increased problem from rerouting effects; on revenue raised it is possible to argue that public transport would be improved or that the money would be wasted; and on safety it can be argued that less traffic will make the roads safer or that less traffic will make the roads more dangerous as cars can drive faster. Given such a spread of views it can be seen why basing strategies on acceptance or non-acceptance would be difficult. Even though different respondents may be using the same category or subcategory, they will assign different dimensions.

Rejecting the Option of Strategies Being the Same as the Categories

The next option that was considered was to have the strategies the same as the categories, i.e., the strategies would become utilitarianism, fairness and sincerity. This was attractive because it was very easy. However, it proved to be implausible.

There was some justification for considering this approach because many arguments seemed to be based on the idea of road pricing improving an overall situation, the fairness of road pricing on certain groups of road-users and whether people could be trusted to pay or the politicians trusted to invest the revenue in transport. These arguments could be classed by the concepts of utilitarianism, fairness and sincerity.

However, this idea for strategies did not hold up to comparison across all the data. It was very common for respondents to argue that they can see the overall environmental advantages of road pricing, although they were worried about some of the fairness implications for people who needed to drive. This involves a combination of utilitarianism and fairness, and their decision about acceptability depends on how they weighed up the dimensions of these. In other words there were situations where the decision about acceptability involves more than one of the categories. Therefore basing strategies (that are meant to reflect whole arguments) on individual categories would have been misguided.

Deciding on the Strategies

The initial ideas for the strategies After these false starts, strategies were discovered that did properly reflect all the arguments. These strategies were derived from a set of ideas in much the same way that stimuli were used to provide ideas for the categories in the open coding stage. However, at this stage of the theory development there was no dictionary to turn to or established theories that might provide clues. Instead the ideas came from three areas:

1 the established categories and subcategories – the concepts that the strategies would be based on were known and by studying these categories some logical ways of grouping them might become apparent;
2 knowledge about the existing arguments about road pricing – from the literature review and from listening to the interviewees the main arguments about road pricing were known;
3 the objective of the strategies to be able to guide planning decisions about road pricing – for the research to achieve its objective of recommending how road pricing could be made more acceptable, the strategies had to feed into the decisions that needed to be made about using a road pricing policy.

Thinking about the categories The categories and subcategories that had been chosen pointed to a logical way of linking themselves together. It was thought that the category of utilitarianism could be reduced to the provision of needs and the sincerity category could be sidelined because it added nothing to the logical debate to say a person needs to believe something is true to give an opinion about it. This meant that the strategies would be centred on the subcategories of the fairness category: provision of needs, payment for services and equality of treatment (from this perspective).

Once the categories of utilitarianism and sincerity had been temporarily sidelined all that was left to do was link the three remaining subcategories together in a way that made some semantic sense. Only three ways were found:

1 equality of treatment in the provision of needs;
2 payment of services for the provision of needs;
3 equality of treatment in the payment for services.

The arguments about road pricing From reading about and listening to the arguments about road pricing it was thought that there were three main arguments. The first two reflect the objectives that road pricing can be used to meet and the third picks up the issue of who should pay:

1   some people argue for road pricing to meet policy objectives by a combination of transport measures (designed to improve the efficiency of transport services and provide environmental alleviation) and traffic restraint (which provides additional benefits by people being priced off the road). The combined effects of new measures and restraint achieves the objectives. In this case, road pricing has the objectives both of traffic restraint itself and of raising revenue to spend on the new measures;

2   there is a second argument that policy objectives should be met by only introducing supplementary transport measures (designed to improve the efficiency of transport services and provide environmental alleviation). In this case, road pricing has the sole objective of providing revenue to meet the cost of the new measures. While the new charge may deter some drivers who can no longer afford the cost of motoring, this is not the objective, and if the same number of people were still driving after the introduction of the charge the objectives would still be met;

3   the third argument is about people saying that it is not fair for their group to pay the charge, because they are essential users.

While the above tripartite division of arguments does not cover the full range of arguments that can be used, it does reflect the main issues that arose in most of the interviews.

Deciding what is acceptable   It was hoped that by linking together the ideas about the logical connections between the categories and the arguments for road pricing, strategies would be formed that could help decide what is acceptable. These strategies were formed by combining the logical ways of linking the categories with a summary of the main arguments about road pricing.

'Equality of treatment in the provision of needs' was linked in with the argument about using road pricing to restrain traffic and so meet transport policy objectives. Both ideas are about using road pricing to meet objectives by paying a charge, although the money does not have to be spent on anything. 'Payment for services for the provision of needs' was linked to the idea of road pricing revenue actually being used to pay for a service that was being used. Finally, 'equality of treatment in the payment for services' was linked in with the idea of the argument about who should pay and when they might be paying too much, or too little.

Grounding these ideas to derive the strategies   The first idea, called equality of treatment in the provision of needs, became the *direct-effect strategy*. This was about using road pricing directly to meet transport policy objectives, such as improving the environment and improving efficiency, by affecting demand. It was realised that the purpose of using road pricing for this objective was to improve the overall situation, as well as for individuals. Therefore the categories involved seemed to be about utilitarianism and fairness. The main arguments connected with these issues were whether meeting the needs of a group affected the needs of the individual. This meant the subcategories involved would be concern about efficiency, concern about the environment, provision of needs and equality of treatment.

The second idea, called payment for services for the provision of needs, became the *indirect-effect strategy*. However, the initial idea for this strategy was expanded to take account of other points. When the use of revenue was mentioned, several respondents linked in the issue of trust of planners. Then it was realised that the trust of planners was also thrown into doubt when the use of information from road pricing was considered (i.e., information on movements from electronic tagging of vehicles). This fitted in with the idea of naming the strategy an indirect-effect strategy – i.e., a strategy that deals with any by-product from road pricing.

As trust about how revenue and information were used was part of the indirect strategy then all the categories were involved in the construction of this strategy. For example, revenue (or information) could be used for the greater good and this involved the utilitarian category. Then revenue involves ideas of fairness about what and whom it is spent on. Finally, concern over the use of revenue and information brings in the sincerity category. However, not all the subcategories were used. In the utilitarian category concern about efficiency and the environment are used because the revenue is spent on measures to improve these objectives. In the fairness category the provision of needs and the payment for services subcategories are used because these reflect that revenue is used for something. Then in the sincerity category, only the trust of planners is used because all the issues relate to this.

Finally, the third idea, called equality of treatment in the payment for services, became the *contribution strategy*. This is because this reflects the idea that drivers are concerned about how much they contribute compared to somebody else. It was also realised that some drivers feel that they would pay too much because other drivers did not pay because they avoided the charge. This brought in the idea of sincerity of other drivers. Consequently the categories in this strategy are fairness and sincerity. The subcategories are the payment for services, equality of treatment and the sincerity of players.

Table 6.3   Summary of the strategies used in the grounded theory of acceptability of urban road pricing

Strategies	1 Direct-effect strategy	2 Indirect-effect strategy	3 Contribution strategy
Main questions that the strategies are applied to	Can road pricing be used to directly meet transport policy objectives?	Can by-products of road pricing (revenue and information) be used to meet any needs?	Is the amount of the road pricing charge that drivers are expected to pay fair?
Grounded theory categories used	• Utilitarianism • Fairness	• Utilitarianism • Fairness • Sincerity	• Fairness • Sincerity
Grounded theory subcategories used	• Efficiency • Environment • Provision of needs • Equality of treatment	• Efficiency • Environment • Provision of needs • Payment for dervices • Trust of planners	• Payment for services • Equality of treatment • Trust of players
How the subcategories are used to form an opinion about the acceptability of road pricing issues	Utilitarian advantages in *efficiency and environment* are weighed against provision *of specific group needs*, and *equality of treatment between different groups.*	Assessment of *payment for services for the provision of needs, efficiency and environmental protection, and whether planners can be trusted* to run the scheme.	Reflects on whether there should be *equality of treatment in drivers' contributions to the payment for services, and if drivers can be trusted* to pay.

To recap, three strategies have been postulated that make use of all the different categories and subcategories; they shown in Table 6.3. The direct-effect strategy deals with any argument about road pricing being used to meet a policy objective by affecting the demand for traffic. The indirect-effect strategy deals with arguments about how by-products of road pricing (revenue and information) can be used. Finally the contribution strategy reflects arguments about how much it is fair for people to pay.

Illustration of the Strategies

Chapters 7, 8, 9 and 10 give many examples of understanding the arguments in terms of the strategies of the grounded theory. Taken together this amounts to substantial evidence that the grounded theory of acceptability of urban road pricing is plausible because amongst all these excerpts (which reflect all the arguments that were recorded) there is not one instance of the grounded theory not being an applicable method of interpretation. However, the purpose of this section is to illustrate the method of interpreting arguments in terms of the grounded theory. Therefore only a few detailed excerpts from the transcripts are used.

Nine excerpts show the beginnings of four interviews. This might seem superfluous but by showing how the conversation goes from an opening question, to consideration of urban road pricing and verbalisation of opinions the full range of an argument (from beginning to crux) is shown. The reader can then see how the grounded theory is used to interpret acceptance of road pricing and if it is sensible. For example, some parts of the conversation are ignored in the grounded theory, and while the researcher may think this is correct, the only way the reader can make up their mind is by looking at those parts of the conversation that are omitted. Also, parts of Excerpts 6.25 and 6.27 have been shown before, in Chapter 5 (Examples 5.2 and 5.1 respectively). The reader can compare the two interpretations and it should be clear that the interpretation given in this final section is more exact.

In Excerpt 6.20 the opening of the interview, aimed at uncovering the level of the respondent's knowledge about road pricing, is shown.

Excerpt 6.20

M   Right. First question is (.) how much do you know about urban road pricing?
I   Not a great deal, I've heard about it talked about but I don't know a great deal about it.

M   So you know=

I   =I know its about getting people err out of the centre of cities, is that the sort of thing you're talking about.

M   Yes

⌈Charging

I   Yes you have a card or something registers something (0.3) something in your vehicle that registers when you pass. Is that right.

M   Yes there are many ways of doing it

⌈well

I   ⌊Well that's the one I've heard of ((laughs))

M   that we'll discuss later. Yes OK that's more or less it. Now if you can look at a typical urban road pricing proposal.

I   Hmm hmm

((Respondent looks at proposal card for 15 seconds))

I   Right

M   The map is on the back.

I   Hmm hmm (0.1) Will the cordon be all of this?

((Respondent points to the ring road around Edinburgh))

M   No the cordon is the yellow bit

⌈there

I   ⌊Oh the green yellow=

M   =So that one in just the old and new towns essentially.

(3.0)

I   OK

M   OK?

I   Hmm hmm

The dialogue shows how the respondent says she does not know much about road pricing and, as if checking what she does know is correct, respondent I starts to describe the purpose of road pricing (to restrain traffic) and a method by which it can be done (electronic meters). The interviewer, M, cuts the flow of the conversation to introduce the typical urban road pricing proposal, which is a description of an inner cordon scheme. The remainder of the excerpt shows how the respondent establishes what the scheme entails. This involves reading and checking where the cordon is. No opinion about the acceptability of road pricing is made in this excerpt. Therefore the grounded theory does not apply and the information in this part of the interview cannot be compartmentalised under the strategies. It does, however, illustrate that the respondent was not led into giving an opinion.

Excerpt 6.21

M   Right. Would you find such a scheme acceptable?

I   Well (.) well (.) I think I need to say now that we're not against that will ((Telephone starts to ring in the background))

M   Do you need to get that?

I   No no that will lessen traffic within the city centre but what we do need to say is that consideration has to be for people with disabilities who have no choice about how they ⌈ travel.

M   ⌊Yes

I   So therefore we would approve of such a scheme if it was designed to suit people with disabilities=

M   =Hmm

I   For instance I have no choice about how I travel

M   ⌈Yes

I   ⌊I can('t) get on a bus.

M   ((Laugh)) OK Do you think other people would find it acceptable?

I   ( ) disabled or anyone.

M   Anyone

I   Oh they would get used to it.

M   Hmm hmm

I   I think there would probably be quite an uproar at the start.

M   Oh yes ((laugh))

I   Because everybody wants to take their car and the number of people you see coming in in the morning with only one person in the car and you know.

M   Yes. What sort of effect do you think that scheme that proposal would have?

I   On?

M   Anything

I   On anything? I think it would make the centre of the city more comfortable to drive for everbody concerned. Less pollution. Less noise. Less danger for pedestrians, cyclists (1.0). But again we'd be interested in what happens to people with disabilities.

M   Yeah, do you think there are any disadvantage.

I   To us there are, people with disabilities. I keep having to emphasise this. There is a definite disadvantage, because car is often the only way we can get into town.
(1.0)

In Excerpt 6.21, which follows directly from Excerpt 6.20, the interviewer, M, asks if the respondent would find the scheme acceptable. Immediately following this first question she gives her opinion. This is based on the balance between less traffic in the city centre and the needs of disabled people. This is a balance between utilitarianism (of the environment for everyone in the city) and the fairness (for the group of disabled people). Therefore it is an example of a direct-effect strategy.

The remainder of the excerpt confirms that this is the strategy she is using. She says that if the needs of disabled people were catered for then she would find the scheme acceptable, further showing how acceptability depends on favourable dimensions to properties in the fairness category. M then asks if other people would find the scheme acceptable. I thinks that they would get used to it after complaining when it was first introduced. This can still be considered part of the direct-effect strategy because those people that drive in separate cars do so because they believe it provides for their needs. Finally, M asks I to identify the effects the scheme might have. In doing this she clarifies the subcategories she is using in the strategy; i.e. she focuses on the advantage to the environment (to everybody) which is the subcategory of utilitarianism; she emphasises the provision of needs for disabled people, which is a subcategory of fairness.

In Excerpt 6.22, the beginning of another interview is shown.

Excerpt 6.22

M   First of all, what's your level of knowledge about road pricing.

II   My level of knowledge is (0.5) limited.

M   OK. Are you aware, you were aware, of the various proposals that were expressed?

II   Oh indeed, yes.

M   OK hmmm. Are you aware of the theory, the economic theory behind road pricing. (1.0) not that I'm going to ask any questions about it ((laugh)).

II   No, no not at all ((small laugh)). The theory. It depends on whose answering that question, and what the final aim is, err, the theory it depends on where it coming from, the theory to (0.2) collect money to recycle into err public transport and so on, one cannot say that's a bad idea, err, but why I need to actually ask a question, why is road pricing required?

M   Yeah, no, errm its

II   ⌈(I mean)

M   ⌊The the the theory I was getting at was the sort of the sort of the academic the economic argument saying that road users should pay the exact cost of their journey rather than try and roughly approximate it and maybe its under in some areas and over in others.

II   ( )

M   That that was the question, it was just sort of just to get at your ( ) to know how much you know about road pricing.

II   OK OK
M   Just an opener really. If you could look at a typical urban road pricing proposal in Edinburgh.
      ((Respondent looks at proposal card for 20 seconds))
II   It's a bit of a bog standard road pricing.
M   The map's on the back. (1.0) The inner cordon covering the old and new towns basically.
II   Hmm hmm

As opposed to Excerpt 6.20, where the respondent did not offer an opinion in the opening remarks, this respondent in Excerpt 6.22 launches into a strategy about road pricing. When the respondent says that he knows something of other road pricing proposals the interviewer probes by asking about the respondent's theoretical knowledge, as a way to gauge the level of knowledge. The respondent seems to interpret this as a cue to enter into debate and he ponders what the interviewer means by the term 'theory'. In verbalising this thought process he says that using money to improve the public transport system is acceptable and a good idea. He further links this in with road pricing as a way to raise revenue. This involves the subcategories of provision of needs (public transport) and payment for services (road pricing). This appears to be starting an indirect-effect strategy.

However, the interviewer does not let the respondent continue to develop the argument at this stage. M explains that he does not want the debate to begin from that starting question on theory and shows the respondent the typical inner cordon proposal. The opinion of the respondent continues in Excerpt 6.23.

Excerpt 6.23

M   OK. The question is would you find such a scheme acceptable.
II   No
M   OK. And why?
II   There should be an alternative to road pricing, public transport could be made more attractive and that doesn't necessarily mean it should be funded by charging vehicles. Err (1.5). There should be a sensible and reasonable number of well err park and ride and walk facilities, oft mentioned, never delivered. That should also be linked with park and ride, which I and I'm wearing my Chamber of Commerce hat, fully agree with. As an alternative there is far too much mention nowadays that road transport's too cheap.
M   Meaning? Travelling by car this is?
II   Or road or or freight as well err (0.5). If there is a sensible and decent public

transport system and everyone says we should have one why is it not being delivered? Bus deregulation has put thousands of buses on the road err some are clapped out wrecks, in Edinburgh we have a modicum of that but we've got a very very good modern fleet of buses, err, but because they have to run at a profit services are lousy at night.

M   Yeah

II   And then we go into the spiral of car usage et cetera et cetera et cetera. Err (0.5). We're going off at a slight tangent perhaps but I mean it's a very interesting

M   ⌈Oh no no

II   ⌊It's a very big topic this one.

M   ⌈Yeah

II   ⌊My gut feeling, to to en encapsulate it for you, before we move on is that that road pricing is only another tax, it is a knee-jerk reaction, lets sort the problem. Lets put some, lets put something on the ground before we get down to more taxation.

M   Yeah

To the question about acceptance the respondent restarts the indirect-effect strategy. He says that he does not think alternatives to the car should be paid for by charging vehicles. This uses the subcategories of provision of needs (alternatives to the car) and payment for services (the money from charging vehicles). He then tries to expand on and justify this argument but, as the respondent himself mentions, goes off at a slight tangent. He mentions two points: firstly, that road transport is too cheap and, secondly, that public transport can be provided by other means. These points are delivered rhetorically and ironically, so care has to be taken in interpretation.

On road transport being too cheap the respondent presents the point in a way that suggests that 'too much' is made out of it. Although the respondent does not answer the question he implies that even if road transport is too cheap it is not as under-priced as opponents make out. Thus he is trying to break the link between road users paying for public transport. On the provision of public transport the respondent mentions that deregulation has tried to achieve this but it has not worked, but unfortunately he does not complete an argument. As not enough subcategories are apparent no strategy can be identified and the argument is incomplete.

In the final paragraph spoken by II he restarts his argument and tries to 'encapsulate it'. He thinks that using road pricing as a tax (subcategory of payment for services) is a knee-jerk reaction (indicating he attaches a low dimension to this subcategory) to providing solutions (subcategory of provision of needs that he indicates he attaches a high importance to). Thus this encapsulation confirms the indirect-effect strategy was being used.

An extension of the indirect-effect strategy is the contribution strategy. While the indirect-effect strategy considers the balance between provision of needs and payments for services to provide needs (as illustrated above) the contribution strategy is subtly different and balances payment for services with equality of treatment. This is illustrated by the respondent in Excerpts 6.24 and 6.25. Although not shown it is also possible for respondents to use both strategies.

Excerpt 6.24

M   What's the level of knowledge about urban road pricing that you have?
III   Right. Well basically most of it has been from what I've read from the press and just talking to the odd individual, but I've never been involved in ideas or schemes
M   ⌈Yeah
III   ⌊Or schemes that are not going to operate.
M   So what you know some of the proposals.
III   I know some of the proposals.
M   Would you say you know the theory behind it.
III   Oh I know the theory
        ⌈I know
M   ⌊OK so you're actually quite
        ⌈knowledgable then
III   ⌊( ) I certainly know what happens in Norway anyway.
M   OK If you could take a look at that typical proposal.
        ((Respondent looks at proposal card for 10 seconds))
M   The map's on the back.
III   Yeah
        ((Respondent looks at proposal card for further 15 seconds))
III   Right OK. That's your suggested idea?
M   Yeah errm
III   And that's roughly the (1.0)
M   Yeah I mean sorry. The old and new towns essentially.
III   OK

In Excerpt 6.24 the new respondent, Number III, begins his interview by answering the questions about level of knowledge about road pricing. As in Excerpt 6.20, but opposed to Excerpt 6.22, the respondent does not offer any opinion about urban road pricing in Excerpt 6.24 and none of the information is considered as part of the respondent's argument about road pricing that is shown in the following excerpt.

Excerpt 6.25

M   Errm. Would you find such a scheme acceptable.

III   Well, obviously I'll be a bit selfish here I'd find anything acceptable that controlled the use of cars in city centres.

M   OK

III   But being realistic and I've I've listened to some of the arguments in you know various (0.5) (areas). I mean nowhere do you mention how you cater for people that actually live there. You know ((softly)). Are they going to be disadvantaged that they have to live inside who live there and maybe commute the opposite way.

M   Yeah

III   Are you going to disadvantage those. They're not really contributing to the congestion because there's nothing opposite at all. Are you going to let them have a resident's ⌈whatever.

M   ⌊Hmm hmm=

II   =a resident's permit or whatever I don't know.

M   Yeah

III   The other drawback is that errm and what I've heard said is is if if these screens are set up it really is a national situation because

M   ⌈Hmm hmm

III   ⌊one of the arguments they'll put up is that everyone will go (and) shop at Falkirk or Stirling or Glasgow. Certainly in some other towns generally Manchester or Yorkshire they're even more attractive because there are a lot of towns close by and they all tend to (0.3)

M   Yeah

III   The other thing is and I maybe going off at a tangent here is that the (0.2) the (0.2) one of the points that people raise is that if they can then reinvest the revenue from that into public transport maybe train whatever one or the other. But that's a catch twenty two. If you're successful in banning cars you're going to reduce your revenue.

M   ⌈Yeah

III   ⌊You can't win. Errm. If they ever would do I don't know. That's some points anyway. Do you want to just keep me going, I don't know but errm.

In the opening remark the respondent says that he would find scheme the acceptable because he finds anything acceptable that reduces traffic in city centres. However, he goes on to argue that even though this is the aim of road pricing he would not find it acceptable. In his first argument he uses the contribution strategy to argue that residents in the city (equality of treatment) would be disadvantaged (a dimension indicating his opinion) because they do not contribute to congestion (which is what the payment is for). Unlike Excerpt

6.23 where the respondent challenged the connection between the need (in that case public transport) and the payment, respondent III is not challenging a payment for congestion but merely questioning whether a certain group (in this case the residents) should be paying for it. Respondent III is not balancing needs with payment, but payment with equality of treatment.

Then, after mentioning the introduction of a resident's permit to overcome this problem (i.e., a permit to exempt, or provide a discount for, residents from the charge) the respondent brings in a second argument. This is based on the impact of the charge on shopping and the worry that people will go and shop at other centres, without the charge. Although the respondent conveys this argument in a shortened manner, enough points can be understood in it to recognise it as part of a direct-effect strategy. Shopping can be understood as a need (subcategory of provision of needs) and the change in travel patterns will affect the opportunities between city centre traders and traders in other towns (subcategory of equality of treatment). Once these two concepts are recognised the argument can be pigeon-holed as a direct-effect strategy.

Then, after saying he is 'going off at a tangent', the respondent introduces a third argument about how the revenue will be used. The respondent argues that if the revenue is spent on public transport, as more people use public transport instead of driving, the revenue will decrease and this will mean that not enough money is available for public transport any more. Although it may seem illogical to reduce the number of people paying the tax, this is far from a fundamental criticism of road pricing. Road pricing might have the objective of reducing traffic in a city, in which case reducing the number of people paying the charge is desirable. Or it might have the objective of funding some infrastructure (such as public transport) and although the number of people driving and thus paying the charge would decline, this is not a problem if the remaining drivers pay a sufficient amount to finance the infrastructure projects. However, respondent III does consider this a problem and this can be classed as an example of the indirect-effect strategy. He focuses on using revenue (payment for services) to provide for public transport (provision of needs).

Excerpt 6.26

M   O.K. What's your level of knowledge about urban road pricing?
IV   Ermm (2.0) it's moderate. I know of some of the proposals of different types of road pricing ...
M   ⌈O.K.
IV   ⌊And that I know there was a proposal to try something out in Edinburgh which Edinburgh weren't even aware of but the government decided it was going to

happen but then it didn't happen (1s) and I know that the (.) is it the Common's Transport Select Committee looked at road pricing in some detail and decided that they hmm weren't quite sure

⌈about it

M ⌊Yes yes

IV And I remember they looked at experience abroad and there isn't a terribly successful model

⌈anywhere.

M ⌊Yeah

IV And that's about it.

M Would you say you know about the theory of it behind it.

IV A little bit.

M Well in fact you're actually quite knowledgeable. You know more than most people. OK we're going to take a look at a typical urban road pricing scheme.

IV Right

((Respondent looks at proposal card for 20 seconds))

IV Right

M OK The map's on the back. If you've seen the proposal you'll probably recognise.

IV No I haven't actually seen the proposal. I've just heard talk of it.

M Yes I imagine they keep it fairly quiet.

But that's what

⌈they're

IV ⌊This is a government proposal as opposed to anything really to do with the council. Is that right?

M It was hmm both = but as far as I know they got to what they call the inception stage where they were thinking about it and thought no we don't want this risk.

IV This was a couple of year's ago wasn't it.

M Initially it was (1.0) floated in nineteen eighty nine but that's when they did the JATES study, looking into integrated transport policies and

⌈that

IV ⌊That's right, but walking isn't transport apparently. Well its not in JATES.

M ((laughing)) Yes yes

IV That's not why I'm very familiar with it, because its before my time. I was actually in Glasgow before ( ) Edinburgh.

M Yeah. Anyway the cordon. Cars cross the cordon ((M points at the map)) that('s) the cordon just covering basically the city centre the old and new towns.

IV Yeah

In Excerpts 6.26, 6.27 and 6.28, respondent IV constructs other arguments for road pricing. In Excerpt 6.26 no strategies are evident and the respondent makes several points in which he tries to place the road pricing proposal in a context. Then in Excerpt 6.27 the respondent starts to formulate an opinion.

Excerpt 6.27

M   OK The question is how acceptable or not would you find such a scheme.
     (4.0)
IV   Well, I'm not sure about the full details of it but I think we would certainly find
     it acceptable as (0.5) an experiment as long as it was phrased in those terms to
     people that it was going to be an experiment
     ⌈ermm
M   ⌊huh huh
IV   Are you saying that every car is going to have to have a meter in? But.
M   In that proposal yes
IV   In that proposal
     ⌈well
M   ⌊But
     I
     ⌈mean
IV   ⌊Certainly with that one we'd argue with but=
M   =OK
IV   but that's a huge investment and someone has got to pay for that ermm. Our line
     on road pricing would simply be that its an interesting idea which has many pros
     and some cons and that we would very much like to see a detailed road pricing
     experiment we'd be very interested to see what happens to the ones happening
     down south we'd like to see one in Scotland and Edinburgh seems like a good
     case but because its only an experiment and it must be something that doesn't
     involve a huge amount of capital to set up and a meter in each vehicle certainly
     seems like a problem in that case. But the idea of the cordon ( ) something like
     the map that's shown here err these timings, this idea of a single central zone I
     think we'd be quite happy with as the basis for an experiment.

The main argument is in the final paragraph and only one point is made
which is about the cost of setting up an experiment using an electronic operating
system. Consideration about the cost of the scheme is a practicality concern,
which fits under the subcategory of efficiency. It is classed under utilitarianism
because it is a concern for everyone. This subcategory is balanced against the
advantages that the respondent can see in the scheme that he mentions when he
says it is an interesting idea. These advantages are clarified in the next excerpt
and reflect utilitarian improvements for the environment. When this is known
the argument can be classified with confidence as a direct-effect strategy.

Excerpt 6.28

M   What do you think some of the pros and some of the cons would actually be?

IV   Well the cons are really just the complexity of it and (.) the cons that the public will see other than simply having to pay for something they didn't pay for before are that certainly the traders will say that they are going to be suffering economic disadvantage particularly if there is a price as high as one pound fifty to go into the city centre. They will say whether its right or wrong that their trade will suffer because people simply won't come into the city centre they will go to the out of town shopping centres.

M   ⌈Hmm hmm

IV   ⌊And since this proposal was put about we've had the Gyle built which is a great large option for people now which has free parking (.) works and very congested roads trying to get to it (.) and (.) they would use the same argument saying that people coming from further a field, people who live in the central belt instead of coming to Edinburgh as they might have done will go to Glasgow instead so they will certainly use that argument and (.) of course there's some truth in that.

M   ⌈Yeah

IV   ⌊That's some of the cons. And then the complexity of it.

M   Yeah I've got the complexity.

IV   The pros. Well obviously that we're, its an attempt to tackle congestion and that it may in fact work in the opposite sense that if the city centre becomes less congested which makes public transport more efficient and makes the pedestrian and cycling environment more pleasant we may find that err retail turnover is actually much increased.

M   Hmm hmm
     (0.5)

IV   So that('s) why we're keen to see an experiment

M   ⌈What

IV   ⌊But we're not committing ourselves to saying this is the answer.

M   Do you think other people would find it acceptable on the whole as an experimental scheme as you say.

IV   I think its becoming it's the kind of thing that's now more acceptable because we've got the Prince's Street experiment going on at the moment so that people are now used to the fact that the Council comes up with some strange ideas and have a go at them (.) and actually they possibly work because. There was a lot of criticism of the idea of the Prince's Street experiment but there is now a lot of positive views expressed about what its actually done its positive benefits seem to far outweigh its negative ones, not that it has (not got some). (.) So (.) I think its more acceptable but I think it is an extremely difficult, still especially with the cost that's proposed here.

M   Yeah

IV   My feeling would be that (.) any kind of experiment like this would initially be subsidised so that the cost would be kept low. Either subsidised in the sense that it only covers its costs and it doesn't actually generate any revenue which this one appears, mentions that this scheme.

M   Yeah

IV   Or it gets a direct subsidy from government so it can raise some revenue but capital costs for instance are paid off. (.) So, but then of course you've got the problem that if you're running an experiment or you're running it at a lower price you're not getting the same answer as if you're running it at the full price.

M   Yeah

IV   So (.) it's a very difficult issue.

The interpretation of Excerpt 6.27 shows that sometimes all the subcategories to form an argument may not actually be spoken. However, there should be a reference to the subcategory that will complete the argument. In this case it is the 'pros and cons'. In Excerpt 6.28 these are talked about. In the first two passages spoken by respondent IV, he mentions more problems. These are about the complexity (subcategory of concern about efficiency) and the loss of trade in the city centre to out-of-town centres (subcategory of provision of needs). He illustrates the loss of trade with the example of the Gyle Centre, which is a large complex on the western outskirts of Edinburgh. Then the respondent talks about the pros and focuses on the public transport efficiency and the environment. These are examples of utilitarianism. At this stage then the strategy is confirmed as a direct-effect strategy, and the respondent's position on acceptability is understood as a trade-off between utilitarian and fairness pros and cons.

As if to confirm this, the respondent draws an analogy with another transport planning issue. This is known as the Prince's Street experiment, where Prince's Street is the main thoroughfare in the city centre of Edinburgh. The experiment involved closing part of the street to traffic and creating a loop system in the city centre. The respondent argues that the predicted problems (such as loss of trade) did not transpire and there are overall benefits. If road pricing is the same then it might be acceptable.

In the last two passages the respondent returns to his worry about the cost. He considers the use of subsidy but realises that this would undermine the objectives of road pricing. He stops his construction of a counter argument to the problems he sees and concludes that it is a difficult issue.

Conclusion

The core category, also known as the phenomenon, is acceptability. An opinion about acceptability is dependent on the categories of utilitarianism, fairness and sincerity. Utilitarianism has the subcategories of concern about efficiency and concern about the environment. Fairness has the subcategories of provision of needs, payment for services and equality of treatment. Sincerity has the subcategories of trust of players and trust of planners. These categories and subcategories are linked together in ways that describe arguments about road pricing. These descriptions are known as strategies and have been summarised in Table 6.3. In part the grounded theory as it stands at this stage is a complete representation of how people argue about road pricing. To recap, they are:

1   direct-effect strategy: not concerned with how the revenue of road pricing is used but the effect of road pricing on travel patterns. This balances concern about efficiency, concern about the environment, provision of needs and equality of treatment. For example, a typical argument would say that even though road pricing might improve the environment the respondent is concerned about the trade of shopkeepers in the charged area;
2   indirect-effect strategy: arguments that are concerned about by-products of road pricing, where by-products can be money or information. This strategy balances concern for efficiency, concern for the environment, payment for services, provision of needs and sincerity of planners. Typical arguments would include advantages seen from spending revenue and concern about how information on drivers' movements could be used;
3   contribution strategy: arguments that involve comparing the amount one group of drivers pay compared to another. This involves payment for services, equality of treatment and sincerity of players. A typical example would be arguing that the residents in a charged area should not have to pay.

In Chapters 7, 8 and 9, selective coding discovers of how acceptability is affected by the different strategies. In these chapters, it is seen which strategies improve acceptability, in order to choose between design options for urban road pricing. Therefore as far as Chapter 6 is concerned, selective coding presents an opportunity to conclude an important step in grounded theory construction. The theory has been constructed to a stage that the concepts and the strategies are able to explain arguments that were recorded.

Chapter 7

Discovering Patterns in the Direct-effect Strategy

Introduction

The direct-effect and indirect-effect strategies relate to how road pricing can be used to meet urban transport policy objectives (such as efficiency and environmental improvements). The direct-effect strategy covers the argument that road pricing can meet policy objectives by influencing the demand for travel (primarily by the increased cost of travel deterring drivers from making trips). The indirect-effect strategy reflects the argument that road pricing can help meet these policy objectives not directly, but by providing revenue to invest in other transport measures that then meet the objectives. Therefore the analysis of consequences of the direct-effect strategy aims to discover the extent to which it is acceptable to meet policy objectives by directly influencing demand through pricing. This is approached by considering each of the main policy objectives in turn and seeing if a direct-effect argument is considered acceptable. A complete answer to the question of acceptability cannot be given though until the indirect-effect strategy has been analysed as well. This is because at some point the two arguments do merge. Therefore, while there is some discussion of the implications of the patterns in the conclusion to this chapter, there is a more complete consideration in the conclusion of Chapter 8.

From the Perspective of Transport Efficiency

Definition of Transport Efficiency

Transport efficiency is about the efficient use of resources in the execution of transportation. The resources can range from money costs (such as the cost of the vehicle being used) and time (such as the time a journey takes) to the impact on the environment. An efficient method of transportation would have an acceptable balance between the different resources that were being used.

For example, if running a car costs more than a person earns then it could be deemed an inefficient form of travel; if the combined impact of drivers ruins the environment it might also be inefficient; but if car travel is affordable and the impact on the environment is outweighed by the time savings then it might be efficient.

Transport economics tries to accurately balance the conflicting benefits and problems of transportation (often time benefits weighed against operating costs and environmental impacts) to determine what is efficient. However, ultimately the balance is a subjective decision because it depends on how individuals decide to value resources such as their time and money (Pearce and Nash, 1981, pp. 8–11). Economics overcomes this problem by aggregating the subjective opinions of individuals. This research approaches the problem by looking at how people talk about efficiency and then finding common themes about how to reach acceptable scenarios.

Because the idea of transport efficiency balances competing resources, it does merge into the other objectives. For instance, accessibility, economic growth and environmental protection can all be included in an assessment of efficiency. However, the respondents in the taped interviews did try to assess the overall balance of objectives as well as comment about the impact of road pricing on specific objectives. This justifies considering transport efficiency as an objective in itself.

When faced with the problem of knowing whether to categorise a quotation under the objective of efficiency a more pragmatic definition can also be used, based on a distinction in Button (1993, p. 94) between pure congestion and pure pollution. If the problem is congestion it afflicts only the users of a transport system, but if the problem is environmental it affects passive victims who are non-users. As congestion is the main indicator of inefficiency, a working definition of efficiency encompasses the idea that only road users and transport providers are afflicted. This type of working definition of efficiency can be seen in May (1997, pp. 45–50).

Two Arguments Using the Direct-effect Strategy

The purpose of this subsection is to show which arguments have been related to the concept of transport efficiency and how the direct-effect strategy can be read into these arguments. In Excerpt 7.1 the direct-effect strategy reflects an argument that road pricing is advantageous because it better reflects the actual cost of driving and allows people to make efficient travel decisions. In Excerpts 7.2–7.4 the direct-effect strategy reflects the argument that if people have to pay an extra charge they will decide not to travel and this will make the system more efficient for other people.

Excerpt 7.1

5   And its a very big thing that car drivers have now. I have a car and the temptation to use the car is tremendous precisely because it has such low marginal cost to it. Average cost of running a car might be quite high but so much of the cost is fixed

M   ⌈yes

5   ⌊apart from depreciation of the thing. But even if you take the other costs your insurance and your road fund licence and all that sort of stuff its all fixed.

M   You're paying then anyway.

5   And even if things like the use of tyres and servicing are partially a marginal cost people don't perceive, the perception isn't that it is a marginal cost. This is ((pointing to the typical urban road pricing proposal)) a better approximation than fuel taxes.

In the first utterance of Excerpt 7.1 the respondent ponders the fact that he owns a car and there is a great temptation to use it. The fact that he chooses the word 'temptation' implies that he may be using his car more than he should, or that the use of the car has a somewhat negative effect. This interpretation is supported in other parts of the interview, where the respondent has linked driving to congestion and environmental problems. Therefore 'temptation' refers to a policy objective and although it is not specifically defined it has been classed as concerned with the idea of using resources efficiently.

Then the respondent explains there is the 'temptation' because there is a low marginal cost to driving. In other words, he is bringing in an economic argument. The respondent goes on to explain why he has linked the problem of 'low marginal costs' to car use. This is because he thinks a lot of the costs associated with running a car are 'fixed' and have to be paid regardless of how much a person uses their car.

The respondent does not say that total costs are not met by the amount people pay in taxes, but he does say, jumping to the last utterance, that the problem is one of discrepancy between fixed and running costs. Because few things are perceived as marginal costs, people drive either because they have paid or because they do not know the true running costs. He considers existing marginal costs for driving, such as fuel taxes, but decides that urban road pricing offers a 'better approximation'. Thus the argument of this respondent can be seen in terms of the direct-effect strategy, because the system of paying for road use, inherent in urban road pricing, will have an overall benefit on efficiency. He does not yet consider the equality implications.

Excerpt 7.2

6   I think that (2.0) speaking as a cab-driver that have been here for 25
      ⌈years
M ⌊O.K.
6   driving in the city. A lot of the reason to why there is congestion in the city, you'll find that basically cars are just in there for one reason and one reason only. They're only there for let's say, to coin a phrase my dad always used to say, because me Great Aunt Fanny's sitting next to them wants to take her picture of Edinburgh Castle as they're walking along as they're driving along ((extra emphasis placed on previous four words)) Prince's Street. They've seen the castle, they've seen the Scott monument, they've seen all they need to see and a wee trip down Holyrood Palace, not interested in going in and having a look at it, just interested in taking a photo and saying right I've seen enough let's get out of here.
M   Yeah
6   ⌈You see
M ⌊Yeah
6   and that basically is the bottom line. And that's what you would find if you would stop half these cars. You know.
M   Yeah
6   Now if you put a barrier up there and you asked them what they were doing in the city centre what business they were doing in it they say oh nothing ((previous two words softly uttered)) I'm just going down to so and so, you know, because the reason, the only reason they're coming in there is to let's run the car, let's go down Prince's Street let's see the castle lit up at night, we've never seen it for a while.

In Excerpt 7.2 the direct-effect strategy is used, but this time the respondent grounds it in congestion problems. The taxi driving respondent begins by establishing the validity of his comments, by saying how long he has been driving, and on the back of this, giving his reason for congestion in the city. He appears to place the blame on capricious tourists, who drive around on whims. Then he says that, perhaps with rhetorical exaggeration, half the cars on the road fall into this category. At this point the respondent brings in the idea of urban road pricing, although a notion of it somewhat different from that portrayed in the typical urban road pricing scheme that was shown to the respondent. He says that if the drivers came to a barrier, where the implication is they have to pay, then many drivers would question what they were doing there. The assumption is that this would reduce traffic because many people would not pay to drive without a proper purpose. This is an example of the direct-effect strategy because the respondent thinks that urban road pricing will produce a benefit to efficiency as road space is freed for drivers with a proper purpose. The respondent has not considered at this stage of the interview the full equity implications of these effects.

Excerpt 7.3

M   So then you wouldn't be opposed
⌈ then
6   ⌊No
M   Purely for the reason it would be stopping non-essential trips?
6   Oh yes oh yes without a shadow of a doubt. There's no way that somebody would come in from the outskirts of the city just to run along Prince's Street and whenever they hit that barrier that yellow circle where there's a barrier and you say you better give me your 50 pence.

In Excerpt 7.3 the interviewer checks that the respondent actually would find road pricing acceptable, in case he might add to his argument. The answer comes back that road pricing is acceptable, and the interviewer summarises the argument, by asking if it is for the reason that road pricing would help stop inessential trips. The respondent agrees and, when saying so in the final section of speech, confirms the parts of the argument that were assumed in the previous paragraph that analysed his strategy.

Excerpt 7.4

6   … or they bill them for whatever it is, you know what I mean. And that's exactly what you know, if people want to use the roads they're going to have to learn to pay for them.
M   OK
6   Its as simple as ABC.

As the respondent had given an argument for road pricing based on a method of charging that is different from the electronic method implied in the typical urban road pricing scheme, the interviewer explained the electronic charging method to the respondent, in place of the physical barrier he was imagining. After this explanation his acceptability did not change, but he used the opportunity to add another point to his argument. This is shown in Excerpt 7.4.

Comparing Excerpts 7.1 and 7.2–7.4, while the arguments are different the strategies are the same. Neither is concerned with how the money from road pricing is spent and both see an overall benefit in using urban road pricing, because some people will decide not to drive. This is what makes both describable in terms of the direct-effect strategy. However, while Excerpt 7.1 expresses how urban road pricing allows a driver to assess the cost of the journey, the responses in Excerpts 7.2–7.4 focus on the aspect that having to pay more will deter people from making trips. In these excerpts both arguments happen to be acceptable to the respondents.

Comparing Other Responses to Decide on the Acceptability of Using the Direct-effect Strategy

Excerpt 7.5

31 So, yes, we do have to genuinely curb and bring back the faster you drive your car the more petrol you, the further the car you drive your car the more petrol that you use, and therefore if you tax petrol you put put a genuine (charge on car use).

M   ( )

In Excerpt 7.5 the respondent has been told about the advantages of urban road pricing to better reflect the costs of driving. Thus he has to provide an answer to the type of argument proffered in Excerpt 7.1. It is no surprise that he chooses to use the same strategy, i.e. the direct-effect strategy about the advantages of urban road pricing, to make a decision about whether to drive (although it does support the plausibility of analysing the discourse by reference to the strategies). Instead of agreeing with this advantage of road pricing, the respondent questions whether road pricing is the best way to achieve this. He argues that petrol tax will achieve the same and the fact there is a mechanism already in place to collect petrol taxation implies that the effort involved in introducing urban road pricing is not needed.

While Excerpt 7.5 serves as an example of an opinion that road pricing is not needed to perceive the cost of driving, it is just one person's view and another, such as in Excerpt 7.1, can have the opinion that road pricing would be superior. What both excerpts have in common though is the idea that drivers need to be able to perceive the costs and at an even more basic level actually pay something to drive. What needs to be defined in both quotations are *the other objectives* for paying the charge, which could define the level of the charge and when it should be paid. Once these are decided it becomes clearer whether road pricing could be a superior option to fuel taxation. Therefore as a preliminary idea for an acceptable pattern in the use of the direct-effect strategy, there could be a role for road pricing to let people assess costs and make efficient decisions.

The other objectives include the extent to which road pricing can be used to reduce traffic to improve efficiency. Unlike the example of perceiving the costs of driving this issue raised more concerns amongst the interviewees.

Excerpt 7.6

M   Would you find it acceptable?
53   Yes I would personally.
M   OK why would you?
53   errm Because I realise that errm there has to be some form of restriction in town centres for vehicles, so I would be prepared to pay if I had to go into town, and it would probably dissuade me from going into town and I would find alternative methods.

Excerpt 7.7

53   And possibly people who go in there less who don't actually need to go in there would pay as much as people who really do need to go in there on a regular basis.
M   But that's a good thing?
53   No I think that's a bad thing.

The respondent in Excerpt 7.6 unequivocally says that road pricing is acceptable, because of its restraining effect on traffic, the amount of which the respondent recognises as problematic. But in Excerpt 7.7 the respondent continues to verbalise his thoughts about road pricing and extends his line of thought to identify problems with road pricing. This time he makes a distinction between people that need to drive to the city and people that do not, and because both sets of people will have to pay the charge he thinks it is bad. This is interpreted to mean that road pricing may interfere with the provision of needs for the essential users, and thus be unfair.

In terms of the direct-effect strategy the respondent is saying that the utilitarian benefits from restraining traffic might have problems when the specific provision of needs of different groups are taken into account. This is a problem that is difficult to answer and an underlying acceptable idea, such as found in the quotations about perceiving costs, cannot immediately be found to resolve the conflict between Excerpts 7.6 and 7.7, and leave open the possibility of road pricing. The problem about the fairness of providing for individual needs is further illustrated when accessibility and economic objectives are considered.

Road Pricing and Accessibility, Economic Growth and Land Use Objectives

Definition of Objectives

Transport efficiency can be understood as a balance between several factors. It is a measure of efficiency to be able to reach chosen destinations or to be able to afford to travel. If accessibility is poor, then instead of changing the transport system it is an option to change land use patterns, to make destinations accessible or affordable. This section considers the objectives that reflect these connections, called accessibility, economic growth and land use patterns.

It can be argued that urban road pricing can meet these objectives by influencing the level of traffic. If there is a charge then there may be less traffic and the improved flow may allow drivers to access destinations more easily than prior to the charge. This improved accessibility might have benefits to business and improve the local economy. From the land use pattern perspective, road pricing may be understood as discouraging traffic in one area and encouraging development in another.

Evidence on the Use of the Direct-Effect Strategy

The evidence is divided into three groups that reflect the objectives and how they overlap. First, accessibility is merged into concerns about economic growth. Then the second and third groups link accessibility and economic growth to land use. This is because there are two land use issues: one about relocation of activities to other sites and the other about rerouting of traffic.

Excerpt 7.8

37   They already complain bitterly about the lack of parking in Central Cambridge, they attribute the loss of trade to the lack of parking.

M   Yeah

37   And we are inevitably involved in this matter of out of town shopping centres.

M   ⌈Yeah

37 ⌊You know. Err. If if you know Mill Road in Cambridge, a very long long
    ⌈road
M   ⌊Yeah
37 with a lot of shops in it, I would imagine, I think I counted them, its probably
    got 120 retail outlets in it you know. By and large they attribute the lack of trade
    to the difficulty in going somewhere near your shop you want to buy from, err,
    and then parking your vehicle when you get there. Throw another disincentive,
    and it will be definitely within your cordon,
M   Hmm hmm
37 Yeah, definitely within your cordon. Throw another disincentive into it and they
    would (0.5) they would regard that as err some of them genuinely will regard
    that, I'm not exaggerating this, as the final nail in the coffin.
M   Yeah yeah

In Excerpt 7.8 the respondent links accessibility to the objective of
maintaining economic growth. Referring to members of his interest group,
he says that they attribute economic problems to lack of parking, which is
another way of saying that if the customers cannot park they cannot access the
shops. He briefly mentions the link of this problem to out-of-town shopping
centres, though he does not expand on this. (Perhaps he is making a connection
that it is easy to park at out of town centres, hence easier to access them, and
they are attracting more customers than city centre traders.) Instead he goes
on to outline the problems of traders in one of the main shopping streets in
Cambridge. He explains the problem of access, created by reduced parking
provision, and says that road pricing is the same style of policy. This will
make access even more difficult and suppress trade even further, causing
some businesses to close. This argument, focusing purely on the restraint
aspect of road pricing, is an example of the direct-effect strategy, where the
respondent has a low opinion that road pricing will meet some of the specific
needs of his members.

Excerpt 7.9

M   Because of that could you find such a scheme acceptable? (1.0) I mean if you
    had to vote on it would you support it?
8   Not being affected on the type of business I run, possibly as an individual yes,
    but as a business person and a representative of a number of small businesses I
    find it very very difficult to get them to accept the principle of this. In reducing
    profit margins, working already to very tight profit margins, its very difficult to
    add another cost on too.

In Excerpt 7.9 the same strategy and type of argument is used. The respondent says that road pricing will not affect his needs, but will affect the economic needs of his members.

Excerpt 7.10

M   Do you think those disadvantages might ever be outweighed by benefits, such as improved environment?

8   We have a problem getting people switched onto environmental ways of things. I think perhaps there is a step before.

M   ( )

8   Disadvantage to small business is how people will look at it.

The same respondent is asked in Excerpt 7.10 if these negative effects could be outweighed by other benefits. While the respondent has given a low opinion about the use of road pricing to provide for business needs, the interviewer has asked about the utilitarian benefits to see if a positive opinion of this concept can outweigh the other. The answer seems to be no. This is because, while issues such as the environment are indubitably important, there is, in the opinion of this respondent, a 'step before' road pricing. (Questions about what the 'step before' were asked but fall outside the use of the direct-effect strategy so are not discussed here.)

Excerpt 7.11

33   Well this whole question of road pricing is a very complex issue in that at the end of the day most business persons, whether they be small, medium or large companies are concerned as to the effect on competitiveness.

M   Yeah

33   And the discussions that we had with members in this region have all come round to the fact that at the end of the day how is it going to affect our competitiveness.

M   Yeah

The respondent in Excerpt 7.11 expands on how the business community will look at the issue of road pricing. He thinks that road pricing reduces purely to the issue of competitiveness. This means that businesses feel that they may be placed at a disadvantage because the road pricing charge will not affect some of their business competitors. In terms of the direct-effect strategy the argument focuses on the equality of treatment between different groups of businesses and the provision of the need for economic growth. While the respondent does not offer an opinion about whether the utilitarian benefits may outweigh the individual provision of needs, he is concerned that road pricing would not treat people equally.

Excerpt 7.12

33 So there will be increasing concern because in this region we have some outposts like Great Yarmouth, Slough, like
⌈Southend.

M ⌊Yeah

33 and and they do feel as they do in Lowestoft, that at the end of the line, and their competitiveness then is is very much in their minds, if it takes such a long time to get there how are they in that very competitive world going to keep their end well and truly up.

M Yeah

The same respondent continues and links the competitiveness problem to issues about land use in Excerpt 7.12. He uses an analogy with towns that are on the outskirts of an economic region to argue that accessibility problems make it difficult for business in these regions. Thus he is implying that accessibility problems affect the economy of the town in favour of somewhere else. This is a continuation of the direct-effect strategy with the focus on equality of treatment between different regions.

Excerpt 7.13

38 In fact I would think that the traders here would go berserk if it was introduced in Cambridge and not anywhere else.

So when someone like the respondent in Excerpt 7.13 says that traders would go 'berserk' if they were the only ones paying, their equality of treatment concerns can be understood, because they are concerned they may lose their share of trade.

Excerpt 7.14

40 My feeling with this ((pointing to the typical urban road pricing proposal)) is that's a broad brush approach with a single cordon, as I say, will create distortion in favour of out-of-town areas.

This problem is not confined to other towns in the region, but to out of town centres as well. This is shown in Excerpt 7.14.

Excerpt 7.15

9   I think long-term wise I would be worried the centre might die out because people wouldn't bother going to use the centre but go to shopping centres out of the centre,

⌈ so

M ⌊Which you wouldn't like to see?

9   No

The same problem is raised in Excerpt 7.15, where the interviewer also asks if 'out-of-town shopping centres' are to be seen as a problem. Unfortunately no clear information was elicited in this interview or others about why out of town shopping centres were seen as a problem. However, it is satisfactory for this research to know that the arguments can be understood in terms of the direct-effect strategy.

Excerpt 7.16

M   Do you see any disadvantage for Cambridge with

46   With road pricing?

M   Yes

46   Yes, Peterborough is the biggest err I think Peterborough has a much better shopping area, much bigger err, you can get to it on the train although I suppose ( ) in their cars aren't going to be doing that. Its its if you I think you could price people out of Cambridge, the ordinary shoppers, and you'd just be left with the tourists.

M   Yes, yes

As well as encouraging changes in land use patterns road pricing can cause rerouting of problems. In Excerpt 7.16 the respondent considers that road pricing might deter shoppers from the centre of Cambridge. This has problems for the vitality of the city, which have been described in the previous excerpts.

Excerpt 7.17

42. Its very difficult because I suspect that if you spoke to various of our members you'd get different responses dependent upon their needs etc.

M   Yeah
42   Errm and the only problem with that is that to, if it is in isolation i.e. this happens at Cambridge but doesn't happen at Peterborough, then you're we're all shooting ourselves in the foot.
M   Yeah
42   What you tend to do is just move the problem.

Then in Excerpt 7.17 another respondent thinks what might happen in Peterborough if people stop going to Cambridge. Not only might the traders lose in Cambridge but the traffic problems that were once in Cambridge would move to Peterborough.

Excerpt 7.18

43   I have to say we we basically don't oppose road pricing errm we know that there is to be a pilot scheme here in Cambridge err we would not be fundamentally opposed to it err there are certain reservations we have about it particularly on certain trunk routes, you know, if you have a route that is a single route from one place to another we think that you shouldn't price that one, if you've got a multiplicity of routes you can then divert people
⌈around
M   ⌊Right
43   through different routes in that sense.

In Excerpt 7.18 this issue about road pricing relocating traffic problems is raised again. The respondent is concerned that road pricing diverts traffic from trunk roads. While this argument is practically more valid when applied to the problem of inter-city road pricing and motorway tolls, it does illustrate the immense rerouting problems faced by introducing road pricing in Britain's particularly dense road network. For example, if a charge is introduced drivers might change destination or route or take an alternative mode instead of paying the charge. This is potentially a significant problem for motorway tolls (Nellthorp, 1994).

Reading a Pattern into the Evidence

The problems perceived in using urban road pricing as part of a package to improve accessibility and economic growth and prevent unwanted land use changes are all interconnected and can be related to the problems associated with using road pricing to improve efficiency by deterring traffic. This has been shown by giving examples where respondents discuss these connections and by noting that the same strategy has been used to argue for and against road pricing meeting these objectives. The strategy that has been used is the direct-effect strategy, where respondents weigh up the influence that road pricing might have on meeting objectives in the context of the concepts of utilitarianism (overall benefit), provision of needs (individuals' ability to meet needs), and equality of treatment (how much it matters that some people might not meet their needs even if there is an overall benefit).

In the interviews there was evidence that these benefits might occur in utilitarian terms. However, when it comes to provision of individual needs, indicated primarily by accessibility, economic growth and what activities people want to do where (land use desires), and whether these needs matter, indicated by assessment of equality of treatment, there are numerous arguments against road pricing.

Therefore a hypothesis seems to be developing that it is 'theoretically unacceptable' to use road pricing to meet the objectives of accessibility, economic growth and land use changes by directly deterring traffic. This is because no pattern has emerged that indicates how the direct-effect strategy, when used to argue about accessibility, economic growth and land use, has the consequence of being unanimously acceptable. This idea of 'theoretical unacceptability' is discussed further in the conclusion.

Environmental Protection

Definition of the Objective of Environmental Protection

As mentioned earlier in this chapter, an assessment of transport efficiency can include environmental impacts. However, environmental protection as an objective does differ from efficiency in that it is concerned with the quality of an environment from the perspective of a passive observer in the environment and not from the perspective of road users. In other words, transport efficiency is an assessment about an activity; environmental protection is an assessment about the environment in which an activity is done. This distinction is also found in the utilitarian subcategories of efficiency and environmental concerns.

In the same way that objectives of accessibility, economic growth and land use patterns can be connected to transport efficiency, the same objectives can be linked to the objective of environmental protection. For example, an assessment about the quality of an environment may include factors such as access to places in that environment, the opportunities for economic growth and land use concerns to optimise environmental protection. In the following subsection, examples of the direct-effect strategy focus on the utilitarian impact of road pricing on the environment balanced against specific concerns of accessibility, economic growth and land use.

Evidence About How the Direct-effect Strategy is Used

The arguments that reflect environmental protection have been divided into two groups. The first (illustrated by Excerpts 7.19–7.21) links accessibility concerns to the quality of the environment by a discussion of parking issues. This illustrates the overlap with other objectives. The next three excerpts (7.22–7.24) cover the arguments that road pricing will discourage car traffic and this will improve the environment.

Excerpt 7.19

23 But the thing is where are they going to provide to park. Because all the residents in the areas will kick up hell about that because they're not going to get to their houses because they're not going to get to their doors. I mean you've got the likes of all the Marchment areas, they're not congested with cars as it is day and night
24 ⌈that true, that true
23 ⌊and that's going to be an area where everyone's going to park.

In Excerpt 7.19, the respondent talks about the issue of parking. This involves a change in land use as people may, he believes, park in the Marchment area of Edinburgh. But it is a problem for residents who, he says, will not be able to get to 'their doors', or in other words access their houses. But he also uses the word congestion and perhaps he is hinting that this efficiency indicator may get worse. Alternatively, and this is what seemed to fit in with other parts of the interview, the respondent was attempting to say there will be a shift in environmental problems. But regardless, he is using the direct-effect strategy by considering if road pricing will meet the needs of a group of residents.

Excerpt 7.20

20 Creating a cordon around the city centre would only move traffic problems

elsewhere. Edinburgh already has controlled parking in the centre, so many commuters drive to the edge of the controlled zone and park just outside it. This creates parking problems and congestion in a ring around the controlled parking zone. Such problems would be made much worse by a road pricing zone.

(Excerpt 7.20 taken from written correspondence.)

In Excerpt 7.20 an almost identical argument is used. This also indicates that the land use concern of rerouting of problems can be understood from an environmental perspective as well as a transport efficiency perspective. However, the direct-effect strategy is being used because the respondent balances the environmental benefits within the charged area with problems outside the area.

Excerpt 7.21

M   Would you find it acceptable?
22 Yes, because you wouldn't get carpark annoy.
M   Sorry I don't understand.
22 Its always a problem to get car park space anyway so I personally don't like driving in in the city.
M   So the charge would be better if you had to drive there because there would be less cars there.
22 Yes

In Excerpt 7.21 the parking issue is again addressed, and while some dimensions of the argument could be classified in terms of efficiency and accessibility, the environment was chosen because the respondent seemed to be trying to achieve a calmer, more pleasant and less aggravating environment.

Excerpt 7.22

47 I know what it is trying to achieve, which is really why I would say it is questionable in in terms of credibility, for example.
M   OK You know the economic theory behind it?
47 My view of it is as a means of controlling the use of the road unnecessary use of the roads, basically as a means of ensuring the benefits of the environment err, its a means of controlling the traffic using the road in any given urban situation.

In Excerpt 7.22 the respondent focuses more clearly on the environment. The excerpt was taken from near the start of an interview, which is why the interviewer asks whether the interviewee knows the theory behind road pricing, because this was one of the introductory questions that was used to ascertain the level of knowledge of the respondents about road pricing. In this case the respondent ignores it to embark on a questioning of whether road pricing, as a means of reducing traffic, should be used to improve the environment. In terms of the grounded theory he begins to ground his argument in the direct-effect strategy by giving his opinion about a property of the utilitarian subcategory of the environment.

Excerpt 7.23

47   I think, going back to the principles why why do you have urban road pricing schemes err, as I said, my view is the reason for an urban road pricing scheme is is to errm maximise or minimise, if you like …

M   Yeah

47   … the the use of the road the unnecessary use of the roads for the benefit of (0.5) the whole.

M   Yes.

47   For the environmental benefits in the the many ways. I mean we aren't just talking about air we're talking about all the various environmental aspects which are involved. And one will accept that, you know, fine.

M   OK

In Excerpt 7.23 the same respondent continues to argue that road pricing may improve the environment overall and actually uses the utilitarian motif, 'for the benefit of the whole'. In other parts of the interview though, he goes on to criticise road pricing for not meeting other objectives on a more personal level. Thus he balances an opinion about the utilitarian advantages of road pricing against specific sets of needs.

Excerpt 7.24

46   Yes it would be fine, if I go into town I always cycle, occasionally get the bus. I suppose occasionally get a lift if I want to take the children and my husband's there, but this would be an incentive to make sure I didn't ever get a lift, and that I did always take the bus on those few occasions. Errm and I guess the same would apply to most people err that the bus services are there for most people. I live near Addenbrook's Hospital.

M   Yeah

46   Err so for people a couple of miles out from the the centre if they can't cycle
or don't want to for some reason there are bus services, they're not terribly
good and I think they're rather expensive. Err so there is the temptation to drive
if you can and I think you know anything which tips the balance away from
driving in favour towards public transport is a good thing.

In Excerpt 7.24 the respondent gives a similar argument that road pricing
would deter her driving with her husband and this has advantages for the
environment. Then the respondent brings in the contribution that public
transport can make to the environment. The respondent implies that public
transport causes less damage on the environment and although public transport
is sometimes inefficient road pricing would help ensure that people took the
more environmentally friendly public transport. This argument is still based
in the direct-effect strategy, though, because the respondent is talking about
influencing the demand for car travel. However, it does bring in another slant
to the argument because instead of merely saying that road pricing deters trips,
she is saying that road pricing encourages a more environmentally sensitive
alternative.

In the excerpts in this subsection two things seem to be happening. When
balancing environmental protection against the issues of accessibility the
arguments do not reflect that the environmental gains from deterring traffic
outweigh problems of individual need. This fits in with the evidence from
the previous section which balanced efficiency gains with other needs. The
second observation is that the environment is important and road pricing is
not discounted as a method of alleviating environmental problems. This is
similar to the argument described earlier, that road pricing could contribute
to efficiency gains. However, in all cases there is still the issue about how to
resolve the conflict between utilitarian gains and fairness in the provision of
other needs. This thesis goes on to suggest that the resolution depends on how
the direct-effect strategy is used with the indirect-effect strategy arguments.

Merging the Direct-effect Strategy with the Indirect-effect Strategy

Connected with the discouragement of car traffic is the role of public
transport. The final set of excerpts explores the argument about improving
the environment from the perspective of encouraging public transport (i.e.,
it is different from the perspective of merely discouraging car trips). While
these arguments have been classified in the direct-effect strategy they are
merging in with the indirect-effect strategy because they begin to consider

how the revenue can fund other measures. Using road pricing to alter the relative demand between public transport and private car use is part of the direct-effect strategy. Meanwhile, using revenue from increased patronage to improve public transport can be interpreted as an indirect-effect strategy because conceptually paying a charge to use public transport is comparable to paying a charge to continue to drive. Whether, the benefits to public transport, and hence the environment, are derived from the direct- or indirect-effects of road pricing are not always clear, as the following excerpts illustrate.

Excerpt 7.25

41   I think I would adopt the same attitude as we did for the bus lanes in Cambridge, that was very controversial, and that is to say it gives public transport an added advantage, it cuts down on pollution which we're all concerned about.

In Excerpt 7.25 a bus company executive discusses his acceptance of road pricing from the constraints of his occupation. The quotation is taken from a section of the interview that addressed if it would be controversial that the bus industry would get a money benefit from road pricing, in terms of extra patronage or direct subsidy. The respondent argues that, seen from the perspective of improving the environment and 'cutting down on pollution', this is acceptable. He is not talking specifically about the indirect-effect of how the money could be spent on improving public transport but about the advantage in deterring car trips. Therefore the argument has been classed as the direct-effect strategy – using road pricing to influence demand and meet the needs of public transport and improve the environment.

Excerpt 7.26

M   So would you find the scheme acceptable? like that
     (1.0)
13   From a railway point of view or a personal point of view?
M   Both, if they're very different.
13   hmm From a railway point of view yes because obviously we want to take as many people out of their cars onto railway services and that's purely a business sense. We would obviously feel that ((pointing at typical urban road pricing proposal)) would discourage people from using their cars. It err would create a greater inconvenience to them and obviously hit them in the pocket and make them more inclined to use rail travel. From a personal point of view, looking at that there and the boundary you're proposing I wouldn't personally have a lot of worry with that err.

M   Right
13   I do feel if it was going out much more you would start to inconvenience people
     you know and hit them for the sake of just hitting them you know ( )

In Excerpt 7.26 a railway executive more blatantly links the business advantage of railways to the aspect of road pricing that is to do with reducing the number of car journeys. Whether this is understood as good in that his business gains, or good in that he believes railways to be more efficient and environmentally friendlier is open to interpretation. It is an argument in the direct-effect strategy, though.

Excerpt 7.27

13   But I believe we've got to start improving the present railway service by
     putting on additional rolling stock. In the mornings we're bringing people in,
     you know, ( ) them in trains, some of the rolling stock we have is 45 years old,
     it is not comfortable stuff to have people travelling in. And there's not enough
     of it.

Finally in Excerpt 7.27 the same respondent talks about the poor impression people can have of the railways because of the old rolling stock. He, a spokesman for the railways, agrees with this problem and says the comfort has to be improved. To use road pricing to do this might involve spending revenue from increased rail patronage or investing the road pricing revenue. The latter case would move into the realm of the indirect-effect strategy.

Conclusion: Acceptable and Unacceptable Consequences of Using the Direct-effect Strategy

This chapter has explored the acceptability of using arguments that are based in the direct-effect strategy of the grounded theory. This has indicated arguments that might be acceptable and, more often, unacceptable. Throughout this descriptive process the analysis has also noted ways that problems of acceptability can be overcome. This helps create suggestions for choosing acceptable objectives. To help this part of the analysis a terminology has been adopted that describes the extent to which an argument can be considered potentially acceptable to use. If problems in an argument cannot be resolved it is considered 'theoretically unacceptable'; if the problems in an argument can be resolved the conditions become 'theoretically acceptable'.

When the objective of efficiency was considered, two main arguments surfaced. First there was the issue about using road pricing to perceive the costs of driving. While there are arguments that road pricing is not needed to perceive the costs, the arguments had in common the assumption that drivers should pay something. This indicates that it is theoretically acceptable that people who do not or cannot pay should not drive. If this is accepted – and there is no evidence to suggest it is not – then road pricing can be considered as method of charging for road use. However, these parts of the argument do not define what the cost of driving should be. This is partially considered in the second argument of the direct-effect strategy which considers the benefits of increasing costs to deter some drivers. In this case the respondents found problems with road pricing not meeting individual needs.

This was illustrated when interviewees considered how road pricing might affect accessibility, economic growth and land use. The respondents indicated that, while there might be utilitarian gains, there would be fairness problems. In terms of the consequences of this evidence the analysis indicated using road pricing to deter traffic directly was 'theoretically unacceptable'. This has to be understood in the light of the evidence about the efficiency category though. If people cannot afford to drive this might adversely affect their individual needs, but it has to be accepted if the charge is acceptable. However, if the charge is there purely to deter traffic, which is one of the arguments that the direct-effect strategy focuses on, the charge is not acceptable. Therefore what people consider 'theoretically unacceptable' is the use of road pricing to purely ration road space as opposed to the principle of some type of charge.

These consequences were also explored in relation to the objective of environmental improvement. When respondents balanced the idea of using pricing to deter traffic directly, the excerpts showed similar problems to the previous section. However, road pricing was clearly considered a method that might contribute to overall environmental improvements. It was indicated that to overcome the problem between utilitarian and fairness the indirect-strategy would need to be explored. This strategy can be used to define how it is acceptable to spend the road pricing revenue and how people might consider road pricing as being theoretically acceptable.

Chapter 8

Discovering Patterns in the Indirect-effect Strategy

Introduction: The Objective of Raising and Using Revenue

Urban road pricing is not simply about influencing the level of demand for car travel; it is also about using the revenue to spend on improving efficiency and the environment. Consequently road pricing is also linked with achieving the objectives of raising and using revenue. Under the grounded theory of acceptability, the argument about raising and using revenue is reflected by the indirect-effect strategy. The indirect-effect strategy is used to argue that the revenue from road pricing can pay for a service that meets some type of need (linking the payment of service subcategory to the subcategories of provision of needs, efficiency and environment).

This chapter finds patterns in the use of the indirect-effect strategy, to discover how its use affects the acceptability of urban road pricing. As in the previous chapter that discovered patterns in the use of the direct-effect strategy, the patterns in the indirect-effect strategy can be used to recommend theoretically acceptable and unacceptable arguments for road pricing. In the penultimate section of this chapter the implications of the direct-effect and indirect-effect strategies are considered together, suggesting how road pricing can be designed around the theoretically acceptable arguments.

Aggregated Data about How to Use Road Pricing Revenue

As described in Chapter 4, on the interview design, all the interviewees were asked how they would spend the revenue from road pricing in order to improve its acceptability to them. The replies to this question have been collated in Table 8.1 and are similar to other research that found an increase in acceptability when revenue is spent on public transport and environmental measures (Jones, 1991), and recommendations to spend the revenue on the triumvirate of car drivers, general environmental protection and public transport (Goodwin, 1989).

These options for spending the revenue meet the needs of the respondents, often in more than one way. For example, public transport investment could improve the efficiency of the transport network and the environment that the transport network is within. In this research no attempt has been made to justify the advantage of one set of uses over another. The grounded theory of acceptability is grounded in the arguments about urban road pricing. To look at the logic of arguments for improved public transportation, over say a programme of road maintenance, would be using the theory in an area for which it has not been tested.

Instead the grounded theory is used to analyse arguments about using the revenue from road pricing, to see if any patterns emerge in the link between the arguments about revenue use and acceptability, rather than trying to specify how the revenue should be spent. In terms of the naturalist methodology, which was discussed in Chapter 3, this can be understood as an attempt to look for hidden connections as opposed to stating the manifest links about how to spend the revenue.

Table 8.1   Number of respondents recommending different options for spending the revenue

Option	Edinburgh	Cambridge
Public transport		
Public transport (general)	26	25
Park and ride	10	22
Measures for car drivers		
Road maintenance	9	0
Car parks	3	3
Road improvements	10	10
General environment policies		
Environmental protection	3	5
Pedestrianisation	10	10
Cycling	1	4
Enforcement (of driving)	9	0
Non-transport use		
General use	10	41.3

Arguments about How to Use the Revenue

The indirect-effect strategy combines all three categories (utilitarianism, fairness and sincerity) but not all the subcategories (only efficiency concerns, environmental concerns, provision of needs, payment for services and sincerity of planners). The subcategories can be related in two main ways:

1 linking payment for services to the provision of needs;
2 trusting that the amount of payment is linked to the cost of providing for those needs and the revenue is not used for unspecified expenses. This brings in the sincerity of planners subcategory.

The following three excerpts illustrate these types of arguments. The first two consider the separate arguments and the third excerpt combines both arguments.

Excerpt 8.1

M But but would you expect Edinburgh to get something out of it?
15 Yes I think politically you would have to in order to make it politically acceptable, particularly if road pricing occurs in Edinburgh and not other cities.

In Excerpt 8.1 the interviewer asks a very simple question about whether the respondent would expect a local benefit in Edinburgh. The respondent replies that there should be in order that road pricing is acceptable and so Edinburgh does not suffer at the expense of other cities. This argument is based on the indirect-effect strategy because the respondent agrees that Edinburgh must have some of the revenue spent on it, presumably to meet needs. Other excerpts explore this issue in greater depth.

Excerpt 8.2

M What would you recommend the the revenue was spent on, in particular in Cambridge?
32 Well I think that there has to be this understanding that it needs to be ring-fenced.
M OK
32 There's no doubt that people are simply not prepared to be taxed and then find that it just goes into the pot.
M Yeah, yes

Excerpt 8.2 illustrates concern about the second issue, trusting the motives of planners. To the question about how to spend the revenue the respondent bypasses the option of proffering opinions about different transport measures and assumes that the revenue needs to be ring-fenced and that people are not prepared to be taxed and not get anything in return. This is the use of the indirect-effect strategy, but this time bringing in the concept of sincerity. As in Excerpt 8.1 he agrees that the revenue needs to be narrowed down to a specific area, in this case ring-fenced for Cambridge. But by saying that people are 'not prepared to be taxed' without reason he implies a lack of trust, and indicates scepticism about road pricing.

Excerpt 8.3

32 So I think that there has to be this much more targeted approach, that the revenue that's going to be raised has got to be very much ring fenced.
M   Right
32 Be like that all the time.
M   And ring-fenced purely for transport improvements?
32 Yes
M   So in other words if maybe err an investment is made in public transport prior to the introduction of road pricing and then the road pricing revenue is used to repay that loan.
32 Yes
M   Similar maybe to the Norwegian model of road pricing.
32 Yes. In a sense it has to be seen that there is a cost but at the end of the day it is being put to the thing that we're having to cope with and its much more smooth running. But we haven't educated people to understand this, that if they are going to be taxed then there can be this ring fencing
⌈ element
M   ⌊hmm hmm
32 and they then feel, well this is fair, we can appreciate that because we know something has to be done.
M   Yeah

In Excerpt 8.3 the same respondent continues to discuss the idea of ring-fencing the revenue. To the suggestion that the revenue can perhaps be used to provide public transport, the respondent agrees, and when he gives the reason for maybe spending the revenue on public transport he assumes the indirect-effect strategy. He says that there is a cost, but the money that is raised should be put to the problems that people have to 'cope with'. He is saying that money should be used for payment for services for the provision of needs; the money provides solutions to problems, whether they are problems connected with service provision for the users, or problems in the environment of non-users. In his last utterance he says that if this is done then road pricing is fair and people can appreciate how the money is spent.

Establishing Patterns in the Use of the Indirect-effect Strategy

Excerpt 8.4

16 Its merely just another exchequer amount. I would be happy to pay if I knew the tax was going to improve the environment or perhaps improve the services that enable me to do my job more efficiently, which is going to mean that the environmental damage I may cause is going to be less, I'm going to be able to get from A to B with less stop and starting.

M Yes

16 You know less application of the brakes, the corners are easier to get around, I'm not going to negotiate parked cars or what have you, I would accept that that would be better if my money were actually ring-fenced in that way. You know, to aid me in that environment. But I wouldn't expect to pay twice.

Similar to Excerpt 8.3, in Excerpt 8.4 the respondent joins the concepts of the indirect-effect strategy together in a way that reflects issues of payment and trust. He opens by saying that 'it', referring to the charge, is just another 'exchequer' amount. The intonation and the context of the interview, that might not be fully reflected in this sentence, is that the respondent is very sceptical of the purpose of the charge and believes that 'it' may just 'disappear' and no connection between payment and use be established. This first utterance indicates that he has a low opinion about the sincerity of the planners. But he goes on to say that if this was not the case he would be 'happy' to pay.

The respondent mentions payment to improve the environment and services that enable him to do his job more 'efficiently'. This reflects that the payment must provide for his needs and the needs of others where they may be affected. If this is done the payment promotes an ideal situation because his personal needs are met, the needs of others are protected and there will be utilitarian efficiency and environmental benefits overall. In the last paragraph he expands on what he means by efficiency, in the context of driving heavy goods vehicles. In his final sentence he returns to the sincerity point that began the excerpt and alludes to the point that these services and alleviation measures should have been paid from existing taxation. Because they have not been, he believes charging will result in him paying twice.

The points made in Excerpt 8.4 illustrate the two main types of argument that have been related to the indirect-effect strategy in the section on linking payment to provision of needs, and payment for services to trust of planners. However, the respondent also implies that if these issues were addressed he 'would be happy to pay'. This interpretation can also be read into the previous excerpts.

From these clues there seemed to be a pattern that if these two issues were addressed respondents would find road pricing acceptable. Even though they found road pricing unacceptable, because they might not trust the planners, or they thought they already paid enough money in motoring taxes, the respondents could not disagree with this underlying logic of the indirect-effect strategy. In short the indirect-effect strategy will have the consequence of being acceptable if the following conditions are met:

1   the payment has to be used for the needs of the users of the transport system, or to protect people in the environment from the impact of the transport system;
2   the payment has to be linked to the amount of money needed for services for the provision of needs.

These two conditions represent a type of logic that people cannot argue against. This is a way of using the indirect-effect strategy that could improve the acceptability of urban road pricing.

More Evidence for Linking Payment to Needs

This section gives further evidence that the revenue from road pricing should be linked to services that provide for the needs of drivers and the needs of people in the environment affected by driving. The implication is that if the payment is spent on other services then the charge would not be acceptable because one has moved away from this rationale of how to spend the revenue.

Excerpt 8.5

M   If it was spent that way ((i.e. on the local area)) would you find the scheme acceptable?

17   Yes, yes
M   Why would you find it acceptable?
17   Err, once again it would it would put the centre of town back on a par with the outside outside shopping areas. Errm. People could come in, they would only come in, they would if they were going to ermm to pay, they would only bring cars in when it was essential.

In Excerpt 8.5 the respondent says that she would find the scheme acceptable if the money was spent on the local area. She extrapolates and says that this would improve the attractiveness of the centre compared to out of town shopping areas. In terms of the indirect-effect strategy this implies the idea that the charge, if needed because there is a traffic problem, and well spent on solutions, is actually a beneficial policy to undertake. In the last utterance, about road pricing encouraging people to drive into Edinburgh only when it was essential, she reverts to part of the direct-effect strategy, about advantages derived from people perceiving the true costs. However, the important point is that the revenue needs to be spent on needs that are related to transport provision and its impact.

Excerpt 8.6

50   You want to cut congestion ermm for two reasons I suppose, raising average transit times and cutting pollution, although (1.5) I'm yet to be convinced that that doing something like this is cutting pollution, for example, electric cars can, everyone says you cut pollution with electric cars but you'd have to charge the batteries and to charge the batteries you'd have to generate electricity and the majority of generation in this country is done from fossil fuels so all you're doing is pumping more and more hydrocarbons into the atmosphere so you know you know, again I personally would say spend it on errm a policy of public transport that actually works and I don't think there is one, I think maybe they have to invent one, come up with something new or err, or research into basically, spend spend, into on cars, things for example, such as you know, they can do it already, you can have have
M   What? Cleaner vehicles?
50   No no yes, that obviously is a by-product of everything, they can make the cleaner vehicles already ( ) and whatever. When they can make more money from cheaper technology they will. Things such as the, they've got schemes running in Japan where they have radar in the car and the car will keep a distance from each other automatically. You know sensors in the road and and that way you could keep a steady flow of traffic.
M   Right

50   The reason you don't get a steady flow of traffic is every time one person
      touches the brake the next 40 people in the queue touch the brake.
M   OK
50   And there's enough room and enough time. In Cambridge its people just not
      driving properly, or just the concertina effect of traffic. If you could just have
      a genuine spacing between cars and the input was taken out of people's hands
      then, I think, things would move a lot more smoothly.

In Excerpt 8.6 another respondent uses a similar argument that supports the
pattern in using the indirect-effect strategy to improve acceptability. He begins
by saying the problems that need solutions are congestion and pollution. He
rambles about the current options that are available, such as electric cars and
improved public transport, and in his verbalised reasoning indicates that he
thinks they will not work. He thinks what is acceptable is spending the revenue
on research into cars. The interviewer asks if this means revenue should be
spent on technology to make vehicles cleaner. But the respondent sees this as
a mere by-product that will happen when companies can make profits from
cleaner technology. Instead he links the solution to the problem, as he sees
it, that is people not driving properly, and if this is solved then the original
problems, congestion and pollution, are solved. In terms of the indirect-effect
strategy he is trying to establish a link between revenue and use (payment
for services and the provision of needs). Regardless of whether one agrees
with his specific options about how to solve the problems, it is impossible to
disagree with the underlying rationale of his argument that revenue is spent
on problems motorists encounter or cause.

Excerpt 8.7

9   Ah yes, but there's an attraction on behalf of the local authorities because its
      seen as a large source of money, and local authorities are getting a steadily
      smaller proportion of the total amount spent on transport.

In Excerpt 8.7 a respondent gives a reason for local authorities wanting to
introduce road pricing. While the respondent does not give specific options he
implies that money is needed to spend on transport related problems because
the local authority is receiving a 'smaller proportion'. This uses the indirect-
effect strategy by linking payment for services to the provision of needs.
Again the important point is that payment for services is linked to transport
related needs.

Excerpt 8.8

34   And Cambridge is not alone, there's Stamford up the road. There are plenty of places who who suffer traffic problems err but at the end of the day the object of an urban community is to to generate err, is to be a centre, is to generate wealth is is a commercial exchange, it's a centre of a community and what people do in a centre of a community is generally exchange money for goods.

M   hmm hmm

34   Now that being the case the goods have got to be there so that means that the means of getting the goods there err become like the means of moving the people to spend the money to buy the goods, an an essential means of transport, you know. There is no other way to do it. ( ) So to to if you like looking at it from from, taking the siege mentality, you're looking at penalising
⌈people

M   OK

34   for that it has really no benefit whatsoever. Its not going to stop that vehicle going into that location because its got to go there for a purpose and the purpose is is to deliver the goods that people want to buy. So you're actually not going to achieve so therefore all it does is, all it becomes is a means of raising revenue. It doesn't, there are no moral grounds for it there at all. Its a purely fiscal issue of raising revenue. Its like the argument, you know, the various arguments you know err err, heaping, err, duty on diesel fuel.

M   Yeah

34   Which is used by all and sundry to move goods on the grounds of being a thinly veiled environmental tax. Its nothing of the sort, its a means of raising revenue.

In Excerpt 8.8 the respondent begins by using the direct-effect strategy. In the first locution he says that Cambridge, like many towns, does have traffic problems. Then he says that within this scenario, commerce – which he sees as one of the main activities of a city – has to go on. In his second locution he says that this means goods and people have to get to the city centre; this is essential for a city to fulfil its purpose. Then, after a short interruption by the interviewer, he goes on to say that 'it', meaning the urban road pricing scheme, is of no help. He expands on this and says that road pricing will actually make it more difficult to deliver goods to the city centre. Thus, he has used the direct-effect strategy, and argued that road pricing will not provide for his business/accessibility needs. This is similar to arguments that were illustrated in Chapter 7.

Then in the final eight lines of Excerpt 8.8 the respondent deviates from the direct-effect strategy into the indirect-effect strategy. He says that he knows what it is really all about, and that is raising revenue. He sees no justification for this, but he provides a gateway into persuading him to find road pricing acceptable, if he can be persuaded that revenue is needed to improve the transport system. The respondent cannot be persuaded that the needs of the environment outweigh the needs of business (which is why he finds road pricing unacceptable from the perspective of the direct-effect strategy); however, he does think there are problems and if road pricing is used to raise revenue it could produce solutions (which uses the indirect-effect strategy). While the direct-effect strategy is morally ambiguous, 'has no moral grounds', the indirect-effect strategy represents a purely fiscal issue of providing money for solutions to problems that the respondent does not disagree with in principle.

Excerpt 8.9

37   The interesting thing about cities and towns is that in our opinion and more specifically my
⌈opinion
M   ⌊hmm hmm
37   towns have to be places to be successful. A town that is quiet or a town that is deserted, do you understand me, isn't a town, it might as well just be the country, do you see what I mean?
M   Yeah
37   The idea of a town is to bring people together.
M   Hmm hmm
37   Obviously in order to trade you don't actually need motor vehicles, the motor vehicle brings the person to it, the conventional market place scenario,
⌈you know
M   ⌊Yeah
37   And therefore if you could reach a situation where you could deliver, ermm, large numbers of people into a city centre, but nowadays without a motor vehicle that would be an ideal solution, how the how you do that in Cambridge is extremely difficult because you've got an established brickwork that you just can't knock down.

In Excerpt 8.9 a different respondent uses a similar argument, that makes the solution to whether road pricing can be acceptable an issue about how the revenue is spent. As in the previous excerpt, the respondent sets the scene by saying what he thinks a city or town is for. Again he sees a town as a place to bring people together, primarily to trade. Then he says that to achieve this 'bringing together' of people the car is not needed, it is simply a tool, and he implies a situation could be imagined where the transport was not the car. But he goes on to say that he cannot imagine a situation, in Cambridge, where the car is not used, and that is 'idealistic' thinking. He is saying that there is no realistic alternative to the car which would achieve this efficient delivery of people into the city centre. In the final sentence, presumably realising there are problems with the existing traffic system, which he has already admitted, he says that he does not know how to achieve this delivery of people within the 'established brickwork'. This is interpreted to mean that he is thinking about the actual provision of the transport services. Thus he is bringing his conception of the issues about road pricing around to how the revenue will be spent.

More Evidence on Linking the Payment to the Cost of Services

As well as linking the payment to services that are needed for the provision of needs the respondents showed that they needed to believe that the money would be spent in the prescribed way. This sub-section runs through some more examples to show that this rationale was accepted amongst all respondents.

Excerpt 8.10

M   What do you think the advantages and disadvantages of such a scheme would be?
     (1.0)
17   Who's the revenue going to go to?
     ((laugh))

In Excerpt 8.10 the respondent begins with a sceptical attitude to the use of the revenue, that betrays a low opinion about the sincerity of planners, which is one of the concepts in the indirect-effect strategy. This betrays the problem of a lack of trust about how the money will be used.

Excerpt 8.11

M   If the revenue was not spent on the area but went to central government, would you find it acceptable then?
17   Spending it in the way we're speaking about is going to be to the benefit of road users in the area. If its going to go to central government coffers there is no, its not going to go to the road, its going to get lost in another budget, and I don't see it should be a general revenue tool.

Excerpt 8.11 is from the same respondent and the interviewer asks whether, if the revenue did not stay in the area, but went to a central government to be redistributed from there, the charge would be acceptable. The respondent stresses that the revenue must be spent on road users in the area, and in doing so enforces the principle of linking the amount of payment to the cost of service provision.

Excerpt 8.12

41   And I wouldn't want to see us going back to what we had prior to deregulation, which was a blanket subsidy given for operating a level of service.

M   Right

41   We should be able to identify exactly what has been paid for.

M   Hmm hmm

41   And then people who pay the money can decide whether they want the service or not, you know,

M   Right

41   Whether they want to subsidise the service or whether they don't want to subsidise the service, subsidise is the wrong word really, whether they want to contract to operate that level of service at that time of night, err, and that way you keep the two things separate, and then you don't get accused by different groups that you're profiteering. You know, you're providing a service when you know you can do to meet the commercial requirements of the company. Err and socially necessary services are provided by the county council.

In Excerpt 8.12 the respondent discusses the problem of taking money from road users in private cars to use on public transport. He says that there must not be a 'blanket subsidy', but a handful of services that need to be provided on top of the usual services. He struggles in the last paragraph to say what he means because he does not want to be mistaken for talking about subsidy, nor the socially necessary services that are provided by the County Council. But he is using the indirect-effect strategy and he is getting close to saying that road users should pay for the alleviation measures and where these are provided by bus services this is acceptable. While one can disagree on whether public transport provides the best solution, it is universally acceptable to the restricted sample of respondents that money gets spent on solutions.

Excerpt 8.13

14   A lot of taxes have started out as having at being directed at certain expenditure but they have a habit of eventually not being related to expenditure.

M   Yes
14   The previous car taxation is one of the things

Excerpt 8.13 shows another articulation about problems in linking revenue to use. Here the respondent is saying that road pricing will end up the same as the other taxes. There is no direct relationship between payment and service provision and if the same happens to road pricing there is no advantage because the link between the people that pay the charge and the services they use is irrelevant. The only way to get over this problem is to make sure the revenue is linked to the cost of solutions to traffic problems. Therefore, although using the indirect-effect strategy to argue against urban road pricing, the respondent is also saying how these problems can be overcome.

Excerpt 8.14

M   How do you think the revenue should be spent to maybe safeguard the interests of your members?
43   As you know if you pay a road fund licence which is still laughably called a road fund licence
M   ((short laugh))
43   it simply gets paid into the exchequer and there is no direct relationship at the moment, even on petrol tax, err or on on road fund licence
M   ⌈Yeah
43   ⌊you know. So it would go somewhat against the established order of things, that if we do start paying for to cross the cordon, that that money somehow is going to be sequestered
M   ⌈Ear-marked
43   ⌊and ring-fenced and not used in other ways. So what you're suggesting I don't think think would happen.

A similar point is made in Excerpt 8.14. The respondent does not find the charge acceptable because he does not believe that the money will be ring-fenced. However, if it was, even though the respondent does not believe it would be, the charge would be acceptable. Again the respondent is using the indirect-effect strategy to argue against road pricing and also showing how the problems can be overcome.

Excerpt 8.15

43   In the public's mind you've got to make an a obvious relationship, look you've bought this system because you've paid for it by crossing the line you know.

M   hmm hmm

43   Because they don't see road fund licence or petrol tax going into anything in particular, which it doesn't.

In Excerpt 8.15 the same respondent confirms that this use of the indirect-effect strategy is acceptable. He does this by stressing the connection between payment and use along the lines that have been mentioned: linking the payment to needs for drivers and those affected by driving and linking the amount of the charge to the cost of the system.

Excerpt 8.16

23   But having said that it should have been done in the past using the road tax and the petrol tax. But its just another form of tax, that's what I say.

M   But it makes sense to spend that tax on the people that are actually paying it? (1.0) Does it not?

23   Err

M   Because otherwise where does this money go?

23   It makes sense, yes, that's fine, but it hasn't happened in the past.

M   So?

23   Not all the money that that people pay in road tax or on petrol tax or whatever other taxes motorists spend it on goes directly to, its all very well saying it makes sense to do it but it it historically has never happened.

M   So you imagine this money will just disappear into government coffers.

23   Yeah yeah

M   But you still find it acceptable even though that might happen.

23   Yes, the overall benefit.

In Excerpt 8.16 another respondent agrees with the logic of transparency and spending revenue on users and alleviation. Although he has the sincerity concern that this will not happen, the excerpt does again illustrate a way that the indirect-effect strategy can be used to improve acceptability.

How to Use the Consequences of the Direct- and Indirect-effect Strategies

The Perspective from which to Interpret the Patterns

In Chapter 1 the philosophical approach of the research was described: a theory was to be developed that takes into account how people create acceptable arguments, and then this theory was to be used to suggest how to design a road pricing scheme that would be acceptable according to the theory. In developing the theory all assumptions and theoretical prejudices – of other people and the analyst – had to be accounted for. This makes the theory as accurate a reflection of acceptability as possible. This same approach is extended to the process of interpreting the theory to derive design options. This is important because the practical use of road pricing is subject to a similar set of theoretical prejudices to the notion of acceptability. Therefore when interpreting how to use the grounded theory to design a road pricing scheme it is important to account for any assumptions. This approach is also similar to naturalist methodology that was described in Chapter 3.

The only assumptions it seems fair to make in the interpretation have been derived from the grounded theory and are based on the patterns that have been derived from the strategies in the grounded theory. If other assumptions were made there would be no evidence to suggest that they are acceptable, other than theoretical prejudices (that the grounded theory was developed in part to overcome). Thus to keep the methodological integrity of the thesis, it is essential that choices between road pricing options are made only using the patterns discovered in the grounded theory.

Summary of Theoretically Acceptable Arguments in the Direct- and Indirect-effect Strategies

In Chapters 7 and 8 the consequences of using the direct- and indirect-effect strategies on acceptability have been analysed. This has delivered a handful of suggestions about arguments that can be seen to be acceptable to all the respondents and arguments that are not. These have been referred to as theoretically acceptable and theoretically unacceptable arguments – where the former are universally acceptable to the restricted sample and the latter are not. To aid the interpretation process, about how to use these patterns, they can be summarised under a number of rules. These rules can be understood as forming the assumptions that are used to suggest how a theoretically acceptable road pricing scheme can be designed.

Rule 1 In the direct-effect strategy the small number of respondents that were interviewed considers that it is acceptable that people who cannot afford to pay what is seen as an acceptable charge do not drive. The question then becomes what is an acceptable charge, and this is assessed in other parts of the direct- and indirect-effect strategies.

Rule 2 Also in the direct-effect strategy, it is argued that the limited set of respondents does not consider it universally acceptable to use road pricing to ration road space. By this it is meant a charge above the cost of service provision and environmental protection, to limit the amount of people driving.

Rule 3 In the indirect-effect strategy it is argued that the respondents find it universally acceptable for people to pay for the cost of their service provision and environmental alleviation measures that they cause a need for. This idea is opposed to rationing because money is spent on solutions.

Rationing, Compensation and Providing Solutions

It is possible to argue that the concepts of rationing (in Rule 2) and providing solutions (in Rule 3) are the same and are united under the idea of compensation. In the case of rationing, the extra money can be spent on compensating the people that are priced out of driving. Thus rationing contributes to a solution because: a) the people that pay more to drive are paying for a scheme that provides for their needs and protects the needs of others; and b) those who have been priced-off have received a service for not driving. A typical example would be paying to drive into a city centre and using the revenue to subsidise park and ride services for those that are priced-off. In the case of providing solutions, the people that pay to drive are actually compensating the people that provide their services and protection measures. Thus, the idea of only providing services incorporates the idea of compensation.

However, there are distinctions between the idea of rationing road space and compensating people who are priced-off (Rule 2), and compensating those people who provide the services that have been considered solutions (Rule 3). In the latter case people have entered into some compensatory monetary mechanism to be able to own a car, buy fuel and pay the excise duties. The road pricing scheme, based on providing solutions, would be a small extension of this behaviour. However, the former case of rationing would involve the drivers entering a competition whereby they had to decide if they would be the ones to pay or the ones to sacrifice their car journey and take the compensation. This has a different context to the idea of using road pricing revenue only to provide solutions.

The pertinent question for this analysis is whether the logic of linking rationing and providing solutions, under the guise of compensation, makes the argument of rationing road space that was used in the direct-effect strategy acceptable. In its favour is the idea that compensatory principles are widely adopted amongst transactions between private individuals, groups and companies. People pay other people for services or products and agree the value according to how much the seller is willing to be compensated and the buyer is willing to pay. That compensatory principles are adopted in the private sphere does not necessarily make them acceptable in the public sphere though. While the buyer and seller may agree levels of compensation, they also have the option not to trade. Therefore in the public sphere an acceptable decision has to take into account of the prerogative of people not to sell something (in the case of road pricing, their right to drive).

From the sociological and theoretical perspective that has been adopted here, a decision about the theoretical acceptability of using rationing with compensation has to be made with *no assumptions*. If it is allowed, it would be based on the *assumption* that it is necessary for people to trade. This cannot be justified from the theoretical standpoint. Furthermore there is no evidence in the data that adequate compensatory arrangements could be arranged: some people would prefer to drive than be compensated.

By not allowing rationing with compensation to be considered theoretically acceptable, one has to answer the criticism that not finding it acceptable is itself an assumption. In other words, do the people who want a system based on rationing not have as much right to organise such a system as those who want a system only based on the cost of providing solutions? A considered answer would be that both groups find the principle of paying for solutions (Rule 3) acceptable, while only one group finds rationing with compensation (a combination of Rules 2 and 3) acceptable. Therefore, although one group may prefer a system based on rationing it is not universally unacceptable to the restricted population of respondents to have a system based on providing solutions only. In short, no assumption is being made then because the argument sticks to the rules of the grounded theory.

The Objectives for Urban Road Pricing

According to the previous subsection, it remains theoretically acceptable to use road pricing to pay for measures that provide services and alleviate environmental damage. It also remains theoretically unacceptable to use road pricing directly to decrease the amount of traffic. This is the case even if the idea is to try to compensate those people that are priced-off. In terms of assigning objectives to urban road pricing, a common practice in transport planning, the objective should therefore be considered as providing finance. As long as the money provides solutions to service provision and alleviation it is acceptable that people will be priced-off. However, these effects are secondary and not the prime objective.

The Far-reaching Implications of Spending Revenue on Solutions

Without specifying the solutions that road pricing can be used to finance, it can be seen that drivers pay a share of the cost of these solutions. The fair contribution that individual road users make is considered under the contribution strategy in the next chapter. If the solution happens to be some type of environmental protection measure (e.g., tunnels in a sensitive area) then drivers pay their contribution. If the solution happens to be the provision of a park and ride service, in the same way, drivers pay their contributions. What is likely in practice is a combination of environmental protection measures and improved public transport services. This allows for the fact that improved public transport services would not be acceptable or practical to everyone – therefore a combination of solutions is needed.

A simple scenario can be postulated where road pricing revenue finances environmental protection measures and park and ride services. Given this scenario, a relevant question is how the charge should be split between the drivers who switch modes to park and ride and those who continue to drive and make use of the environmental alleviation measures. If one makes no assumptions, other than that drivers should pay for their services, the fairest way to split the cost would be evenly amongst all the drivers (including the drivers who use park and ride). This is imagining that there is a collective of drivers and a package of solutions, and no distinction is being made between the different road users or the measures in the package. From this perspective, then, there is no contradiction of the grounded theory rules.

Some people might argue that road users in high-polluting vehicles should pay more than those in low-polluting vehicles. Jumping ahead to the next chapter, this is justifiable and is covered under the patterns of the contribution strategy. However, this argument does not justify road users who use park and ride paying a different rate from those who continue to drive and use the alleviation measures, if the set of solutions is still seen as a package of measures. Rather, the people who drive high-polluting vehicles before the implementation of the solutions pay a greater share, regardless of whether they choose to continue to drive or use park and ride.

But then some might argue that the road users who use the park and ride service should pay less than those drivers who continue to drive and make use of the environmental alleviation measures. This is disaggregating both the collective of drivers and the package of measures. This can be argued from two perspectives: first, park and ride users do not make as much use of the alleviation measure as the people who drive; second, the people who continue to drive get a benefit by people opting to use the park and ride service.

In the first perspective, the people who use park and ride can argue that they do not make use of the alleviation measures that the drivers use. Therefore, the park and ride users say that they should not pay for these measures, the need for which is caused by the drivers. In this way the park and ride users are distancing themselves from the car drivers and saying that they should not pay for the solutions for the people who still drive. However, if the park and ride users can say this, then the people who still drive can say that they should not support the park and ride facility which they do not use.

Given this scenario two further situations are imaginable:

1   the park and ride users and people who drive agree to pay their separate costs. This could be chosen where it was financially advantageous (i.e., the road pricing charge would decrease) to one or both groups;
2   the park and ride users and the people who drive realise that they are mutually and financially dependent. That is, the charges for park and ride users and for people who continue to drive would increase if there was no cross-subsidy.

Therefore from this first perspective, if the park and ride users are going to rely on some subsidy from the people who continue to drive, both sets of drivers should pay the same charge (allowing for different contributions for how polluting their vehicles are).

In the second perspective, it is argued that drivers get a benefit from people choosing to use the park and ride facility. If people use park and ride they do not drive, and this means that the cost of possibly providing more alleviation measures for the people who continue to drive has been saved. This argument could then be used to justify park and ride facilities being subsidised by people who continue to drive, with those who continue to drive paying more by an amount equivalent to the benefit that they gain. Furthermore, if the situation is such that it is not possible to construct actual physical alleviation measures, then the option might be to have a ban on driving, thus the people who continue to drive should perhaps pay the time benefits that they gain by driving over using the park and ride.

In either case it can be seen that it is in the interest of the people who continue to drive to support the people that use park and ride. (How one calculates the amount of the difference in payment is a separate issue.) Looking at it from the perspective of the rules of the grounded theory, though, these types of arguments contradict the second rule about rationing road space and, in particular, the scenario of rationing road space and compensating those priced off. It is impossible to say that the people who use park and ride would do so voluntarily because continuing to drive would be more expensive. Thus the people who pay more to continue to drive are in essence paying the people who use park and ride not to continue to drive. This has already been shown to be theoretically unacceptable because the road users do not get a choice about wanting to enter the competition for road space.

Therefore, in this simple example of a hypothetical scenario where road pricing revenue is spent on a package of park and ride and environmental alleviation measures, the rules of the grounded theory point to a couple of acceptable ways of splitting the cost between the road users:

1   arguing that it is not in the interest of park and ride users, or people who continue to drive, to subsidise each other. In this case the two groups would each pay the amount needed to cover the cost of their own service provision and alleviation measures;
2   arguing that it is in the interest of park and ride users and people who continue to drive to subsidise each other. In this case, though, the two groups have to pay the same amount of money, that covers the cost of park and ride and alleviation measures.

Within these two situations the high-polluting road users would have to pay a greater contribution because they would have contributed to a greater need for the set of solutions. These issues are covered in the next chapter.

To draw a general rule out of this example, one might say that if revenue from road pricing is used to support other modes then there must be a reciprocal agreement whereby the cost of using either mode is the same. If it is in the interest of both modes then this is acceptable. The most obvious case for reciprocal agreements is between private and public transport. This type of argument, though, would need further investigation. What is important in terms of the thesis is to see that the grounded theory can be used to suggest design options.

Problems with the Acceptable Objectives

The 'theoretically acceptable' objectives about raising and using revenue are difficult to meet. The previous section showed that many respondents thought that they already paid enough in motoring taxes or that they were sceptical that road pricing revenue would be related to transport expenditure. However, the difficulty in achieving them does not negate their importance; although respondents think that the money they pay is wasted or they pay too much, it does not mean that any new money raised from urban road pricing schemes should not be spent according to the theoretical rules of acceptability. Rather, more effort should be made to make sure that it is spent in a theoretically acceptable way.

Road pricing revenue can possibly be related to transport expenditure by legal regulations to ring-fence or hypothecate the revenue for specific purposes (as is the British government's intention: Department of the Environment, Transport and the Regions, 1998). One has to hope that the electorate trusts the planners. At the end of the day this trust has to be established not just in the arena of transport and the grounded theory can give no more insight into how to achieve it.

The issue about motorists paying enough in taxation is more difficult. Existing taxation paid by motorists is not hypothecated to the cost of transport expenditure and is not specifically a charge. However, if the motorists have to accept higher taxes on the activity of motoring compared to other activities, then they might assume that the extra taxation should be spent on something connected with motoring. If there is no connection then the motorists could (and do) claim to be unfairly treated compared to other groups of taxpayers.

To answer this question, the amount that motorists actually pay and how the money is spent needs to be compared. This issue is not directly addressed in this book. This is because it goes outside the bounds of the grounded theory of the acceptability of urban road pricing and into the domain of general taxation. However, allusions are made to the issues in Chapter 11, where further research ideas are explored.

The practical problems of achieving the theoretically acceptable objectives do not, however, undermine the value of the grounded theory of acceptability and the contribution of the book's thesis. The grounded theory is the first step in developing a set of ideas about how road pricing can acceptably be used. It is part of the social science process that the theory is reworked and rigorously tested, and during this process the theoretically acceptable objectives might alter. But the point of the thesis is to show how a theory can be developed about acceptability and how the ideas of the theory can suggest design options. It does not matter if the suggestions are difficult to implement or lie uncomfortably with current thought; what matters is that a first attempt has been made to develop a theory that has some practical relevance has been made. On this basis this chapter has shown that the method of grounded theorising is achieving the thesis objectives.

Conclusion

This chapter has uncovered a pattern in the use of the indirect-effect strategy that appears to be acceptable amongst all the interview data. Namely, that it is acceptable for people to pay for the cost of service provision and environmental alleviation measures. This chapter also combines this pattern with the pattern that was discovered in the previous chapter, that it is theoretically unacceptable to use road pricing directly to decrease the amount of traffic. These rules are used to infer that the acceptable objective of an urban road pricing should be considered as providing finance, as long as the money provides solutions to service provision and alleviation. Although some people will be priced off, these effects are secondary and not to be considered the prime objective.

If this theoretically acceptable approach to designing road pricing schemes were to be adopted it could also be used to argue that it is theoretically acceptable that people who continue to drive under road pricing and people who use public transport, if revenue from road pricing has been used to improve the public transport services, should pay the same rate of charge. These ideas for applying the rules of the grounded theory are put to one side in the next chapter, while the contribution strategy, concerned with the amount that individuals and groups of drivers should pay compared to each other, is explored. They are returned to in detail in Chapter 11.

Chapter 9

Discovering Patterns in the Contribution Strategy

Introduction

In Chapter 9, the same process of analysis as in Chapters 7 and 8 is extended to the contribution strategy, which has not been discussed in detail so far. This involves uncovering patterns in the use of the contribution strategy and deciding what the patterns mean for the design options of granting certain groups of road users discounts or exemptions from the charge. Aggregated data from the questionnaire are presented which give an overview about how respondents imagined dividing the burden of road charges. Then the discourse is analysed to understand what is an acceptable way of deciding who should be exempt from the charge or have a reduced charge. This analysis uses the contribution strategy to uncover patterns in the arguments that can suggest consequences for the issue of acceptability. The chapter goes on to use the information about the contribution strategy to make recommendations about who should pay. This shows how the grounded theory can help decide between design options for a road pricing scheme. In addition, these recommendations for exemptions and discounts are briefly compared with those from the London congestion charging research programme (The MVA Consultancy, 1995).

Spread of Opinion about Discounts and Exemptions

Transport practitioners have recognised the potential for increasing the acceptability of road pricing by giving certain groups exemptions or discounts. The discounts could be administered by allowing groups of users to pay a lower rate, perhaps allowing a certain number of free journeys per month, or only charging for a pre-set number of journeys. These last two options have been called credits and caps (ibid.).

In the interviews the respondents were asked to consider which groups might merit exemptions or discounts. Their replies have been aggregated in Table 9.1.

Table 9.1   Number of respondents that thought it was acceptable to give discounts or exemptions to groups of road users

Options	Edinburgh		Cambridge		Total	
	Sure	*Unsure*	*Sure*	*Unsure*	*Sure*	*Unsure*
Emergency vehicles	29	1	30	–	59	1
Utility vehicles	19	1	19	–	38	1
Scheduled buses	27	2	30	–	57	2
Coaches	8	2	17	1	25	3
Taxis	14	7	18	7	32	14
Heavy goods vehicles	7	–	10	–	17	-
Light goods vehicles	7	2	10	–	17	2
Residents within boundary	14	1	24	–	38	1
Residents on boundary	9	2	10	2	19	4
Tourists and visitors	2	–	2	1	4	1
Mobility impaired drivers	20	–	22	–	42	–
Motorcycles	14	–	12	–	26	–

From Table 9.1, the groups that gain most support for some type of exemption or discount are:

1   emergency vehicles (98 per cent of total number of respondents);
2   scheduled buses (95 per cent);
3   disabled people (70 per cent);
4   utility vehicles (63 per cent);
5   residents within boundary (63 per cent);
6   taxis (53 per cent).

Other groups gain less than 50 per cent support from the respondents for some type of discount or exemption. Taken together, the results indicate that consideration of discounts and exemptions is important to the respondents and that they want the charge to reflect the differences between groups. This issue is reflected in the grounded theory of acceptability by the contribution strategy and to help understand how decisions about exemptions and discounts are reached the next section looks for patterns in its use.

Deriving Patterns in the Contribution Strategy

The Contribution Strategy

The contribution strategy links the categories of fairness and sincerity, but it does not consider utilitarianism. In other words, it is concerned with fairness and honesty when drivers pay a road pricing charge, but not with the actual provision of any needs such as efficiency or environmental protection. Consequently the contribution strategy uses the subcategories of payment for services, equality of treatment and trust of players.

The payment for services category refers to the amount of the charge that the respondent thinks a group of users should pay. The payment is not linked to any particular service and merely reflects that a charge is being paid. The equality of treatment subcategory reflects parts of the arguments that recognise that one group should be treated differently, and that doing so does not create any equality of treatment problems. For example, respondents might think that certain groups make different contributions to traffic problems or that road pricing affects these groups differently. In these situations it is unfair to treat these groups the same. The final subcategory that is used is the trust of players subcategory, which reflects concern that certain groups of users may abuse the system and claim exemptions or discounts fraudulently.

In the contribution strategy it was most common for the payment for services subcategory to be linked to the equality of treatment category. For example, a respondent might say that a certain group should pay less because they are different from other groups and if this is done road pricing is more acceptable. The sincerity subcategory was less used. In Chapter 6 the rationale of linking these subcategories together was given.

This section now explores the different ways of using the contribution strategy, in relation to the design option of whom to charge. The objective, as already mentioned, is to uncover patterns in the use of the contribution strategy. To do this the main groups of users and vehicles which might be treated differently are examined in turn. As the analysis progresses, patterns in the use of the contribution strategy emerge. It will also be seen that the reasons for giving exemption or discount (that form the patterns in the contribution strategy) are transferable between these groups.

Emergency and Utility Vehicles

In Excerpt 9.1, the respondent considers emergency vehicles and thinks that they should be exempt.

Excerpt 9.1

55   Because they shouldn't have to pay for doing their vital to life job

In terms of the contribution strategy the respondent uses the equality of treatment subcategory (indicated by the fact that he is referring to how emergency vehicles are treated compared to other users) and the payment for services category (indicated by considering the amount that should be paid). The property of the equality of treatment subcategory on which he makes the decision is about how 'vital to life' are their journeys.

Excerpt 9.2

14   Well, well the main reason is that they [emergency vehicles] are, like our own case, essential users. I think utility vehicles are providing a service again, err, they've got to be there, they're not doing it for fun, and they are providing a service anyway.

M   Yes, yes

14   So yes, I think that they should be exempt.

In Excerpt 9.2 the subcategories of equality of treatment and payment for services are used again. This time the respondent uses the phrase 'essential users' and qualifies it as the provision of a service that is not done 'for fun'. Because 'essential' and 'vital' are similar in context these form the first pattern in the reasons for exemption. In Excerpt 9.2 the respondent also applies the reason about being an essential user to his own case (business) and to the case of utility vehicles. Therefore this reason appears to be transferable to other groups of users.

Excerpt 9.3

40   Emergency vehicles, I would not give them a discount, because an awful lot of their movements are not emergency movements.

M   OK

40 I would make them pay. I mean there would have to be a mechanism for charging it back, but at least err.

M OK

40 Utility vehicles I would make pay.

M Why?

40 How do you identify utility vehicles today? There is no such thing as the gas company any more is there? Now a lot of the work is done by contractors.

M OK

In Excerpt 9.3 a different approach to thinking about the contribution of emergency and utility vehicles is given. The respondent thinks that emergency vehicles should pay for their journeys because many of them are not emergencies and are no different from the journeys made by other groups. The respondent extends the same argument to utility companies and says that they could not be distinguished from other businesses. However, this argument can still be understood in terms of the pattern of assessing the essentiality of a trip. In this excerpt the respondent avoids any potential relativity in defining essential users by making everyone pay. Thus the property that is assigned to equality of treatment is still about how essential trips are, but his opinion is different. This opinion is based on avoiding relativity problems. However, he does admit that at times emergency vehicles would have to have the money returned. This can be seen as admitting they might be more essential than utility vehicles.

Excerpt 9.4

38 Well one would presume that emergency vehicles should be exempt

M OK

38 And utility vehicles
⌈err

M ⌊If you can just give a reason with each one as well

38 Well emergency vehicles I think that people already feel that err you know they pay through err various systems for those services provided and it should not be that they pay pay again. So I think emergency vehicles are exempt.

M Yeah

38 Utility vehicles I think err (0.3) they probably should err pay if they've got to be in those areas at that time but with discounts

M OK

In Excerpt 9.4 the respondent begins by saying that emergency vehicles should be exempt but does not give a reason. The interviewer reminds the interviewee to give a reason and the respondent says that people 'feel' that they have paid for 'those services' and it should not be that they 'pay again'. In terms of the contribution strategy the subcategories of equality of treatment and payment for services are still being used. The respondent has said that emergency vehicles should be exempt and that indicates a difference from other classes of user, and the payment for services subcategory is used to reflect that the payment is not needed from the emergency services. Therefore this reason is different and does not fit into the pattern that was being established in the previous excerpts.

The respondent in Excerpt 9.4 goes on to give utility vehicles discounts because they 'have got to be in those areas'. Again, the equality of treatment and payment for services subcategories are used. This time the reason for discount is closer to how essential are the trips.

Excerpt 9.5

48   Emergency vehicles need to be exempt.
M   Why? (.) Even though it may seem obvious but.
48   Well its obvious, no, well, I think its unnecessary, its a small its a very small part of traffic on the road. Utility vehicles (2.0) is in is in a more marginal ( ) if I were generous I might offer them a discount errm but they could be exempt.

In Excerpt 9.5 another respondent thinks that emergency vehicles should be exempt and that utility vehicles could be discounted because they are a 'small part of traffic on the road'. In terms of the contribution strategy the respondent thinks that these groups need to be treated differently because they do not make a large contribution to the traffic problem. Again this is a different reason from the essentiality of trips.

Excerpt 9.6

36   All these bastards [utility companies] make millions of money, being monopoly suppliers, they can damn well pay.
35   They'll pass it onto the customer of course.
36   Oh they can try, but that's up to the customer.

Finally in Excerpt 9.6, the rarer case of using the sincerity category is shown. The first respondent thinks that the utility companies should pay because they can afford to. Thus if they pay their needs will be met the same as with other groups and they will not be disadvantaged. However, the other respondent in the interview raises the problem that the utility companies may pass the charge on to the customers. This brings in the subcategory of the trust of players and the second respondent is worried that the 'customer' will have to pay the charge instead of the utility company, and this is unfair because the utility company can afford to pay it. The first respondent says that it is 'up to the customer' to resist and implies it is not an excuse for exemption.

Drawing together the strands of the arguments leads to the following preliminary conclusions about the reasons for exemptions and discounts.

1   users warrant exemptions and discounts if their trips are deemed 'essential';
2   users merit exemptions or discounts if they have already paid;
3   users can have exemptions or discounts if they do not contribute much to the traffic related problems;
4   users could be given exemptions or discounts if there is a threat that they can unfairly pass the charge on to other people.

From the data, the most frequently used, and hence most important reason seems to be 1). The next subsections build on these reasons in the hope of uncovering patterns that can help decide on how to award exemptions and discounts.

Public Transport: Scheduled Buses, Coaches and Taxis

Excerpt 9.7

37   Utility vehicles these days are businesses.
M   Hmm hmm
37   I think they ought to be discounted, buses are businesses, as are coaches and taxis, so they should also be discounted.
M   OK. OK. For they're businesses you're driving at, because they have a purpose to be there.
37   Correct, for a certain extent they don't get the choice do they, if I jump in your taxi you have to take me where I want to go.

In Excerpt 9.7 the respondent decides to give discount to several groups because they are businesses and 'have a purpose to be there' (in the charged area) and do not have a 'choice'. This reason can be classified under essentiality of trips. Furthermore, it shows that the same reason is transferable between utility vehicles, businesses and importantly for this section, buses, coaches and taxis.

Again, in Excerpt 9.8 the respondent gives scheduled buses exemption because they are 'essential users'. Then he has difficulty deciding on coaches. He considers that coaches charge people to come in (yet scheduled buses also charge people to travel) and he truncates this line of argument. Then he thinks that they are providing a service that is in some way essential because it encourages business.

Excerpt 9.8

44   Err scheduled buses, I think they should be exempt, again they're a essential user err. Coaches? That's an arguable one.

M   Yes, like tourist coaches coming in, that's what I'm driving at.

44   I suppose there could be a perhaps a discounted charge.

M   ⌈OK

44   ⌊For tourist coaches. You have to bear in mind that tourist coaches are coming in there (.) it's a difficult one really err they don't have to be there they could go somewhere else, I mean they are making a charge for bringing people in so its difficult then for me to argue, isn't it?

M   Oh yes, please say you don't know

44   Difficult to say on coaches err. They provide a service and bring business err it would have to be either exempt or discount, somewhere in between the two I think. Err taxis err, well again they are providing a service, and how would people get about if there weren't taxis, would they go presumably on scheduled buses.

M   Hmm hmm

44   Errm. There's a convenience factor for for using the taxi, is it a tax on convenience? You know err (.) I think perhaps a discounted one for taxis.

However, for an unnamed reason he does not consider coaches as deserving as buses and only offers them a discount. The respondent goes on to consider taxis and realises that they also are providing a service and decides on a discount. This shows that even though the respondent is not completely sure about the validity of the cases for exemptions for different groups, he wants to create a scale about the merit of different trip purposes.

Excerpt 9.9 (on exemption for scheduled buses)

M   What reason?

52   Because they are there to reduce the traffic.

In Excerpt 9.9 a respondent thinks that scheduled buses should be given exemption from the charge. This is for a new reason about contributing to a solution for traffic problems.

Excerpt 9.10 (on taxis)

52　Yeah, I'd exempt them because they're just bringing people into town and dropping them off, there're no parking problems although they do drive into town errm, but they would reduce parking problems.

The same respondent later extends this argument to taxis and gives them a full exemption because they help to reduce parking problems.

Excerpt 9.11

38　As far as scheduled buses are concerned well presumably they (3.0) we're wanting those people to use the err public transport so you can hardly feel it is fair if if there is a payment.
M　Yeah
38　So you would have to say they come under the exempt category. As far as coaches are concerned well
　　⌈err
M　⌊They are coach loads of tourists, that sort of thing=
38　=they are part of the problem so therefore there has to be some kind of appreciation by tourist boards that coaches only come in at the free times. So I don't think they actually come into this. As far as taxis are concerned, well (0.5) I think that that's a difficult area. Some of these taxis are used because there is no other way of transporting yourself there, so I think they're in a particularly difficult category now I I think they should really be err
M　If you don't know just say
38　Well
M　If you don't know just say
38　No.

The respondent in Excerpt 9.11 considers the position of scheduled buses and decides that it is an objective to use buses more and considers it unfair if 'there is payment'. This is similar to Excerpts 9.9 and 9.10, where the respondent bases the decision on whether the vehicle is providing solutions to traffic-related problems. Then the respondent considers coaches and taxis. He thinks that coaches should not come under the influence of an urban road pricing scheme because they should only come into the charged area 'at the free times'. But instead of saying that coaches should pay if they are in the charged area he by-passes proffering an opinion and says that they 'do not come into this'. Thus no strategy can be read into this. For taxis the respondent thinks that they are a 'difficult category' because there is 'no other way of transporting yourself'. While the respondent does not offer an opinion he has pondered the issue that taxis are a service, like scheduled buses, and a decision would need to be made about how to treat their payment. Here the respondent indicates that he is going to use the contribution strategy but does not carry it through.

To the question of public transport exemption, some respondents also mentioned giving exemption to buses with the cleanest engines. If the buses had poorly maintained diesel engines they could be seen as contributing a larger part to the need for protection measures, despite being seen as a solution. Therefore there is further potential for different charge levels based on cleanliness of vehicle engines. Unfortunately, excerpts where respondents argued this for buses were not tape-recorded (because these questions were asked near the end of the interviews when, sometimes, the tape had finished), but were written down in the note taking that accompanied the recording process.

Consideration about public transport adds the following reasons to the comparison:

1   public transport trips can be viewed as essential;
2   public transport trips can be interpreted as part of a solution to traffic related problems;
3   different vehicles can be given different rates of discount depending how clean or polluting are their engines.

Goods Vehicles

Goods vehicles were one of the least popular groups and many people thought they should contribute.

Excerpt 9.12

38   Well light goods vehicles heavy goods vehicles they should pay because there are times when when they can be in the area, as a right.
M   Yes

In Excerpt 9.12 the respondent says that heavy goods vehicles and light goods vehicles should pay. They either have the option of being in the city when there is no charge in operation or when there is a charge they should be discouraged. Thus the respondent thinks that there are no equality of treatment problems if these groups have to pay.

Excerpt 9.13

40 Light goods vehicles, heavy goods vehicles, I think have to pay otherwise there is no disincentive err. Clearly there are all sorts of arguments about it, but I would have thought the attraction about making them pay is that one single movement rather than multiple movements must be more attractive err. That might encourage a retailer to have all his goods coming in on a limited number of deliveries, rather than, you know, clearly perishables have got to be brought in every day. But then you see what, you might, I mean I would be inclined to give exemption to goods vehicles if it was 24 hour charging, for example, to give the exemption at times that would encourage them to come in you know, at user friendly times, like midnight to six a.m. or something.

M Yeah

In Excerpt 9.13 the respondent thinks that goods vehicles should pay to act as a disincentive to travel. This is using the charge to meet the objective of reducing traffic. He continues to explain how the charge can be used to encourage more efficient delivery procedures and contemplates giving exemptions in certain time windows to encourage goods movements at those times. In terms of the contribution strategy though he seems to be saying that goods vehicles should pay unless it is at 'friendly times' when they do not contribute to traffic-related problems.

Excerpt 9.14

42 Light goods, the goods vehicles (2.0) err yeah the goods vehicles would pay heavy goods vehicles would probably pay I I it might be tempting to say pay more for that. I mean I think ((he sighs)) you you would end up with lots of little goods vehicles, you know, so there is probably no great advantage.

In Excerpt 9.14 a respondent decides light and heavy goods vehicles should pay. He considers that the heavy goods vehicles should pay more but is concerned that more light goods vehicles would replace them, 'so there is probably no great advantage'.

Excerpt 9.15

33   Being business orientated I would say both light and heavy I would like to see discounted, because many of our members will require heavy goods vehicles to come and many of them operate light goods vehicles.

In Excerpt 9.15 the respondent bases his decision on the needs of the members of his interest group. These are business needs, and to these people just as important as the needs of other groups. This uses the already familiar assessment of discount based on how essential are trips.

In terms of the list of reasons for discounts and exemptions, the arguments about goods vehicles support previously-seen reasons:

1   exemptions can be given at times when they do not contribute to the problem;
2   discounts and exemptions can be considered if their trips are essential.

Motorcyclists

Excerpt 9.16

47   Motorcycles could have a discount. They cause (0.7) less congestion because taking up less space.

Motorcyclists tended not to have much popularity, but they were the one group that got support for discounts based on the fact that they do not contribute to the need for transport services as much as others. This is shown in Excerpt 9.16: they take up less space and should therefore pay less for the services.

Excerpt 9.17

35   Motorcycles yes
36   Why?
35   Why not? Because cars have to I don't see why motorcycles should not.
36   But they take up so little space.
35   I don't think its errm
36   But they take up so little space ( )
35   ⌈True
36   ⌊They don't clog the place up, they can get through the traffic, and they're good guys and I've got one.

35 Ahh well that's why you've got a special plea then. Errm no I don't see why errm.

36 If everyone rode a motorbike we'd all go around much more quickly.

35 This is true, and we'd all have much higher accident costs.

36 Not necessarily, no its not motorbikes that collide into each other its, stupid car drivers that don't appreciate the problem of being on a motorbike.

35 I think we're getting far from the point here.

M OK we've got both views.

In Excerpt 9.17 respondent number 35 thinks that motorcycles should pay and respondent number 36 thinks that they merit discount or exemption. Both arguments depend on opinions about equality of treatment in the contribution strategy. Number 35 thinks they are no different from car drivers and when countered with the argument that they use less road space, he says that they increase accident costs. Number 36 counters this claim by placing the blame for accidents back on car drivers. Unlike decisions about relative need, the apportionment of blame and contribution to problems can be partially calculated and a solution to the disagreement found.

In terms of adding to the pattern of use of the contribution strategy, the case of motorcyclists illustrates the distinction between exemptions based on type of user and those based on type of vehicle. Reductions are given on the basis of motorcycles contributing to the problem of traffic to a lesser extent than other vehicles, irrespective of trip purpose. In previous cases, for example, for buses and goods vehicles, trip purpose and impact have been intertwined.

Disabled Drivers

Excerpt 9.18

37 Disabled drivers have to be exempt because they don't get any choice

In the case of disabled drivers, many respondents thought that they deserved discount or exemption. A typical response is shown in Excerpt 9.18 where the respondent thinks disabled drivers should be exempt because they do not 'get any choice' about their decision to travel by car. This reason is similar to that about being an 'essential' user.

Excerpt 9.19

M Would you find such a scheme acceptable?

(1.0)
39   I've got to say on the basis of the exemptions on your card no
M   ⌈OK
39   ⌊because that would price out very large numbers of disabled people
     completely.
M   Right.
39   There is an exemption to public transport without any commitment to accessible
     public transport.
M   OK

Excerpt 9.20

39   The other thing that puzzles surprises me about it is the fact we talk about a
     crude method of charging of £1.50 every time you cross the boundary.
M   Yes
39   Now, that seems to me that (0.5) its also ( ) against a person who may have short
     duration visits. If someone's stamina is low they may actually choose not to
     make one three hour visit to a location and do everything in one trip a fortnight,
     they may actually choose to make four or five trips each of only half an hour's
     duration, because their maybe
     ⌈( )
M   ⌊Right.

In Excerpts 9.19 and 9.20 a respondent who is more knowledgeable about
the requirements of disabled people says that road pricing is not acceptable
because a large number of disabled people will be priced out. Furthermore,
in Excerpt 9.20, when considering a cordon scheme, the same respondent
considers road pricing to be unfair because it affects those disabled people with
limited stamina. These excerpts show that disabled drivers have a particular set
of accessibility problems and that driving partially solves them. This solution
has been encouraged with the provision of grants to purchase vehicles and
orange badges to give priority for some parking spaces. This can be interpreted
as basing the reasons for exemption on essentiality again.

Excerpt 9.21

39   Making it too easy [for disabled people] and making no price rather does away
     the point of road pricing. What one would end up with is seeing more orange
     badges go by, two buses, one police car and also a paying person, click £1.50 at
     last. There is the counter problem.

In Excerpt 9.21 the same respondent recognises that being disabled does not automatically qualify drivers for exemption. They should pay for the contribution that they make to the cost of solutions to traffic problems the same as everyone else. However, because some disabled people do not have the same opportunities as other drivers, it would be fair to consider some type of priority. The quotation also begins to touch on the issue about trust of players. There is a chance that people may falsely claim a disabled status in order to qualify for exemption.

In contrast with motorcyclists, who warrant discounts because of the smaller impact that their vehicles make, disabled drivers are given exemption or discount because it is considered essential that they have the option to drive, to maintain their mobility. This fits into the classification about how essential the trips are.

Residents, Locals and Visitors

The bulk of people who might be subjected to road pricing come under the group of people living in the charged area, people living in the vicinity of the charged area and visitors.

Excerpt 9.22

40 Drivers living within the charged area ought to be exempt because once again they don't have the choice, it seems a bit odd to price them out of returning to their own place of residence.
M   OK

The respondent in Excerpt 9.22 thinks those residents living in the charged area do not 'have a choice' about paying the charge and should be exempt. As in the previous sections this phraseology indicates that the decisions about exemptions are based on a measure of how essential it is to drive.

Excerpt 9.23

32 It's it's for debate but it is a real problem, you've chosen to live in that area for very special reasons and err I think it's very hard if you're then going to be disadvantaged.
M   Yes
32 All drivers resident in Cambridge, well I think that they should have discounts if they have to come to Cambridge. Don't forget that within our colleges we

have many fellows and err and tutors who are there because of their work and they do need to somehow to be somewhat accommodated.

M   Yes

In Excerpt 9.23 another respondent extends the same argument to people that work in the centre of the city of Cambridge.

Excerpt 9.24

54   Well, road pricing may make me go to Huntingdon and St Ives instead, you know, so we have to pay, if I'm going to cross into Cambridge its going to cost me money, I still though have the option of not going to Cambridge, so I could go elsewhere, so even me, those living on the borders should be charged.

In Excerpt 9.24 this transferability is shown again when a respondent considers the fairness about residents on the border of a city paying. He says that residents on the border should pay because they 'have the option of not going'.

Excerpt 9.25

M   What, so its tough luck if you live just outside the boundary.

56   Well I would hope like I said before there would be park and ride possibilities so they wouldn't have to use the car anyway.

In Excerpt 9.25 another respondent had made similar points about residents being exempt and those on the border of the charged area paying. The interviewer asks if insisting that they pay the full charge is fair. The respondent says that those people will have the services such as park and ride that the revenue should have been spent on. Thus it is not essential that they drive because they have other travel options. This means that the respondent can argue it is fair to treat the residents and those on the border differently because park and ride provides alternatives for those drivers on the border, but not for residents. Hence, how essential it is that the two different groups have the option to drive is different.

Excerpt 9.26

52   I I possibly think that they should be exempt because of the err difficulty of setting up the system because you have to have a thing in your car.

M   OK
52   So it wouldn't be practical. So possibly they should be exempt.

Excerpt 9.27

53   I definitely think visitors must pay because every resident would be very upset if visitors just shoot around.
52   Well if its practical to do it maybe they should pay.

In Excerpts 9.26 and 9.27 two respondents are considering the position of visitors. In Excerpt 9.26 the view is expressed that they should not be charged because of the difficulty of setting up the system. In the interval between excerpts the interviewer explains how the scheme could be adapted for visitors; by directing visitors to park and ride sites and then giving them an option of taking a bus or renting an in-car meter for the duration of their stay. With this new information the respondents agree that visitors should pay if 'it's practical'. The other respondent stresses that the visitors must pay to ensure equality of treatment. These arguments show that a measure of essentiality of travel has been used to compare visitors with residents, and also that one respondent tried to counter this with the reason about practicality.

Excerpt 9.28

23   You have to charge them
M   Hmm hmm
23   Because you wouldn't let a visitor or a tourist into a museum without charging them, what have you, no you'd have to charge them.

In Excerpt 9.28 the respondent uses the contribution strategy to argue that visitors use a service and should pay for it. This was the most common view.

In terms of the patterns of the contribution strategy, the primary rationale for giving exemptions to residents, locals and visitors seems to be based in how essential are their trips. The only supplementary argument brought in a practicality issue.

Summary of Patterns in the Contribution Strategy

When the respondents were deciding how much a group of users should contribute, the most common argument was to gauge how essential their trips were compared to other groups. This can be understood as comparing their equality of treatment based on their need to drive. In every group, except for motorcyclists, this was the dominant reason for granting exemptions or discounts. But, more importantly in terms of deriving the pattern, respondents showed that this argument was transferable between different groups. Therefore the primary pattern for calculating acceptable contributions involves assessing how essential are users' trips.

If this becomes one of the criteria to calculate the level of the charge it creates the problem about how to decide between the 'relative' essentiality of the trips. Despite this subjectivity, though, the respondents showed that there was considerable agreement about who should be exempt. This was illustrated in Table 9.1. For example, the respondents thought that trips made by emergency vehicles are more essential than those by goods vehicles, and trips made by goods vehicles are more essential than those by visitors.

A second reason for discounts and exemptions was based on the impact that a class of vehicle makes. This is separate and additional to how essential the trip might be. This reason was used to argue for discounts for motorcycles, and buses and goods vehicles that had cleaner engines. It can also be imagined that other vehicles that made less impact could pay less if they were subject to the charge. Unlike assessing how essential trips are, the impact can be calculated by objective measurement.

A third reason, mentioned in the public transport subsection, was that these vehicles deserved charge privileges because they were part of the solution to traffic problems. This can be subsumed, though, under the previous two reasons of granting discounts, based on essentiality of use and creating a lesser impact. Some respondents imagine that buses produce less pollution and take up less road space than cars, per passenger carried. Therefore public transport can be charged at a different rate from the average car user. However, because public transport can be seen as contributing to solving environmental and congestion problems, some respondents might say it is essential that this group pays a lesser charge because it is a sustainable form of transport and more important in the long term, perhaps, than car use.

As well as basing equality of treatment on essentiality and vehicle impact, other reasons were used in the data. Some respondents said that if groups had already paid they should not contribute and that there are sincerity problems arising from trusting certain groups to pay. These reasons do not form patterns that can explain acceptability, though, because they were used irregularly and they did not affect the established patterns.

Combining the Patterns into a Method to Calculate Exemptions and Discounts

Two main contribution issues have been raised: the impact of vehicles and how essential it is that a person has the option of driving. This section uses these ideas to suggest ways to improve the acceptability of dividing up the charge among different groups. However, it does not offer definitive recommendations, rather suggestions about issues that need to be resolved to derive the most acceptable charge levels.

In the conclusion to Chapter 8, where patterns in the direct- and indirect-effect strategies were used to suggest policy objectives that could be used to design an urban road pricing scheme, the link between the patterns and policy suggestions was close. In Chapter 10, the link between these patterns and actual recommendations is more obscure. This is methodologically interesting because it illustrates a different type of pattern, and hence a different style of practical suggestion that a grounded theory can make. The contribution strategy of the grounded theory points to issues that have to be resolved in order for road pricing to be acceptable, rather than to conditions that must be met.

The first issue to be resolved is to calculate the amount that different vehicles contribute to the need to solve traffic problems. For example, heavy good vehicles take up more road space and often have larger engines that can produce more pollution. Based on this, they should pay a larger amount. While it is recognised that exact calculations of impacts are difficult, and when effects of vehicles are assessed the findings are readily challenged, the contribution strategy reflects a desire to apportion responsibility. Although it may not be achievable at the present time and other inaccurate charges might have to be accepted for lack of an alternative, it is acceptable to try and it might be, conversely, unacceptable not to try.

However, for the majority of vehicles, which are cars, these calculations would probably only make marginal changes to the amount that each driver contributes. The most significant changes to the amount people should contribute would probably be based on the second issue of how essential were their trips. This presents the difficult problem about how to assess an essential trip.

The respondents are clear that certain trips are more essential than others. Yet decisions have to be made that some of these trips warrant exemptions from the charge or a reduced rate, and others do not. To aid this decision it can be imagined that trips can fall into different groups, the first group given exemption, the second the lowest discounted rate, the third a slightly higher rate, etc.

The order of distributing the trips could be based on the aggregated opinions of the respondents, with the most popular groups for exemption falling into the first exempted group. From Table 9.1, this might be emergency and utility vehicles, scheduled buses and disabled drivers. However, this is would be a political division of trips; this book is looking for an inherent division that can be derived from rules of the discourse that people use when discussing road pricing.

Unfortunately, as alluded to, clear-cut rules have not been derived. However, the combination of qualitative and quantitative data can be used to suggest where some of these rules might lie. It would have to be left to further research to try to better establish their plausibility.

The common theme between essential trips, argued by everyone, is that they are trips done for a person, by a person or that a person accepts a commitment for supporting this set of trips. For example, trips by emergency and utility vehicles are not done by the drivers who were interviewed, yet they can accept exempting them because their trips can be understood as sometimes done on behalf of these drivers. Similarly, trips by scheduled buses can be seen to warrant exemption because the drivers might use the buses, or can see a benefit for themselves in other people using public transport. In the case of granting exemptions to disabled drivers, the data illustrates that the respondents accepted the commitment to allow some free trips (as long as the privilege was not abused).

As all respondents seemed to agree that the above groups should warrant exemptions, it can be imagined that they could be placed in the first group receiving exemption. However, this still leaves the remaining trips to be divided into different levels of essentiality and for this there is no common agreement. For example, should residents pay a lower rate than people on the border of the charged area, or should business visitors pay less than tourists? For these issues, the answer is likely to change according to who one asks and whether that respondent interprets one of the trips as more essential than another.

In the data it seemed to be assumed that people with a social or economic purpose in the area should warrant discounts or exemptions above visitors. For example, people argued that trips by residents and people on the border, deliveries for businesses and commuting trips could be exempt, yet trips by tourists should be paid for. Further research would be needed to establish the order of priority amongst the aforementioned groups, which would involve answering the following questions:

1   should residents who work in the charged area be given more free trips than people who live in the area, and work elsewhere;

2   should commuters be subject to the same charge as residents;
3   should businesses and residents be given the same priority?

This research has not been able to answer these questions. However, it has pointed to a method for resolving them by analysing how people talk about the issues.

Comparison of Suggestions with Research in London

The approach to deriving patterns in the contribution strategy and suggesting how the information can stimulate acceptable solutions to distributing exemptions and discounts has been kept separate from the other strategies of the grounded theory and the objectives road pricing might be used for. This is because the contribution strategy is free-standing and can help to increase the acceptability of road pricing even if the objectives are not those that are recommended by the grounded theory. Because of the independence of these recommendations, the opportunity is taken in this section to compare them with work from the London congestion charging research programme (The MVA Consultancy, 1995), which commented on awarding discounts and exemptions.

The London research programme concurs with the grounded theory recommendations that discounts and exemptions can be given on the basis of who is making the trip and the type of vehicle used. However, unlike the discussion in this chapter, the London study takes a more practical view of the decisions and focuses on opportunities for abuse of systems of discounts and difficulties in operation. The grounded theory took a more theoretical line and was not concerned with what is technically possible, but simply how people imagined what they would like to happen.

On who should receive exemptions, the London study first mentions mobility-handicapped people who are exempt from paying for vehicle excise duty. It foresees problems if the exemptions were extended to all orange badge holders, though, because of the greater number of these people. It also mentions exemptions for scheduled buses and emergency vehicles.

> While it may well be possible to make cases for other user categories, as the list of exemptions is extended, so it becomes increasingly difficult to defend it against further extensions. It may also be more difficult to establish arrangements which prevent abuse or fraudulent use of the privilege. We strongly believe exemptions should be kept to a minimum (ibid., pp. 7/25).

Other groups that the study considers might deserve exemptions or discounts are residents and commercial vehicles based close to cordons. However, it does not give exemptions or discounts to these groups in the tests that it carried out. In comparison, with the grounded theory recommendations, the London study considers a similar set of groups. What it does not do, because of its practical concern, is give such an imaginative description about how exemptions could be divided amongst a hierarchy of users, as was stimulated by the grounded theory.

In the case of awarding discounts by vehicle type the London study agrees that there is economic rationale for varying the charges. However, it goes on to say that there are policy considerations for limiting differentials. In the case of commercial vehicles:

> Although higher charges could be justified on the basis that some commercial vehicles have a greater effect on congestion and the environment than cars, higher charges are unlikely to bring direct relief to either, and would add to business costs [and] charges by vehicle type make enforcement more complicated (ibid., pp. 11/4).

In the case of motorcycles, the London study decided to grant exemptions because 'the number of motorcycles is relatively small and we anticipate technical difficulties in having an effective charge collection system for them' (ibid., pp. 11/5). Therefore, while agreeing with the reasons of the grounded theory that the charges can vary by vehicle type, the study backs away from administering systems for political concerns about increasing business costs, and practical worries about enforcement.

Conclusion

In this chapter arguments for awarding exemptions and discounts to different groups of drivers have been analysed by looking for patterns in the use of the contribution strategy. It was found that arguments for charge privileges are typically based on the size of impact of a vehicle and the how essential it is that a person has the option of driving. Awarding discounts and exemptions would involve calculating the relative impact a vehicle makes compared to other vehicles and assessing the relative essentiality of trip purpose.

These findings concur with the London research programme approach that discounts and exemptions should be given on the basis of who is making the trip and the type of vehicle used. However, unlike the grounded theory suggestions, the London study takes a more practical view of the decisions and focuses on opportunities for abuse of systems of discounts and difficulties in operation. The grounded theory took a more theoretical line and was not concerned with what is technically possible now, but simply how people imagined what they would like to happen.

Chapter 10

Using the Grounded Theory to Decide between Area, Time and Charging Structure Design Options

Introduction

In Chapters 7, 8 and 9 patterns were found in the different strategies of the grounded theory that had consequences for acceptability. This provided guidelines about setting the objectives of an urban road pricing scheme and choosing who should pay or be entitled to discounts or exemption. In Chapter 10 these guidelines are used to suggest 'theoretically acceptable' alternatives in other sets of design options. Although excerpts from the data are still used to illustrate that the grounded theory applies to these sets of decisions, this chapter differs from the others because no patterns in the use of the strategies are being uncovered.

The design options about where and when to operate the urban road pricing scheme are explored. Next the design options about the charging structures are investigated; where charging structures reflect the choice between time-, distance- or cordon-based charging. Then the applicability of the grounded theory to deciding between options for operating technology are considered. A summary, which draws together all the recommendations that have been made about acceptability is given at the beginning of Chapter 11.

Area, Time and Differential Charging

Background

One of the important sets of design options for urban road pricing involves the extent of the scheme. This includes the area that the scheme encompasses and the time during which the scheme operates. Within any broad decision about area and time there is also the potential to choose to alter the charge level in different areas or at different times of the day. This is known as differential charging.

In the second section of the interviews respondents were asked to choose, in their opinion, the most acceptable area and time for urban road pricing. As in other parts of the interviews, they were encouraged to explain their decisions and to feel free to choose other options not presented in the prescribed options of the interview.

For the choice of area, all respondents had to choose between a city centre only scheme and a whole city (citywide) scheme. Some of the respondents could also choose a citywide scheme with an extra charge for travel in the city centre. Only the people that favoured cordon-pricing were given this option though.

Similarly, for the time of operation, all respondents had to choose between peak hours only and all day charging. Respondents who opted for all day charging were then asked if the charge should be more in the peak hours, to elicit an opinion about differential charging.

In Table 10.1, answers to the question that asked respondents to choose the area of the scheme are collated. The citywide scheme has slightly more support, for reasons of breadth of the traffic problem and of equity between different parts of the cities, as explained in the following subsection.

Table 10.1 Number of respondents and the charged area they found more acceptable

Option	Edinburgh	Cambridge	Total
City centre only	10	13	23
Citywide	17	16	33
Wider than citywide	2	0	2
Only on radial routes	1	0	1
Unsure	0	1	1

The potential for differential charging by area is shown in Table 10.2, where the number of respondents who chose to have cordon-pricing covering the whole city and have an extra cordon charge for travel in the city centre is shown. This option was only given to the majority of respondents who chose cordon-pricing (in total 43 out of 60 respondents) – it was assumed that respondents who opted for the time based pricing would understand that travel in the congested city centres would be more expensive. Of the people who answered the question, 40 per cent thought that a more expensive cordon

Table 10.2   Number of respondents who thought differential charging by area and time of day was more acceptable

Options		Edinburgh	Cambridge	Total
Citywide cordon pricing	Yes	11	6	17
with an extra cordon charge	No	14	12	26
for travel in city centre	Not asked	5	12	17
Peak time	Yes	13	16	29
only charge	No	17	14	31
If no, more expensive	Yes	3	3	6
charge for travel in	No	13	9	22
peak time	Not asked	1	2	3

charge in the city centre would be acceptable, and 60 per cent thought there should not be an additional charge.

Table 10.2 also illustrates opinions about acceptable times of operation and the potential for differential charging. Twenty-nine out of 60 respondents thought that the scheme should be operated in the peak time only. Of the remainder who favoured an all day charge, 22 preferred keeping the charge at the same rate throughout the day, while six answered that the charge could be increased at peak times, while still being in force all day. The main reasons for not wanting the charge differentiated were simplicity and prevention of peak spreading.

Discourse Analysis

The quotations in this subsection illustrate the arguments that were given to support the respondents' choices. The analysis that accompanies them shows how they can be interpreted in terms of the strategies of the grounded theory and if the theoretically acceptable guidelines, about how acceptably to use the strategies, offer ways of deciding between design options.

Excerpt 10.1

53   If you just did it in the centre it would not make much difference actually.

In Excerpt 10.1 the respondent thinks a charge limited to the city centre would not make much difference. The underlying reason about not making 'much difference' could be interpreted as part of the direct-effect strategy or part of the indirect-effect strategy. It depends whether the respondent sees the objectives as influencing demand or raising revenue to invest in transport measures.

Excerpt 10.2

50   Knowing Cambridge, the problem in Cambridge is this area. I don't know if it extends too much beyond that ring road. That really is the problem area in Cambridge, that central area err.

In Excerpt 10.2 the same ambiguity is found and the opposite view is expressed that the charge should be in the central 'problem area' only: from the perspective of the direct-effect strategy the respondent implies that traffic levels should only be influenced where there is a problem; from the perspective of the indirect-effect strategy the respondent implies that revenue should only be collected to be spent on solutions in the problem area. This difference in opinion about the extent of the problem area, and hence what the charged area should be, is common (see Tables 10.1 and 10.2, where no opinion was dominant).

In using the grounded theory to help choose between the options, the indirect-effect strategy is the most appropriate perspective from which to look at the quotations – because the indirect strategy defines an acceptable charge as one that covers the cost of measures needed to solve solutions to traffic-related problems. An acceptable area should then be one that facilitates the charging of drivers who cause the need for services in the problem area. Usually respondents supposed that the charged area and the problem area – where money is spent on solutions – would be the same. However, charging drivers outside the problem area might be considered, if it was clear these drivers caused problems in the problem area. Beyond this rather obvious linkage between charged area and problem area, though, the grounded theory cannot be used to decide on extent of a charged area – because it depends on how the revenue is spent. However, it is a useful guideline because it reinforces the theoretically acceptable objectives, which can get distorted in discussions about how to use road pricing. The next two excerpts illustrate this point.

Excerpt 10.3

37   I think has to be the outer cordon and I'll tell you why. On the inner cordon, and I'm talking specifically about Cambridge

M ⌈Yeah

37 ⌊there is insufficient room to go on any park and rides or to put up anything adequate to answer the question, so therefore you are by definition forced into a situation where you've got to go outside the outer cordon, which in our case is the M11 and the AA14 and all the rest of it.

M hmm hmm

37 Because you've only physically, you see yes there are some spaces, oh perhaps I'm wrong, you could I suppose, yes there are spaces, you can see them.

M Yes

37 You know, but I suppose, let me rethink that for a moment.

(Interviewer 'M' points out the existing park and ride sites in Cambridge, that are just inside the proposed outer cordon, in the break between the excerpts.)

Excerpt 10.4

37 Yes, I would say crossing the inner cordon should be the way to price it, because there is the ability to put adequate sites as available just outside the inner cordon.

M OK

37 If that ( ) were fully filled with buildings then you'd have to cross this one and say right we're going to have to put it out here in truth nearly to Bar Hill.

M Yeah

37 Because there's Bar Hill there. And err so you'd have to put a site here somewhere wouldn't you. Yes so it's got to be crossing the inner cordon errr would have to be the answer to your question, inner cordon only, map 3a.

In the first part of Excerpt 10.3 the respondent uses a combination of direct- and indirect-effect strategies to argue for the outer cordon. His argument rests on spending the revenue on park and ride facilities to give drivers the option of not driving, and having the cordon placed near the facilities to encourage their use. As there is no room (in his opinion) for park and ride sites between inner and outer cordons, he thinks that such sites need to be placed just outside the outer cordon. Then the interviewer corrects the respondent, by pointing out the existing park and ride sites which are located within the outer cordon. Following the correction the respondent changes his opinion, in Excerpt 10.4, and decides on the inner cordon. This is based on the same logic.

From the perspective of the indirect-effect strategy, these excerpts indicate a link between the charged area and where the money is spent: in Excerpt 10.3 the respondent imagines that the park and ride site serves the whole city and thus it makes sense to have the charge citywide; in Excerpt 10.4 he says that the park and ride site could just serve the city centre, thus the charged area should be the city centre.

However, the respondent also says that the charged area cannot encompass the park and ride site, otherwise people that take the park and ride would also pay to drive. This illustrates that although the respondent's discourse has the patterns of acceptability in it from the indirect-strategy (about spending revenue on solutions), he is willing to distort them in favour of having drivers that use park and ride (and previously caused the traffic problems) use the service for free. As explained in Chapter 8, this would be theoretically unacceptable, and the park and ride drivers and people who continue to drive should be expected to pay the same charge, if the scheme was designed around the theoretically acceptable principle of the grounded theory.

Excerpt 10.5

55 To be totally fair probably 3d ((laugh)) with screenlines.
M   Why?
55 Just because I think there are different areas in the city that have quite different characters and people are going to be moving around in there in a different way. I think some of the residential areas should be treated differently to the main drags into town that all the commuters come in on.
M   Right
55 But if I had to choose something a lot simpler I'd go for the outer cordon as a straight forward practical thing to introduce.

A rare argument in support of the citywide cordon scheme with screenlines is shown in Excerpt 10.5. It is rare in the interview data because most respondents who opted for cordon pricing (in preference to time-based and distance pricing) did so for simplicity and were unlikely to then opt for the most complex cordon pricing scheme. The respondent can accept that different areas should have different charges because the people driving in the different areas are contributing different amounts to the problem. The respondent draws on the example of the 'main drags' that the commuters use. At the end of the excerpt the respondent recognises that this fairness in the distribution of costs has to be balanced against simplicity. But if the technical problems can be overcome, there is no reason that some differentiation of charges by area could not be acceptable. From the perspective of the indirect-effect strategy, the respondent is linking contribution to the cost of measures in different areas. This 'theoretically acceptable' guideline then can be used to support differential charging by area.

Excerpt 10.6

32   It is the city centre that is the (0.5) crucial point. Throughout the whole city, I suppose that many would say it should be, but when you really come down to the constraints that are going to have to be addressed I think you'll want as tight an area as possible, and it is in the city centre that is err the difficulty, and there has to be a peak time, and err eight to 10 would be.

M   OK. So the morning is the worst then?

32   Throughout the two, the morning peak and morning and evening peak you have to accept that the school scenario in the centre of Cambridge is a very important element and if that was somehow addressed you will find that the business community would have the easier run throughout the year, that they have end of July, the whole of August and over the Christmas holiday period, than they do at present.

In the first part of Excerpt 10.6 the respondent considers the area of the scheme. The respondent recognises the argument of the whole city, but balances that against the area of the more severe problems, and practical concerns. This can be understood in terms of the direct- or indirect-effect strategies, and linking the charge to the problem area.

The respondent goes on to give his opinion about the time of operation. This is based on the same logic as the decision about area – essentially where the problem is. Then the respondent clarifies his views and says that if the peak problem of transporting children to school was solved the 'business community' would have a better 'run'. This is moving into the indirect-strategy of solving the problem by providing solutions and 'addressing' the issue.

Excerpt 10.7

40   I suspect in reality if only the morning peak was charged it would have the desired effect.

In Excerpt 10.7 the respondent alludes to the 'desired effect' instead of the 'problem area'. This still can be understood as combining the direct and indirect-effect strategies and shows that the arguments about time of charge are similar to those about charged area.

Excerpt 10.8

48   I suppose therefore the logical answer to your question is the morning eight to 10.

M   Yeah
48   You would then capture all the incomers and then after then after them you do allow the delivery drivers to go about their business from that point on.
M   OK
48   Because by far the majority of vehicles you have already caught.

In Excerpt 10.8 a more substantive argument is given. The respondent is bothered about getting the majority of vehicles to pay, and then letting other vehicles go about their business. This is using the charge to achieve direct and indirect-effects, and then trying to minimise the direct-effect for drivers travelling between the peaks. However, there is the issue that the drivers using the road after the peak time will be using the services free of charge. This would be contrary to what is seen as fair in the indirect-effect strategy. The counter argument would be that the drivers in the peak time are responsible for the implementation of new measures and should be the ones to bear the cost. The resolution of these issues depends on the time of the problems (that caused the need for measures) and which measures have been implemented. This can be juxtaposed with the interpretation about arguments for the area of the charge.

Excerpt 10.9

52   I'd say all day.
M   For what main reason?
52   Because errm although it would probably delay the rush hour I don't think it would stop the rush hour because people would just change their times and you'd still get the same amount of cars so you'd get another rush hour
M   ⌈Hmm hmm
52   ⌊before eight o'clock or after six o'clock.

In Except 10.9 the same issue is seen from a different perspective. The respondent is worried that the peak time charge would cause peak spreading and it is necessary to have the scheme operate all day to prevent this. However, some users would claim that the charge is the responsibility of the drivers travelling during the peak. If the peak spreading did occur, though, additional measures might be needed for the drivers now travelling outside the traditional peak hours, because of peak spreading. Therefore, the decision about the time of the charge has to be fairly flexible and take account of changes in peak travel times to ensure that the charge is linked to the people causing the need for the extra expenditure. In the same way as the decision about area, 'theoretically acceptable' guidelines cannot decide between all day and differential charging.

Excerpt 10.10

54   I suppose if the shops were concerned you could turn it off during after err during the day so the shoppers didn't have to pay, but I think it should be on all the time and people don't get confused so they're not worrying oh is it off what am I going to do.

In Excerpt 10.10 the respondent is not sure whether the all day scheme is better for simplicity, or the peak time scheme is better for not impinging on shopping habits. This shows that within the decision about when to charge there are practical concerns. Even if the respondent thinks that shoppers should not contribute, for whatever reason, the favoured charging times have to be balanced against simplicity. Therefore with 'theoretically acceptable' arguments there is leeway about when to operate the charge. The respondent seemed to accept that the fairest distribution might not be practical.

Theoretically Acceptable Options about Where and When to Charge

From the above discussion it can be seen that the issues can be analysed in terms of the grounded theory strategies. Also the consequences about what is 'theoretically acceptable' seem to apply. In simple terms this links the charge to the charged area and time. This makes complete sense because, if the 'theoretically acceptable' objective of road pricing is to raise and use the revenue, the 'theoretically acceptable' design options should link where and when the charge is raised to where and when it is used.

Beyond this surface level explanation of choosing the extent of the charged area or time the grounded theory can also be used to explore scenarios and interpret whether they fit the theoretically acceptable principles. Chapter 8 described how this can be done, in the case of deciding between charging people that continue to drive more money than people that switch to park and ride – the theoretically acceptable decision should be to charge them the same.

If the charged area or time is not directly the same as where or when the revenue is spent on solutions to traffic problems, the grounded theory stresses that the link between the people that pay the charge and the cost of solutions to problems they cause needs to be firmly established. Care has to be taken that such differences between charged area and time, and where and when the money is spent, do not surreptitiously invoke the direct-effect strategy of trying to price drivers out by charging above the cost of measures that are needed to overcome the problems that they cause. This is similar to the reason for charging park and ride users and drivers the same rate.

In the case of choosing differentials the decisions can also be helped by a similar use of the grounded theory. Imagine splitting the charged area in two, and having a high rate in one and a low rate in the other. According to the grounded theory this is justified if the money needed to solve problems in one area is greater than the other area. However, it might be predicted that such a differential could lead to greater problems in the area with the lesser charge; and thus the charge in that area might have to be raised in order to fund solutions to the problems. If the cost of having the differential increases the amount that the one of the areas has to pay above the amount it would have to pay if it shared the revenue, then it would seem sensible for there to be no differential. Another example might be if the cost of administering differentials actually increased the cost to an area, above accepting the same charge without differentials.

In such ways, interpreting the choices solely in terms of the grounded theory guidelines, theoretically acceptable solutions can be found. However, it would not be expected that the respondents would answer the questions in the same way because the grounded theory uncovers unverbalised rules about how the respondents construct acceptability. As the respondents would not necessarily follow all the rules that are being considered universally acceptable to them, at the same time, their answers would be different.

Comparing the aggregated replies in Table 10.2 illustrates this. In the case of differential charging by area, 40 per cent of respondents thought an extra city centre charge was acceptable – and on the grounded theory interpretation this reflects a greater cost of problems in the city centre. However, when differentials by time were considered, only 10 per cent of those asked said that the peak-time should attract an extra charge – in terms of the grounded theory this shows that people thought that peak spreading, as people changed travel time to avoid the charged time period, would increase the costs more than having the same charge all day. None of the respondents, as shown earlier, got close to offering the above critique about using differentials, but they did give reasons that fitted in with different parts of the grounded theory. All the interpretation does is go beneath these disparate surface level explanations and respecify them in terms of the theoretical framework about what is acceptable– thus illuminating why more people can find differential charging by area more acceptable than differential charging by time.

Types of Charging Structure

Background

In the second half of the interviews the respondents were asked about the type of charging structure that they preferred. They were given information about the differences between congestion time-based pricing, time-based pricing, distance pricing and cordon charges. As in other questions they were encouraged to explain why their preferred option was more acceptable than the others.

Table 10.3 shows the number of respondents who said each of the charging structures was more acceptable. The clear favourite was the cordon charging option, primarily for simplicity. The second favourite was distance pricing, which appealed to people because of its fairness in distributing the costs based on how much people used the system. With least support were time-based pricing and time-based congestion pricing. These appealed to those respondents who thought it a fair way to make those who use the road network more pay more. However, they lost support for reasons of complexity, unfairness in charging people to be in congestion when it may not be their fault, and encouraging dangerous driving.

Table 10.3   Number of respondents by the type of charging structure they found more acceptable

Option	Edinburgh	Cambridge	Total
Congestion	1	3	4
Time-based	2	0	2
Distance	2	9	11
Cordon	25	18	43
Unsure	0	0	0

Discourse Analysis

As in the previous section, the purpose of the discourse analysis subsection is to isolate 'theoretically acceptable' arguments and to see if they can determine the choice of charging structure.

Congestion time-based pricing and time-based pricing   In Excerpt 10.11 the direct-effect strategy is used to support the congestion time-based pricing option. The key phrase is in the third line, where the respondent says that the charge will 'encourage people to get out of their cars when we most need them to'.

Excerpt 10.11

40   I think time-based congestion pricing

M   OK Can I ask you the reason for that.

40   Because it will encourage people to get out of their cars when we most need them to.

M   OK Do you think there is any problems with that being maybe over complicated and maybe a simple cordon charge would be more more apt?

40   A simple cordon charge is obviously easier to administer, errm and. (4.0) It depends how what method is used, obviously if it is transponder type thing that clicked money off a meter as you went across or whatever errm then fair enough but cordon pricing seems to suggest a man sitting in a box taking the money.

M   Right

40   Not really I think what we would look for.

M   OK

After focusing on this advantage of road pricing, the interviewer asks him if there would be any problems, and suggests the practicality concern of over-complication. Although this question is leading it does prompt the respondent to verbalise how he imagines the cordon pricing system operating. He imagines a manual system where people stop at a tollgate and pay the charge. This would have practicality implications, which would come under the concept of efficiency. These then would create unwanted direct-effects. (In practice the cordon charging system could operate electronically though.)

Excerpt 10.12

33   Well the time based congestion pricing where people are charged the length of time they spend in the congestion

M   ⌈Yeah

33   ⌊does have some appeal because initially you're still going to have the difficulty of knowing how long their journey is going to take.

M   Yes

33   So I think that I would go initially for the time-based congestion pricing because hopefully most people will recognise that if they are in that congested

area for a specific length of time and if they're going to be unloading in times within that hopefully you know things will be organised so that they can very swiftly unload and move out. So there will be a willingness within the business community for both parties to work together to ensure that when a vehicle has arrived it's quickly turned around.

M   Right

33   And the difficulty for retailers who are going to be in areas where you know customers are required, this whole business of well, you know, many times people do need their car reasonably handy, because shopping is something that has got to be looked at.

M   Yes

33   Its its difficult, but err. I think that time-based congestion pricing issue will be the one.

M   OK

In Excerpt 10.12 the respondent chooses the time-based option and again presents his argument in terms of the direct-effect strategy. He rejects the congestion pricing option because of the difficulty in calculating the amount of the charge in advance. (In another section of the interview he says that this is important for businesses to be able to budget, use their resources efficiently and know how much to quote customers for work.) He then argues that the time-based charging system is the best because it encourages efficient use of the road network. He gives the example of businesses improving delivery procedures. In the respondent's penultimate utterance he goes on to balance this utilitarian efficiency gain with the provision of needs of specific people in certain areas. Thus in terms of the direct-effect strategy the respondent finds problems with both congestion and time-based pricing.

Excerpt 10.13

35   You should be charged, most of us in this life, if you have two or three pints of beer you're expected to pay more than if you had one pint.

M   Yeah

35   So it would be nice to think of a system that in many ways where you are charged according to the amount of err time you use the product, or the distance.

In Excerpt 10.13 the indirect-effect strategy is used to support the case of paying by time. This involves arguing that people that spend more time on the road should pay more. The respondent also realises that the same argument could be applied to distance pricing.

Then in Excerpt 10.14 the same respondent continues to ponder the problem and puts forward the counter-argument that time-based pricing would be difficult if the driver was caught in a queue. Although, he does not expand on this point it can be interpreted as saying that the congestion may not be the fault of the driver, or it is unfair to pay more for worse efficiency.

Excerpt 10.14

35 Time of course is awkward if you're sitting fuming in the queue.
M Yes it would.
35 But but how far they travel, I suppose that's pretty fair. It took me ten hours to drive the mile, it only cost me five pee.
   ((laughs))
36 And again it comes down to what one is trying to achieve by this, if it is to try to get people away from using it, that's rather different from saying what is a fair system of trying to cope with the problem. Hmm.

The respondent thinks that distance charging would not have this disadvantage and consequently can be seen as fair. Then in the final part, the respondent provides evidence that the charging structure depends on the policy objectives of road pricing. If the objective is restraint, that would presuppose a different charging structure from a fair way of distributing the cost. As the 'theoretically acceptable' objective is to raise revenue and deal with the problem by financing other measures, this excerpt supports the view that time-based pricing may not be 'theoretically acceptable', yet distance pricing might be. This fits in with the previous excerpts which only support time-based or congestion pricing as a way of directly affecting traffic levels, and not the promotion of fair contributions.

Excerpt 10.15

12 So I think you know probably for ease of, I know this is not meant to be done for ease, you're thinking of, to charge somebody for spending time in congestion I don't really see that being a you know you've got a lot of comeback, what if somebody breaks down in front of you and you're spent in that congestion you know err.
M Yeah
12 Makes it very difficult to price someone on that. Certainly I wouldn't be in favour of that of that type. Time-based pricing. Yes that's more, again how much time their journey takes. It's like the one above. You could get caught up in things that you didn't want to. Distance pricing. How would you do that?

In Excerpt 10.15 another respondent considers the fairness implication of paying more in congestion, and expands on the reasons more than the respondent in Excerpt 10.14 does. With an argument based in the indirect-effect strategy, the respondent raises the problem of paying more when the congestion is someone else's fault. Even though the respondent might see the logic of having to pay more to use urban roads at congested times, he also expects to get something in return for the payment. In his next statement he realises that time-based pricing might have the same distribution of blame problem. He then moves on to consider distance pricing and raises a practicality concern. This excerpt supports the previous ones, though, because the respondent is questioning the ability of congestion and time-based pricing to reflect the 'theoretically acceptable' objective of linking payment to expenditure.

Excerpt 10.16

39 I've got to say I would personally think that time-based pricing is the preferable one. I think the problem with congestion pricing is that the charge to the user, and I'm assuming here that disabled people are paying something even if they might be paying 10 per cent of the rate or something.

M   Hmm hmm

39 That the problem then is that you may well go in not expecting congestion, not predictable congestion but there may be an accident and as a result, or somebody unloading building materials or something and the result is it doesn't take long for considerable congestion to build up some distance away from the cause errmm its a bit rum with people having to pay because pay extra for the use of the road simply because there was a pile up on the road errm.

M   Yes

39 Time-based reflects the fact that the amount of time they spend in the congested area, inside the cordon area is charged for. You remove this incentive to leave the vehicle in once you've got it in there.

M   Right

39 Distance (0.3) I suppose has a similar impact actually. I think distance or time doesn't I can't see that it makes a major difference err distance might be better it might discourage the the teenage yobbo from going to take his escort SR5 through can I get it through in 15 seconds from boundary to boundary.

M   With time-based of course if you do get caught in congestion then it does amount to the same thing.

39 Yes, I appreciate. Yes the point. Yes and on that basis you might be right and distance might be. Yes the advantage of distance is that you're not paying for congestion at all then, you're only paying for distance err. Cordon pricing has I've said earlier I have this concern that it does militate against a number of issues for several people.

M So which ones will it be between?
39 Thinking about it now as I read. I think distance pricing is probably the one I would opt for.

In Excerpt 10.16 another respondent considers all the types of charging structures. In the first three statements the respondent argues for the use of time-based charging and against congestion time-based charging. He then considers distance pricing and, with a prompt from the interviewer, realises that the disadvantage of congestion pricing also applies to time-based pricing. He finally decides on distance pricing, because it is fairer than cordon pricing.

In his first criticism of congestion pricing he essentially says there may be occasions when it is not fair because congestion may be the fault of somebody else. At this stage, though, he thinks that time-based pricing is fair because it reflects the amount of time a person spends in the congested area. He links this in with the direct-effect strategy by saying it removes the incentive to stay in the area. When he considers distance pricing he realises that this also reflects the amount a driver uses the road. He then realises it may have an advantage over time-based pricing because the latter could encourage speeding. This safety concern can be categorised under the utilitarian concern of the environment. It can also be interpreted in the same way as the previous arguments though; congestion and time based pricing do not reflect a fair contribution if some drivers will recklessly speed through the charged area – hence paying less.

The interviewer does not explore the safety concern but is more concerned why the respondent does not see that time-based pricing has the same apportionment of blame problem as congestion pricing. After thinking, the respondent realises it does, which leaves him the choice between cordon and distance pricing. Because of a number of issues that the respondent had mentioned in the first section of the interview, when a typical cordon pricing scheme was discussed, he decides for distance pricing. These issues were mainly concerned with rough justice for people on the boundary of the cordon, so again distance pricing can be understood as the fairest way to distribute costs among drivers.

Distance pricing Other respondents who favoured distance pricing cited similar advantages about distance pricing being the fairest way to distribute the cost of road pricing amongst drivers.

Excerpt 10.17

52   I think distance pricing.
M   You would go for distance pricing?
52   Yes, definitely.
M   (You)
53   Same
M   Honestly? Do want to just say why.
52   It just seems the fairer option to me. All the others, errm errm I mean possibly
     you have the rush hour in the morning but it just seems the fairest way to do it
     to me.
M   OK

Excerpts 10.17 and 10.18 are from different respondents in the same interview. In the first excerpt the respondent says that distance pricing is fairer, and this is interpreted as use of the contribution strategy. However, he does balance this by a realisation of higher costs when people are in congestion, such as the peak hour.

Excerpt 10.18

53   Errm time-based congestion doesn't really make sense to me because you're
     sort of punished by being in the congestion anyway so I can't see how that
     would work and the time based pricing could lead to people just rushing even
     more, so I mean there will be problems with speeding and that sort of thing, and
     the cordon pricing, again I'm a bit worried that certain certain areas would die
     out so that's why I come to distance pricing.

Then in Excerpt 10.18 the other respondent explains how she decided on distance pricing, which is by a process of faults with the other methods of charging. With congestion pricing she thinks that the driver is being punished anyway so it does not make 'sense' to charge. This is using the direct-effect strategy to argue that congestion pricing is not fair. Then the time-based pricing option is criticised for encouraging speeding. This, as mentioned above, is a problem based on the direct-effect strategy, but does have implications on fairness in contributions. The final argument draws on the problem of road pricing encouraging out of town development. Unfortunately the respondent does not really specify the advantage of distance over cordon pricing to prevent this. It might be that distance pricing encourages drivers to think how far they travel; if this is the case then it could be subsumed under the direct-effect strategy of implications of road pricing.

Excerpt 10.19

47   The distance one I guess would be OK because it would solve the problem of the the short journey one. [i.e. rough justice]

The final important argument that was associated with distance pricing is shown in Excerpt 10.19. The respondent argues that distance pricing overcomes problems of rough justice that arise when people have to make a short journey and the place they live means they may have to cross over a cordon boundary. This fits in with 'theoretically acceptable' guidelines and further indicates that distance pricing might be 'theoretically acceptable'.

Cordon charging Despite the arguments that have been shown in favour of congestion, time and distance pricing, the overwhelming favourite amongst all the respondents was cordon charging. Cordons were seen as more feasible, practical or simple than the other options. This implies that it will be more efficient and not lead to negative problems such as the encouragement of speeding. However, cordon pricing still has problems. These are unfairness implications because of 'rough justice' to people who live on the cordon and potential for rerouting problems as drivers try to avoid the cordon. These problems were mentioned in detail in Chapter 7, when the cordon pricing scheme was the example for general discussion. By moving to distance pricing and multiple cordons these problems are reduced, but at the expense of simplicity and practicality.

In terms of the indirect-effect strategy cordon pricing can be seen to relate cost of provision of services to the area that is surrounded by the cordon. In this case it is superior to some more arbitrary taxation systems (for example, taxation on fuel or national vehicle licensing).

Excerpt 10.20

44   For simplicity, I mean at the end of the day a system has got to be workable. If its overly overly complicated then its going to be err I mean the object of the exercise is to raise revenue for the benefit of the environment, if you spend all the revenue on an enormously complex system err it really hasn't achieved anything its just throwing money from one pocket to another isn't it.

M   Yes

44   It isn't achieving anything. No. And to achieve something its got to be simple and I would have thought to be honest the simplest thing is cordon pricing.

M   Hmm

In Excerpt 10.20 the respondent talks about the advantages of simplicity. He is concerned that the system is workable for the purpose of 'raising revenue for the benefit of the environment'. He says it is no good if the system is so complex that the revenue is all spent on the system. Thus he focuses on the theoretically acceptable objective, and then ensures that money is not wasted by making the system as user efficient as possible.

Excerpt 10.21

13   You've got to think how would kit all these vehicles out. Yeah.
M   So you'd go for the cordon?
13   Yeah, the cordon.

In Excerpt 10.21 the respondent is concerned about practicality. He believes the only viable option will be cordon pricing because it is too complex to install electronic meters in all vehicles to operate the more complex charging structures. As in the previous excerpt, the respondent balances the policy objectives with efficiency.

Excerpt 10.22

55   Because I think that time and distance charging cause people to drive unsafely. That's my experience.

In Excerpt 10.22 the respondent rules out the other options because they encourage dangerous driving. Thus the other systems of charging might adversely affect the environment. In terms of the time-based charge this is in agreement with previous opinions and the theoretical ideas. However, applying the same argument to distance pricing was unusual. Unfortunately this issue was not explored, so it might be a mistake on the part of the respondent or part of a logical argument, such as the encouragement of short cuts.

Excerpt 10.23

35   Cordon pricing I think at first glance.
M   For the main reason? For this.
35   It is the least bureaucratic, err, it (0.5) err it. In terms of measuring your time I take my car in to see a company that happens to be in this area I find somewhere to park, either on their premises, or in the public car park or wherever, on street parking errm, and I am still paying more in addition for the time that it takes me

to do my business. That has got to be penal hasn't it. Errm, how far they travel. Well again that means you've got some sort of tachometer, you've got to be recording. Again infringement of civil liberty and all sorts of things.

In Excerpt 10.23 another respondent constructs an argument for road pricing using a series of mistaken opinions. When considering time-based pricing the respondent is mistaken in thinking that he will continue to pay when he has parked his car to conduct his 'business'. The interviewer did correct him at a later stage, although it did not change his opinion about the level of bureaucracy needed for systems of charging other than road pricing. His next opinion concerns distance pricing and is about the civil liberty issues. Depending on the communications technology, this could be a valid issue, but would apply to all types of urban road pricing systems and not exclusively to distance pricing. Bureaucracy, conjuring up the image of inefficiency, and unfairness of paying while parked are linked with the idea of paying more than is needed for the cost of solutions to problems that are caused by the driver. Meanwhile, civil liberty concerns are about the trust of planners and government and this is part of the indirect-effect strategy also, albeit about how information is used, instead of money.

Excerpt 10.24

49 The first three are difficult because I cannot determine how long I spend in the congested area because if it gets gridlocked it isn't in my control how long I stay there is it?
M Yeah
49 Therefore the time my journey takes is not in my control.
M Yeah
49 Err. How far they travel, is almost a misnomer because by definition you ain't going to travel far inside, your cordon is only about two miles no three miles across it.
M Yeah
49 Err, you're almost forced into this cordon pricing thing, when you cross the cordon. So I suppose I think I'll go for that.
M OK

In Excerpt 10.24 another respondent uses more than one argument, with correct assumptions to conclude in favour of cordon pricing. He does this in way that supports the 'theoretically acceptable' guidelines. He rejects the time-based options because they do not reflect the link between charge and the cost of solutions, and then questions the practicality of distance pricing if the charged area is small. This shows that distance pricing, although maybe fairer, still has to be balanced against practicality concerns.

Deriving a 'Theoretically Acceptable' Charging Structure

It has been established that the objective of a road pricing scheme should be to raise revenue, then spend the money on measures to improve services for the drivers and the surrounding environment for other people. To carry out this process the grounded theory provides guidelines:

1   revenue use should be linked to improvements that drivers need and measures to alleviate the environmental impact that they make;
2   the contribution that drivers make should reflect the cost of the measures and the amount drivers contribute to the need for the measures.

The amount of money that is needed would have to be calculated in advance, and then a charge calculated on the favoured charging structure. In cordon charging the charge would be determined by dividing the revenue needed by the number of vehicles crossing into an area, in distance by distance vehicles travelled, in time-based by time travelled and in congestion time-based charging by the time spent in congestion. It can be also argued that if the transport system operated predictably all these alternative options would meet an interpretation of the guidelines. As revenue can be used for a set of transport improvements, they are all in some way fair ways of splitting the contribution. However, if the transport system does not operate predictably, cordon and distance pricing still meet the guidelines, but congestion time-based and time-based pricing do not. If journeys take longer than predicted for some reason, drivers in cordon and distance charging still pay the same amount. This means revenue is still linked to improvements and they are still making a fair contribution. With the time-based options, though, the drivers will be paying more. This serves to break the link between connecting revenue raised with the measures implemented. Furthermore, it will create a feeling of unfair contributions because the drivers who pay more are getting a worse service.

Despite the move away from time-based and time-in-congestion pricing, cordon and distance pricing can still be used to charge more in congested areas to reflect the extra cost of the measures needed to provide solutions. This is 'theoretically acceptable', as was shown earlier in this chapter when the case of differential charging was explored.

When respondents had to decide between cordon and distance pricing, the issues seemed to be about complexity and fairness. Some people thought that cordon pricing was simpler (hence more efficient), while others thought that distance pricing would be fairer, especially for people travelling short distances. Cordon pricing might be efficient to administer but the charge might be seen as unfairly high for people travelling a short distance. Distance pricing overcomes these problems, but at the expense of efficiency, because the scheme would be more complex to administer.

The best solution depends on the needs of individual cities and no reasons could be found to choose between them. However, the grounded theory can be used to suggest a guideline by looking beneath the surface-level reasons that have been given so far. Earlier it was described how it can be theoretically acceptable to have differential charging by area as long as having a difference in charge does not cause one of the areas to have to charge more than it would have to if there was no differential (perhaps due to rerouting effects or administrative costs). This reasoning can be transposed to the decision about distance pricing by imagining that it is the same as creating a series of cordon charges in adjacent areas. If the cost of solving traffic-related problems is less for drivers that travel through fewer of the adjacent areas, and the cost of collecting revenue by distance pricing does not increase the costs above those by not having distance pricing, then distance pricing could be theoretically acceptable. However, if having distance pricing increased the cost, compared to having one cordon charge, then it would be unacceptable.

Deciding between Technology Options

Background

The charging systems may also be operated by different technologies. These have been described as ranging between:

1   high technology – cars fitted with electronic meters that respond to roadside beacons;
2   low technology – manual systems of operation, such as vignettes in car windscreens.

Although the low technology system could only be used in conjunction with cordon pricing, all respondents were asked to decide between high and low technology options, and to give reasons for their choices. The aggregated results are shown in Table 10.4. It can be seen that no clear favourite option emerges, and in Edinburgh the respondents were evenly split.

Table 10.4   Number of respondents and their preferred technology option for scheme operation

Option	Edinburgh	Cambridge	Total
Low technology	15	10	25
High technology	15	17	32
No preference	0	3	3

Discourse Analysis

In the discourse analysis the opinions of people can be understood in terms of the grounded theory.

Excerpt 10.25

42   I think aside from the civil liberties concerns over tracking people's every move I wouldn't have any strong preferences, probably whatever is most cost effective.

In Excerpt 10.25, the respondent says he is not concerned about the technology used, as long as it is cost-effective and civil liberties are protected. This reflects the indirect-strategy, as the respondent wants to make sure that the money is not wasted and that information is not abused.

Excerpt 10.26

40   Obviously you've got to be. Most people would I think pay (.) the way they were happy that everyone else was paying. And
⌈that's
M   ⌊right=
40   =and that's that's very important so its got to be simple, or you could again use use maybe the difficulty of actually buying your credits too as a further deterrent
M   ⌈hmm
40   ⌊to using your car, that's a way of doing it hmm. Lots of people still don't have

cheque books or credit cards or or bank accounts so you'd need to be careful about payment and so on.

M   Yes

40   Hmm vehicle identification I I guess is (.) open to you know it does smell of big big brother. You know, someone using something like a phone card, its there, its not linked to anything else, I guess would be more acceptable errm

M   Yes

Meanwhile in Excerpt 10.26 the respondent exhibits this same urge to ensure efficiency and protect civil liberties, and recommends that people should be able to pay in more than one way. However, he does counter with a thought that perhaps the objective should be to make it difficult to pay. Given that the 'theoretically acceptable' objective of road pricing is to raise revenue to spend on solutions this is not relevant though.

Deciding on Theoretically Acceptable Technology

If the objective of road pricing is to raise revenue then the technology must promote this. Both high and low technologies can achieve this. For the more complex cordon charging options (i.e. with screenlines) and distance pricing, high technology would have to be used though to be feasible. Meanwhile, for simple cordon structures both high and low technologies could be used.

Conclusion

This chapter has shown that the grounded theory of acceptability of urban road pricing can be used to understand the parts of the interviews where respondents considered different design options. In terms of helping to decide between the options, the grounded theory has helped define 'acceptable' criteria on which the choices should be based. Although the choices of design options will change from city to city, depending on the extent of the traffic problems and the solutions that are chosen, the 'acceptable' criteria will be the same. Chapter 11 begins with a summary of how to choose between design options.

Comparison of the Grounded Theory of Acceptability Recommendations with Other Research

Introduction

Purpose and Structure of Chapter

In Chapters 7, 8, 9 and 10 the grounded theory has been used to develop three distinct sets of recommendations: about policy objectives, whom to charge and design options. These recommendations have been summarised in Table 11.1, along with a brief explanation as to why each recommendation was made. The table is followed by a description of the rationale for each of these suggestions.

The recommendations were derived by interpreting the responses of the sample and finding 'theoretically acceptable' arguments that were common throughout. Therefore the recommendations need to be compared with research that has explored reasons about the acceptability of urban road pricing. This will be able to support or question the interpretation presented in this book.

In the case of the recommendations about which policy objectives road pricing should meet there is a considerable body of research that considers the acceptability of road pricing with respect to broad policy objectives. This comparison forms the main body of this chapter and is important because it shows whether the grounded theory is justifiable in its contention that road pricing should only be used for the objective of raising finance. These objectives also determine some of the design options, such as the extent of the road pricing scheme.

However, in the case of the recommendations to be derived from the contribution strategy there is less research with which to compare the suggestions about who to charge. These recommendations have been compared in the conclusion of Chapter 9, and are left free-standing, to be accepted or rejected as useful or superfluous to practitioners and social scientists.

Table 11.1 Summary of the theoretically acceptable recommendations

Transport planning decision	'Acceptable' option	Reason
Which objectives to use road pricing to meet	To provide finance only	In the grounded theory restraining demand by pricing is not universally acceptable to the respondents. However, using road pricing to raise revenue to finance other transport measures can be found to be universally acceptable to the respondents.
How to spend the revenue	On measures to solve transport problems	To be universally acceptable to the respondents road pricing revenue must be spent on measures that solve the transport problems or alleviate the environmental impacts caused by road users who pay the charge.
Should discounts and exemptions be given	Give an allowance of 'free trips' to essential users and discounts to low polluting vehicles	The contribution strategy showed that the respondents created a hierarchy for exemptions based on how essential trips were seen to be and a hierarchy about the physical impact of vehicles.
Charged area	Where the solutions financed by the revenue are applied	To ensure that the revenue is used to provide solutions to problems caused by the people paying the charge.
Charged time	When the road users that cause the need for solutions travel	To allow for the fact that people that travel out of peak hours may not contribute as much to the need for solutions.
Scope for differential charging	Yes	Contributions vary according to area and time.
Type of charging system	Distance or cordon charging	These options link the revenue to the solution. It is unfair to use the time-based options because the drivers could be paying more for a worse service.
Technology to operate the scheme	Any	Other than being cost-effective and protecting privacy the grounded theory has no specific recommendations. Perhaps providing more than one payment option would be advantageous.

Thus, after the summary of the grounded theory recommendations, this chapter compares the grounded theory ideas with research from the US which focuses specifically on the acceptability of using road pricing to reduce congestion directly. Then the comparison moves to Britain and compares the grounded theory with general and case specific research that has considered road pricing in a broader context. Finally, there is consideration of the implications of the grounded theory for economic theory in a general sense.

Rationale behind the Grounded Theory of Acceptability Recommendations

Policy objectives   In Chapters 7 and 8 patterns in the direct-effect and indirect-effect strategies were uncovered and used to recommend that the only theoretically acceptable objective for urban road pricing is to finance solutions to transport problems, as opposed to restraining traffic. In the direct-effect strategy it is not universally acceptable to the limited number of respondents to price people out of driving by charging a fee beyond that seen as an acceptable amount. Then in the indirect-effect strategy, a universally acceptable amount for driving with respect to this restricted population of respondents was defined as that needed to provide services for driving and protect people in the environment from the impact of driving.

In Chapter 8 it was also suggested that these patterns could be used to define what constitutes a solution and overcome a criticism that there is an exception to the guidelines. Namely, it is acceptable to price people out of driving when the revenue is used to compensate those people who have been priced out. An example of such a combination of strategies might be where drivers pay a charge and the revenue is used to fund a park and ride service, which drivers can use instead of paying to drive – thus park and ride is used to compensate those people priced out of continuing to drive. Based on such logic it would also be possible to spend the revenue on non-transport-related measures, as long as they satisfied the people who were priced-off; for example, subsidised schools and hospitals. And if such logic is acceptable, the grounded theory guidelines are undermined because all measures become potentially acceptable and proving a causal link with transport becomes unnecessary.

However, in Chapter 8 it was shown that the compensatory position could not be upheld unless other assumptions were brought in to support it. Namely, the compensatory argument assumes that people want to enter a compensatory game. In support of this assumption is the fact that they have bought a car, paid road tax and purchased fuel, which shows that they have entered into an arrangement with another party where they have received a commodity and compensated the supplier for it. However, in these arrangements the purchaser and supplier agreed to cooperate – one to be supplied and one to be compensated – and they had the option not to trade. In the case of implementing road pricing there is no option 'not to trade' and 'not play the compensatory game'.

As any assumptions for a theoretically acceptable road pricing strategy must be based in the grounded theory patterns about what makes road pricing acceptable, the compensatory case must be rejected because it brings in other assumptions. This then defines the solution not as something that satisfies a person who can no longer afford to drive, but rather as a measure that improves services for drivers or protects the people in the environment from the effects of driving. This might range from the provision of park and ride services through new road surfaces to facilities to work at home. The point is that the services solve problems caused by people who intend to drive and should be paid by these people.

In Chapter 8, the case that people who switch to park and ride instead of continuing to drive should pay less was also examined, where the park and ride scheme is considered a solution. It was argued that the people who continue to drive and drivers who switched to park and ride should continue to pay the same amount, if the park and ride service receives subsidy from the people who continue to drive.

There are two arguments for giving park and ride users discount (based on the direct- and indirect-effect strategies, not the contribution strategy): firstly that they cause less damage than car drivers do and if some measures are shared by park and ride users and drivers, the former can claim that they should pay a reduced amount; secondly, people who want to continue to drive get a benefit from people opting to use park and ride.

The first argument is countered by the requirement to adhere to the indirect-effect strategy rule that it is theoretically acceptable that drivers pay for the cost of measures needed to drive and to protect others from the impact they make. If park and ride is lumped in with a package of measures then it is theoretically acceptable that the people who intend to drive, whether they end up using park and ride or not, pay for the package of measures. However, if park and ride is separated from the other package of measures, then it can be said that people who use park and ride should pay only for park and ride use. If this is done, though, the people who do not use park and ride can say that they should only pay for the other measures that they use. Therefore, it is only advantageous for park and ride users to claim separate treatment if they do not need to rely on subsidy from people who continue to drive. If they do need subsidy, and still want discount from the full road pricing charge, then the people who continue to drive can argue that they should not fund park and ride, which is theoretically acceptable, according to the indirect-effect strategy pattern. If this is done, then the cost of park and ride would rise instead of being reduced. Therefore the first argument is countered by a principle of reciprocal agreement between groups of users.

In the second argument, the compensatory principle that was discussed above is used – where park and ride users are accepting compensation from car drivers switching modes. Therefore, the direct-effect strategy rule, about not using road pricing to ration road space, is broken if benefits for people who continue to drive are taken into account. For example, if it is argued that car drivers save time by people using park and ride, it could not be justified that the money saved should be used to subsidise park and ride use.

Whom to charge   In Chapter 9 patterns in the contribution strategy were uncovered and used to recommend a hierarchy of charge levels based on who is driving and the impact of the vehicle being driven on the transport problem. In the first hierarchy, emergency vehicles, utility vehicles, residents and public transport, would have a priority for making trips over visitors, for example. If there are diseconomies of scale in transport provision, where the cost of providing for a few trips is cheaper than providing for more trips, then the higher priority groups could make a theoretically acceptable argument that they should pay less than the lower priority groups – because the cost of providing for their limited number of trips would be less if the other people did not drive. In the second hierarchy, the relative contribution that different types of vehicle made to the need for solutions to transport problems would be assessed. Accordingly, motorcyclists may conceivably pay less than car drivers, and heavy goods drivers more.

The potential for discounts and exemptions, though, is in addition to the guidelines about policy objectives. In the case of providing discounts to park and ride users, where park and ride receives subsidy, it does not contradict the advice in the previous subsection, which said that park and ride users and car drivers should pay the same fee. This is because it is the mode that the driver intended to travel by that counts – once a driver pays the road pricing fee, which funds a set of solutions, they can use any of the solutions. Drivers who intend to travel by public transport or by a less polluting mode would be entitled to discounts if the mode by which they intended to travel did not receive subsidy from the other groups paying the road pricing charge.

Other design options In Chapter 10 the recommendations to be derived from the direct- and indirect-effect were combined to suggest acceptable charging structures and how to decide on the charged area and time. The more acceptable charging structures seem to be cordon- and distance-based charging; the choice depends on which solutions the revenue is being used to fund. The charged area and time again depends upon which solutions road pricing revenue is used to finance, but should also reflect the contribution to problems drivers make at different times and in different urban areas.

Again the grounded theory can be used to suggest guidelines beyond these surface level recommendations. This uses the same arguments that have run through the previous discussions, and reflects strict adherence to the grounded theory guidelines. In the case of choosing the area of the charge, the reciprocal agreement discussed between park and ride users and people who continue to drive can be extended to the choice of area. In this case a sub-area might be imagined as a set of park and ride users who are claiming discount because the measures they need are less expensive than other users/other areas. Thus if a sub-area of the charged area claims discount, it is only worth doing if the sub-area can raise the money needed by itself. It may happen that by having such a differential, traffic diverts to the cheaper sub-area – and perhaps increases the money needed back to the original level or above – or the cost of operating a differential increases the cost above not having one. In these cases differentials might not be beneficial. Also, the same principle of reciprocal agreement could be used to assess the outer boundary of the charged area – where the charged area will not cause the cost of measures to increase in the non-charged area, beyond the amount of money that is available anyway (through conventional sources).

The same principle of reciprocity can also be applied to the choice of time that the road pricing scheme operates, and the choice between distance and cordon pricing. If the cost of measures are proportional to the distance that people travel and it is cost-effective to have a system of distance pricing, it would be fairer to use than cordon pricing – because the drivers would pay an amount closer to their contribution to the cost of services. If the cost of measures is not proportional to the distance travelled, then cordon pricing might be more appropriate.

Acceptability of Urban Road Pricing as a Congestion Charge in the USA

Background to the Comparison

In 1992 the journal *Transportation* published a special issue on using road pricing to impose 'charges on moving traffic that are substantially higher at congested times and places than at other times and places, for the explicit purpose of reducing congestion' (Editorial, 1992, pp. 288–9). In other words the articles are concerned with using road pricing for the specific objective of improving congestion by influencing traffic levels, rather than using road pricing to finance measures that help reduce congestion.

As the grounded theory of acceptability has been used to argue that road pricing cannot 'acceptably' be used for the objective of directly reducing congestion (but only financing other measures) it is valuable to compare the thoughts in these articles with the recommendations of the grounded theory. This provides a way of checking that the grounded theory has not omitted any important points that could reconcile the problems of finding a universally acceptable consensus, amongst the limited set of respondents, when they use the direct-effect strategy.

The Comparison

Giuliano (1992) assesses the 'political acceptability of congestion pricing'. She gives the reasons why congestion pricing is opposed in the city of Los Angeles and then suggests politically acceptable pricing alternatives to overcome these problems. The reasons for opposition are as follows.

1 High tolls produce winners and losers: in Los Angeles an 'economically efficient toll' would be high. This would mean people with a high value of time who continued to drive might gain at the expense of those with a low value of time that continued to drive or were priced off the tolled road onto another facility. And while some of the people who lose may be recipients of toll revenues others may not be.

2 Equity and fairness: these issues depend on how the revenue is redistributed. 'If it is assumed that revenues are not redistributed in any way, congestion tolls will generally result in gains for upper income groups and losses for lower income groups' (ibid., p. 348). Thus how the revenue is spent is seen as crucial to equity and fairness concerns. However, Giuliano

thinks that 'no matter how revenues may be redistributed, some individuals may still be made worse off, since congestion tolls do not lead to Pareto improvements' (ibid., p. 348). Giuliano's pragmatic response is to say that 'equity does not appear to be a major public policy issue' (ibid.) in the US and people who use this argument are 'motivated by other reasons' (ibid., p. 349).

3   The problems of toll revenue: Giuliano considers the revenue a 'political mixed blessing' in the context of acceptability (ibid.). She sees a pressure to spend the money on specific transportation projects to increase acceptability instead of using the revenue to 'offset toll impacts on low income groups' (ibid., p. 350). In this way she begins to form an argument that instead of agreeing with the public that revenue from road pricing needs to be earmarked for service provision or alleviation measures, it should be used to try to limit the losses for low-income groups.

4   Scepticism and uncertainty regarding congestion pricing outcome: Giuliano thinks that the principle of congestion charging is correct and that the public have not been adequately informed of the concept or interest groups have misinformed the public. Therefore she suggests that 'once the concept is properly communicated, the public will support congestion pricing' (ibid., p. 351).

In the above points Giuliano has tried to keep the principle of this form of congestion charging as *a priori* 'acceptable' and to develop her assessment of improving acceptability around this unassailable principle. However, the result is that she is not able to say how congestion pricing could be made acceptable. In (1) she admits that there will be winners and losers, then in (2) says that it is impossible to distribute the revenue to avoid this problem. In (3) she confounds the problem by recognising that the pressure to spend the revenue on transport projects will not improve equity and fairness. Finally, in (4) she says despite these problems, to which she offers no solutions, the principle of this form of road pricing is still acceptable.

In contrast, grounded theory was used to recommend that urban road pricing should not be used directly to improve congestion because there would be losers, for the same reasons Giuliano recognises. Then the grounded theory focused on financing, and asserts that it is acceptable to use pricing to pay for measures that alleviate congestion and environmental problems. If this is what the revenue is spent on there are no equity problems because the restricted set of respondents consider that it is 'universally acceptable' that people pay for the services they use or to protect others from their impact. While some drivers may be priced off, and in economic terms lose, it is not a specific problem for acceptability. Giuliano does not counter this argument, nor does she give an alternative reason for believing road pricing should be used to affect congestion levels directly. In fact, in the conclusion of her article she seems to move closer to the grounded theory position and says that acceptability is more likely 'if pricing is linked with added capacity ... even if some of the economic efficiency benefits are lost in the process' (ibid., p. 355).

Decorla-Souza and Kane (1992, p. 307) also argue that the principle of congestion pricing is correct. Thus when revenue exceeds highway infrastructure needs it should be spent on 'non-auto travel options' to 'compensate those "tolled-off" the highways (usually low income users) for benefits lost to them'. Similarly Poole (1992, p. 395) accepts the rationale of this congestion pricing argument and says it is increasingly common 'to pay higher rates for (presumably) better service'. Both these views fail to reconcile the grounded theory view that a fair payment is linked to the cost of the service one receives (including the cost of environmental protection to others). Decorla-Souza and Kane see the revenue as being used for compensation. This is problematic because they do not describe how people can be adequately compensated. Meanwhile, Poole links the cost of the service to the quality of the service but does not assess whether there is a fairness issue in increasing prices beyond the cost of the service provision.

Small (1992) tries to argue a way out of this dilemma, by considering how to use the revenue from congestion pricing and in doing so he comes closer to the grounded theory recommendations about using road pricing. This indicates that, in terms of acceptability, the grounded theory recommendations are commensurate with practical resolutions to congestion pricing problems. He thinks that it is possible 'to more than fully compensate the majority' (ibid., p. 367) by allocating the revenue in three areas:

1   reimbursement to travellers as a group;
2   substituting general taxes used to pay for transportation services, and;
3   new transportation services.

In the grounded theory it was recommended that road pricing should be used to pay for transportation services by those who used them. This is essentially what (2) and (3) do. However, (1) tries to compensate drivers who need to travel and might not have an alternative. This, as explained before, is contrary to the grounded theory view. Yet despite offering the idea in (1), Small goes on to say that compensation would not be satisfactory and 'someone will be made worse off no matter how the program is designed' (ibid., p. 378). Therefore he ends up agreeing that the compensation could not be arranged to be 'universally acceptable' and concurs with the grounded theory.

Further research in the US agreed: 'Inevitably, some individuals will be disadvantaged' (Transportation Research Board, 1994, p. 78). This led the TRB to suggest that a more acceptable form of congestion pricing 'would be for the government to distribute "tradeable peak driving permits," which individuals or groups could use or sell' (ibid., p. 95). Thus 'instead of being "tolled-off" a user with a low value of time could be "bought-off"' (ibid., pp. 95–6); it is up to the individual whether or not he wants to sell the 'permit'. Whether this form of pricing could be acceptable is outside the scope of grounded theory of acceptability, and would probably raise a new set of problems. However, it indicates that the idea of congestion pricing can mutate into another form of pricing which does not immediately contradict the grounded theory recommendations – and agrees with the arguments given in Chapter 8 and repeated in this chapter, about compensatory agreements being acceptable when all parties agree to trade.

Urban Road Pricing in Britain

General Research

In Britain the idea of road pricing has been treated more flexibly and has not stuck to the economic congestion pricing principles as firmly as has previous work from the US. May (1992) describes how road pricing has come to incorporate additional goals such as environmental improvement and infrastructure finance. Jones (1995, p. 7) writes that there are a 'number of policy objectives that can be served by urban road pricing' and 'focusing on "congestion charging" would be too narrow'.

In this climate road pricing can be seen to have the dual objectives of reducing traffic to improve congestion and the environment and of raising revenue to finance other measures (Jones, 1998). This has transpired because research has found that the acceptability of road pricing increases when the money is used to improve public transport and make other transport and environmental improvements (Jones, 1991). Thus the concept of road pricing has had to take on board the fact that people view it more favourably when they think it is a form of charge for a service – in line with the grounded theory recommendations.

Jones and Grieco (1994) consider the importance of this point when there is no agreement about using road pricing to ration road space, but there is acceptance that money needs to be raised. They use the term 'road pricing' to refer to the rationing idea, and 'tolling' for the idea of funding services for the drivers:

> In such a context, planners and policy-makers may find it useful to blur the distinction between tolling and road pricing. Such an ambiguity can be functional where tolling has a higher political acceptability than road pricing; in this case, initially introducing the technology for eventual road pricing within a tolling framework can provide a more acceptable, though more gradual, path towards road pricing. Thus, whilst analytically, tolling and road pricing have different aims and purposes, politically, it may be necessary for transport planners to forge links between these two transparent organisation practices as part of a strategy of gaining gradual acceptance for the new more radical policy of road pricing (ibid., p. 1522).

Jones and Grieco illustrate this strategy by describing how road pricing plans in the Netherlands have been reduced to a tolling scheme and the tolling scheme in Trondheiåm is moving towards implementing road pricing. For Britain, though, Jones and Grieco do not explicitly state how the blurring between tolling and road pricing should progress; whether road pricing should be marketed as a toll first, with the technological possibility of being used for road pricing later, or if road pricing should be a combination of tolling and road pricing from the outset.

Commentary about the Acceptability of Implementing Road Pricing

Other commentary and research that has explicitly considered acceptability has suggested more of an emphasis on the finance objective as a first step to implementation. Richards (1998) argues that the original economic objective of road pricing is well founded, however, the real interest in introducing road pricing will be to raise revenue for local authority investment in transport. Similarly, Begg (1998) shows commitment to the economic rationale for road pricing, yet argues for road pricing to be given the objective more akin to tolling:

> The political acceptability of congestion charging will be enhanced if the investment in alternatives takes place in advance of any charges being introduced. Even then, however, road pricing has all the potential to be a

political minefield. As a first stage we must build on the strong support that exists for better public transport in our towns and cities and engage the public in a debate about how the improvements are to be paid for (ibid.).

This seems to suggest that road pricing should have the objective of only raising revenue as a 'first stage' and the intention would be to use road pricing for other objectives later on. A similar reasoning can be found in Tyson (1998). As a first stage for an implementation policy the grounded theory and this genre of opinion are in agreement. However, the grounded theory of acceptability of road pricing can be understood as going one step further than these types of arguments. The grounded theory takes the bold move and says that the economic principle that underlies using road pricing to ration road space can never be universally acceptable, because the analysis of the arguments of the limited set of respondents found it unacceptable, and consequently road pricing cannot be used as a tool to reduce traffic directly, even in a second stage of implementation. It is not a question of time before people become educated to the economic rationale, but a fundamental stumbling block, because the economic rationale is not reflected as a universal rule in the discourse of the respondents that made up the sample for the derivation of the grounded theory. Therefore the grounded theory agrees that the first step to introducing road pricing should be to finance improvement, but this should also be the last step. Support for this position comes from outside academic circles, such as Dawson (1998):

> It is not realistic to approach road pricing as a tax measure – to have any chance of acceptance it must be approached as a transport measure, e.g. it should be neutral in revenue with one payment replacing another ... Motorists don't recognise price as rationing tool – they understand about paying something to get something in return ... The AA has said that in principle there is an argument to move towards pay as you drive. In principle, it could help manage our existing road space better and help investment and environmental management.

Despite the universal logic of the grounded theory with respect to the limited population of respondents, and the recommendations of some leading practitioners to use road pricing primarily to finance new measures, definitely as a first step to implementation, it is interesting to note that this has not been made transparent in government policy and has not been an option that has been tested in road pricing experiments in Britain. The policy and experiments have always seen road pricing as a way to both reduce traffic and finance new measures at the same time.

Government Policy

The previous government's response to the Third Report of the Transport Select Committee (1995) that investigated road pricing does not draw the distinction between using road pricing to raise revenue and using it to restrain car use. This ambiguity continues in the first White Paper of the current government to support road pricing (Department for Environment, Transport and the Regions, 1998, p. 115).

> We will therefore introduce legislation to allow local authorities to charge road users so as to reduce congestion, as part of a package of measures in a local transport plan that would include improving public transport. The use of revenues to benefit transport serving the area where charges apply, which in many cases will mean supporting projects in more than one local authority area, will be critical to the success of such schemes.

From the above quotation it is unclear whether road pricing will have the objective of raising revenue, thereby indirectly reducing congestion, or whether it will be allowed a combination of objectives which include directly reducing car use. The government hints that road pricing should be focused on revenue raising in some parts:

> Charging will provide a guaranteed income stream to improve transport and support the renaissance of our towns and cities. The availability of a revenue stream will also open up the scope for greater involvement of the private sector working in partnership with local authorities (ibid.).

Yet the government also shows commitment to using road pricing directly to influence car use:

> We already use duty on different fuels as a way of influencing demand for road transport and as an incentive to consumers to buy more fuel efficient and less polluting vehicles. We are looking at ways of using taxation on vehicles to achieve similar results. More direct charges can also be very effective in influencing demand for travel or the choice of mode (ibid., p. 119).

Thus the government can be seen to be keeping the options for implementation of urban road pricing open. Another reason might be that if road pricing were to be put forward as a financing policy only, there would be greater pressure put on the government to make its accounting procedures more transparent so road users could see where their existing taxes are spent. As mentioned in Chapter 8, this would be a necessary accompaniment to using urban road pricing as a financing tool, to maximise its acceptability.

Edinburgh

The Joint Authorities Transportation and Environmental Study incorporated road pricing into some of the transport policy scenarios that it tested. 'In such integrated strategies, the revenue raising potential of road pricing plays an important part in facilitating the financing of other strategy elements' (The MVA Consultancy, 1991, p. 8). It also reinforces a 'package of measures designed to achieve a combination of efficiency, environmental, accessibility and equity objectives' (ibid.).

However, from the point of view of this chapter, it is unclear whether road pricing has the primary objective of finance or a combination of economic/ efficiency objectives and finance. The actual scenarios that were tested show that the intention was probably the latter. For example, the road pricing revenue was hypothetically assigned to transport projects outside the area in which the charge was being collected (ibid., p. 70). Therefore it can be seen as contributing to solving problems that were not caused by some of the people who would pay the charge. A fuller explanation about how this contradicts the grounded theory rules was given in Chapter 10, and earlier in this chapter.

Cambridge

Cambridgeshire County Council investigated the potential for using road pricing and ran a small-scale experiment where some drivers were equipped with meters in their cars and given some money. They were then charged, at different rates, and if they avoided the charges they could keep the money they did not spend. This provided information on technical feasibility and behaviour. This experiment was supplemented by surveys to calculate the value of time (WS Atkins Planning Consultants, 1994) and modelling to assess the optimum charging structures (Smith et al., 1994).

The objectives of road pricing for Cambridgeshire County Council were a combination of economic vitality, efficiency, environmental protection, equity and providing finance for a light rapid transit system. They chose to try a congestion metering scheme where the 'on-board metering device would only commence charging when a combination of speed and distance travelled indicated that the vehicle was in a congested situation' (Ison, 1996). Therefore the scenarios that were imagined were not solely aimed at providing finance but at reflecting the cost of externalities.

Ison (ibid., pp. 118–19) gives reasons why the idea of road pricing lost favour in Cambridge:

1   'one of the key operational requirements is "transparency" in that the price should be readily ascertainable by road users before a journey is undertaken';
2   safety concerns about drivers speeding to avoid paying the charge;
3   dealing with road works and accidents that will delay drivers but not be their fault and be perceived as unfair to pay for.

These reasons can be understood in the context of the grounded theory that was used to explain why congestion metering would not be acceptable, because it breaks with the common logic that people use when discussing road pricing. After the road pricing experiment Cambridgeshire County Council has put more emphasis on 'public transport policies, with the bus playing a key role in combating congestion.' However, they have not publicly supported road pricing, even as a method of financing these public transport measures.

Bristol

The Avon Traffic Restraint Study looked at how to use road pricing to help reduce congestion and improve the environment in Bristol. However, as the title of the study implies it looks at how road pricing (and parking restraint and fuel price increases) can be used to restrain traffic. It does not consider in-depth how road pricing can support other policies. The study finds that:

> High charge levels ranging between £1.20 and £1.90 per cordon at 1991 prices are necessary to significantly contribute to the objectives of the Avon Area Traffic Plan. These levels are much higher than the public, particularly motorists, currently perceive as acceptable ... There is, therefore, a need for more widespread public consultation on the subject before a decision is made ... One clear message is that it will be necessary to apply the revenues to improve public transport as a condition of public acceptability (Ove Arup and Partners 1997, pp. 53–4).

Thus, like other studies, road pricing has not been considered originally as a solely financing measure, but the conclusion suggests that acceptability would be improved if it were.

Leicester

The Leicester Environmental Road Tolling Scheme experimented with road pricing. A major feature of the experiment was to provide an attractive public transport alternative to car travel and 'a large part of the scheme's costs have gone towards a transport infrastructure that comprises a purpose built park and ride site, a dedicated bus service, and a public transport priority route to the city centre' (Smith, 1998). Thus the experiment can be seen as focusing on using road pricing to finance other measures. However, in the scenarios tested by participants in a trial, the design reflected both the objectives of restraining traffic and raising finance.

For example, the park and ride site was located outside the cordon and drivers paid either to drive, or parked and used the park and ride facility. The park and ride had a charge as well and the participants could pay using the same smartcard that they used to pay to drive. If the charge to use the park and ride was the same as the cost to drive then road pricing could solely be seen as a means to raise revenue and drivers used the mode that was most convenient. However, this scenario was never tested, and there was always a differential between the toll and the park and ride fee of between £0.20 and £10.00. This shows that there was always an element of the restraint objective in the design and it was never solely considered as a method to raise revenue to finance solutions to problems caused by road users. See Chapter 8 and this chapter for fuller explanation on why differential charging between park and ride and driving are theoretically unacceptable, if the park and ride service is subsidised by the drivers.

In conclusion, though, the Leicester study finds that there is a 'significant latent demand for the park and ride service amongst the general public, without the application of road tolling'. Therefore they think that the drivers may be willing to switch modes and say 'there is now a general acceptance that road pricing is a viable proposition, but on the clear understanding that quality alternative public transport systems are in place beforehand' (ibid.) Current thinking thus places the emphasis on hypothecating the revenue to pay for the alternative transport system. In common with the other studies, making road pricing acceptable seems to reduce to using it to a way to finance transport and environmental measures.

Recommendation for Objectives of Using Road Pricing

Research in Britain has focused on using road pricing to meet the objectives of efficiency, environmental improvement and raising revenue to finance other transport measures. Each of the studies that considered acceptability has recognised the potential of increasing the acceptability by using the revenue to finance other transport measures and the unacceptability of using pricing to directly restrain traffic. In this they are commensurate with the grounded theory recommendations.

However, unlike the grounded theory they showed that there is still a belief that using pricing directly to restrain traffic could be found acceptable in the long term. Perhaps for this reason government policy and road pricing experiments have backed away from using pricing only as a finance tool. This is indicated by the government arguments and the UK experiments that have been described above.

The grounded theory goes a step further and says that the emphasis should be placed on using road pricing solely to finance transport measures in both the short and long terms. The grounded theory has been used to recommend this course of action because it argues there is no universal logic in the discourse of the limited set of respondents that could find using road pricing for other objectives acceptable. Therefore the grounded theory can be used to recommend that scenarios that use road pricing solely as a finance measure should be tested in future.

The Grounded Theory and Welfare Economics

Realising the Cost of Externalities

The previous two sections have dealt with the case of using road pricing to ration road space and raise finance. The case of rationing road space has been associated with economic principles which argue that the revenue should compensate those 'priced off' the roads. This short section reminds the reader that, while the grounded theory is a rejection of a specific case of a set of economic arguments, it is not a rejection of the entire set of economic arguments about using road pricing. These are subtler, and at most the grounded theory can be seen as a way of modifying these arguments to be seen as a way of financing solutions to problems.

One of the main arguments for road pricing is that it can be used to make drivers cover the cost of their externalities. These are elements such as the cost of congestion, accidents and the environmental damage and can be counted on top of the taxes and charges that motorists already pay. They can be calculated to be between £29.3–36.9 billion per annum (Newbery, 1995; Pearce, 1993). One of the effects of making drivers pay these charges would be to reduce traffic. Thus the argument is often linked into the idea of rationing road space. However, from this economic perspective, making drivers pay for externalities goes beyond the objective of rationing road space: it is something that drivers should be doing anyway. The following subsections explore this economic idea, which was introduced in Chapter 2, by interpreting it in terms of the grounded theory. Firstly, the acceptability of paying for externalities, ignoring how the money is spent, is investigated. Secondly, the acceptability of paying for externalities when the use of the revenue is taken into account is explored.

Paying the Full Cost of Externalities

Assuming fair competition exists, the economically efficient price to charge for driving should include the full marginal social cost that drivers make on such things as congestion and the environment. Thus people will only make decisions to drive if they are 'willing to pay' for congestion and environmental effects of their journeys, which is a more efficient basis for making a decision to drive than if drivers did not have to pay these costs. This argument was given in Chapter 2.

It is possible to use this argument to say that it is acceptable for drivers to pay the full cost of externalities. This might offer a way of undermining the grounded theory of acceptability because the grounded theory is used to defend that it is only universally acceptable to the restricted population of respondents to charge drivers for the cost of services and environmental alleviation measures.

If people have to pay the full marginal cost of their trips then they will drive only if they value their journey by car more than the level of congestion and environmental damage to which their trips contribute. This reflects an economically efficient use of resources. However, this argument assumes that the environment and congestion can be worsened if someone is willing to pay to do so. This is against the principle of the grounded theory which sees it as being universally unacceptable to the restricted population of respondents to affect another person's ability to meet their needs. It does not reflect that some people might value their environment or congestion-free conditions extremely highly and thus think that pricing is not protecting their interests.

Furthermore, it is an assumption that conflicting needs can be balanced by making a decision in the medium of money. This is only one method through which decisions can be reached and one which can favour those people who have a vested interest in making decisions about money. The grounded theory, on the other hand, does not make such an assumption and can be considered more holistic and reflective of the variety of ways of making decisions about how to use resources. For example, under the utilitarian category of the grounded theory, subcategory concepts of efficiency and environment reflect ways that people might establish an acceptable balance of needs for a whole society. One of these ways might be through economic efficiency principles, but equally it might be done through setting environmental standards. When the direct- and indirect-effect strategies – which include the subcategories of the utilitarian category – are used, the grounded theory balances these views with other subcategories classified under the fairness category. Within these strategies the marginal economic efficiency argument is only one technique that people use to reach a decision about an acceptable price for driving. Thus it is not argued that it represents a universally acceptable argument – one that is necessarily acceptable to all respondents – because there are clearly some people who find it acceptable to balance utilitarian and fairness subcategories in a different way.

Also, in order to cost externalities it is necessary to ascertain how much congestion-free travel and a traffic-free environment are worth, or to value how much congestion and environmental damage cost. Not surprisingly, different people will place different values on efficiency and the environment. This means that whichever aggregate value for externalities is decided on, it will be an undervalue for some and an overvalue for others. An assumption would have to be made that it is acceptable for drivers to pay the aggregate value and not the value that a group might think travel is worth.

However, one thing that is universally acceptable to the restricted population of respondents, on which the grounded theory is based, is that a road pricing charge reflects the cost of measures needed to provide services to drivers and protect those in the environment from the impact of driving. This overcomes the three criticisms, given in the above three paragraphs, of the marginal economic argument. The charge is not being linked with any assumptions about how to balance competing needs of individuals (which cannot satisfactorily be resolved) other than drawing on the universally acceptable principle, derived from the restricted sample of respondents' views on road pricing, that the individuals should be free to meet their needs, and where this interferes with ability of others to meet their needs, solutions to the conflicting interests should be found. Also, the grounded theory interpretation of acceptability avoids the criticism that environment and congestion-free conditions can be traded-off if drivers are willing to pay.

The marginal economic argument can be altered, though, to take on board the grounded theory criticisms about how it fails to address acceptability holistically, by arguing that the money raised from charging for externalities should be used to minimise those externalities. However, before addressing this issue a more sophisticated use of the marginal economics argument is examined which links it with the idea that people are willing to sell perfect efficiency and environmental conditions if they get something in return. Thus paying for externalities is more akin to the objective of financing without the precondition of trying to minimise externalities.

The Welfare Economics Argument

A simple exposition of the welfare economics argument can be found in Parkin et al. (1997). In an uncomplicated situation a consumer buys a service from a provider and the price the consumer pays should equal the cost of that service. This is fair because the consumer is willing to buy the service at the given price and the provider is willing to sell the service at the agreed price. For example, if provider P owns a landfill site and consumer C wants to put rubbish into the landfill then P and C agree the price. Assuming no one else is involved or affected, then there are no externalities.

However, there are more complex situations where other people are involved. In the landfill example, the rubbish C buries may cause pollution outside the area that is owned by P and so affect other people. Unlike P, who is getting paid for the use of his landfill site, the others are not getting paid for suffering the pollution. This pollution is an externality. If these people were willing to be paid to suffer the pollution (in the same way P agrees to sell the use of his landfill site) then C should pay this additional cost. This additional cost represents the money cost of the externality.

In transport there are many of these externalities. For example, cars make noise and this affects other people, travelling at peak time contributes to congestion and slows down other people and driving causes accidents and a feeling of danger that severely affect the lives of others. If the government, which is the provider of the roads, merely charged for the construction and maintenance cost of the road, then none of the externalities would be paid for by the motorists.

This would be a problem because the drivers would be affecting other people, who were getting nothing in return. Therefore, the government, so the welfare economics argument goes, should act as an agent for these people and find out how much money they would be willing to accept in compensation for the inconvenience suffered at the hands of motorists. Then it should redistribute the money to those affected.

However, because of the pervasiveness of the impacts of driving, the government would not know to whom to give the money. Instead it should continue to act as the agent for the money from externalities and invest it in projects that have net social gains. For example, although a community may suffer from the environmental impacts of a road, the money from payment for externalities could provide a new school. If the money has been well spent the value the people in the community place on a school should outweigh the value they place on the inconvenience from the traffic.

Even though some people value the environment more highly than others, an average value can be placed on the externalities. This is acceptable based on the logic that society needs to combine the views of its individuals. Thus the welfare economics argument recommends that drivers should pay for the construction and maintenance costs of the road (in economics these are called private costs) and the cost of the externalities (social costs). The role of the government then is to make sure the cost of the roads is met and to invest the rest of the money in projects with a net social gain. The welfare economics argument does not define how to spend the money because it assumes that the people are willing to trade the environmental impacts for other services. Again, on average they are.

In the case of driving there are other private costs, such as the cost of the vehicle and the fuel. However, the government does not need to take these costs into its calculation of the tax that motorists pay because private companies provide these goods. However, it is convenient to place a tax on these commodities on top of the value-added tax (which is levied on most commodities). The welfare economics argument recommends that the value of this tax should cover the expenditure on the road network and the cost of externalities. But if urban road pricing were introduced to pay for costs of infrastructure provision in urban areas it would also be possible to use this pricing mechanism to charge for the cost of externalities in urban areas.

In this way the welfare economics argument is more subtle than the crude 'rationing of road space argument' which has been used in the previous two sections and more holistic than the simple marginal economic argument described in the previous subsection, because it looks at how the revenue from pricing can be used as well.

Appending Ideas from the Grounded Theory

The indirect-effect strategy is the relevant part of the grounded theory to compare with the aims of this part of the welfare economics argument. In the strategy it was claimed that the only universally acceptable use for revenue, which the restricted population of respondents backed, would be to spend it on measures to solve the problems that drivers inflicted on others. It would not be acceptable to spend the money on compensatory measures because some people would not want to be compensated and some may not be sufficiently compensated.

The welfare economics response would be to explain that the argument is based on another universal principle perhaps ignored by the grounded theory. Coase (1960) implies that when one person wants to pursue an activity that will affect another, he agrees with that person an acceptable price to pay to carry out the activity. This could be considered to be a universally acceptable principle. Therefore it is possible to infer that the welfare economics argument takes this universal principle and expands it across a society.

The grounded theory is not challenging that private agreements between consenting groups of people might be universally acceptable. Rather, it is saying that in the bounded case of charging for urban road use there are groups of people who will not consent to have compensation paid. Therefore the aggregation that is essential to applying the welfare economics argument to road pricing in urban areas is not appropriate in this case. The only universally acceptable course of action, as derived from analysis of the discourse of the restricted population of respondents, would be to raise revenue to solve the problem. This is explained in Chapter 8 and earlier in this chapter.

In order for the welfare economic argument to adapt to the grounded theory of acceptability, thus taking on board the above criticisms, money raised should not be about providing compensation but about minimising the cost of externalities. Even if it proves impossible to eliminate the effect that gives rise to externalities completely, the universally acceptable course of action, according to analysis of the discourse of the restricted population of respondents, is to try.

A General Statement about Using Grounded Theory and Welfare Economics Arguments

When there is an environmental problem there are several courses of action. A government can:

1   live with the problem – this might be done where the benefits outweigh the problems;
2   make the offenders pay the cost of the externalities – this money may be used to compensate the people affected;
3   ration the activity to return to an acceptable level;
4   ban the activity in question – an example of this is pedestrianisation;
5   invest in solving the problem.

Urban road pricing can cover (2), (3) and (5). If the charge is used as a method of rationing or to cover the cost of externalities this is not universally acceptable to the restricted population of respondents, according to the grounded theory. However, if urban road pricing is used to finance solutions to problems that are caused by the people paying the charge then it is universally acceptable to the limited set of respondents.

In the case of transport, though, the case for charging for externalities to then invest in projects that have a net social gain could be mistaken for being the option that the respondents would find universally acceptable. It may be that the grounded theory is wrong in its contention about what is universally acceptable to the restricted population of respondents, and this can be tested. However, it does raise the question of whether the increasingly unchallenged welfare economics argument should be put forward quite so dominantly and in a way that ignores its political bias – i.e., it is putting forward a view that is acceptable only to a few.

The issue is not a question about which option meets social, environmental and efficiency objectives most effectively. It is more a question about ensuring that the system that is being used reflects what human beings want. And what they want to do, as reflected in their use of language, is to be free to do what they will and if their activities interfere with others, to solve the problems. It is contended that the grounded theory reflects this better than welfare economics.

It is possible to link this idea in with Habermas' communicative theory (1984) which focuses on how human beings historically have the tendency to create systems that trap them and do not reflect their actual needs. The grounded theory recommendations can be seen as an example of what human beings want, whereas the welfare economics approach can be seen as a system that may not deliver this.

However, to go on and discuss the implications of this would require leaving the bounds of the grounded theory. It is sufficient to say that there is incongruence between the grounded theory and welfare economics and this could be important because some social and historical research has noted the tendency for systems to not reflect what human beings want. However, at this stage this can merely be a suggestion for further research.

Conclusion

In the first section of this chapter the recommendations that have been made from the derivation of the grounded theory were outlined. The most important and controversial recommendation was that urban road pricing should only be used to finance solutions to transport problems. This formed the central theme for the next three sections.

The following section considered the specific case of using road pricing to relieve congestion. The literature that was compared was not able undermine the grounded theory's contention. Then, research in Britain supported using road pricing to raise revenue to finance solutions. However, government policy and road pricing experiments did not consider the use of road pricing solely as a method of financing. This can be explained by the dominance of the economic logic for road pricing. So, in the next section, the subtleties of the welfare economics argument were detailed. But in the case of urban road pricing the full economic argument did not cast doubt upon the grounded theoretical idea about acceptability.

By way of conclusion, it was suggested making drivers pay for externalities would not be universally acceptable to the population of respondents from whose opinions the grounded theory was derived. The only universally acceptable option to this restricted population is to use road pricing to pay for solutions to the problems that drivers face or cause. This is because this rationale is intrinsic to the arguments that all the respondents used in the interviews.

Chapter 12

Conclusion

Summary of Research

Research Approach and Objectives

In Chapter 1, the role of using a sociological theory to mediate between conflicting opinions about urban road pricing and the choice of design options was described. If people's arguments are recorded then a theory can be developed that explains and understands how these arguments are constructed. The theory can then be used to establish rules about which arguments are universally acceptable amongst all respondents and to choose between the options for road pricing, according to these rules. Figure 1.1 in Chapter 1 illustrates this process.

The research objectives, from a practical planning perspective, were to use sociological theory to decide: for which policy objectives it is acceptable to use road pricing; if there are constraints on how it is used as part of an integrated package of measures; and to decide on design options that acceptably meet these objectives. From a sociological perspective it is necessary to ensure that the theory is not based on notions of acceptability that are not relevant to road pricing. Therefore the methodological objectives were to ground the theory in opinions about road pricing. To achieve this, the method of grounded theorising was applied.

Recap of Chapters

Chapter 2 provided a background to urban road pricing and established that a theory, applicable to choosing between road pricing scenarios, did not exist. In Chapter 3, it was argued that the best method to develop a theory would be using qualitative sociological research techniques. The grounded theorising approach was favoured because it places greater emphasis than other techniques on keeping a theory relevant to practical research problems. As the development of the grounded theory would involve collecting data about people's reactions to a full range of road pricing options, and no such data was available, Chapter 4 describes the process of data collection. The case studies were carried out in Cambridge and Edinburgh; the sample comprised 60 interviews with interest groups and individuals in the case-study areas; these in-depth interviews covered the general idea of road pricing and specific design options. In Chapters 5 and 6, the data is analysed, making use of excerpts from transcripts to enhance reflexivity, to develop a grounded theory of the acceptability of urban road pricing. The main feature of the theory is that it identifies strategies that people use when constructing arguments about road pricing. In Chapters 7, 8, 9 and 10, patterns in how respondents use the strategies are discovered, which reflect arguments that all respondents find acceptable. These patterns are used to postulate rules about what is universally acceptable to this limited set of respondents and to decide between design options. In Chapter 11, these theoretical ideas are compared with other research into the acceptability of urban road pricing.

Findings

Theory Development

Concepts The grounded theory that was developed says that arguments relating to acceptability use three main concepts, called categories in grounded theorising terminology: utilitarianism, fairness, and sincerity. These categories are divided into subcategories, to improve precision. Utilitarianism is split into concern about the ability of road pricing to make an overall improvement to efficiency and to the environment. Fairness is split into three subcategories that reflect its wide meaning; provision of needs, payment for services and equality of treatment. Sincerity is subdivided into trust of planners and trust of players, where the latter refers to the drivers that pay the charge. This hierarchy of concepts is illustrated in Figure 6.1 and examples of each of the subcategories, known as properties, are shown in Table 6.1.

Strategies Arguments about the acceptability of road pricing, according to the grounded theory, use combinations of the concepts. Three combinations were identified, called strategies. The direct-effect strategy balances utilitarian advantages in *efficiency* and *environment* of using pricing to influence demand, against the *provision of specific group needs*, and *equality of treatment* between different groups. The indirect-effect strategy questions whether road pricing is needed to provide revenue *to pay for services* for the *provision of needs* and if *planners can be trusted* to use the revenue as needed. The contribution strategy addresses whether there should be *equality of treatment* in *payment for services* and the problem of not being able to *trust drivers* to contribute. The strategies are summarised in Table 6.3.

Theoretically acceptable rules When the respondents used the direct-effect strategy, two rules with implications for acceptability were postulated. Firstly, it is acceptable that drivers who do not pay what is seen as an acceptable charge do not drive. Secondly, an acceptable charge is not one that uses pricing to ration road use, by raising it above what is seen as an acceptable amount. After analysis of patterns in the use of the indirect-effect strategy a third rule was hypothesised that it is universally acceptable to the respondents for drivers to pay for the cost of service provision and environmental alleviation measures. This idea is different to rationing because money is spent on solutions.

In contrast, analysis of arguments in the contribution strategy did not provide such concrete rules about acceptability as the analysis of patterns in the direct- and indirect-strategies. It did, however, suggest that contributions could change to take account of the extent to which different vehicles contributed to the need to solve traffic problems, for example, high polluting vehicles paying more than cleaner vehicles. Also respondents found it acceptable to alter the amount drivers pay according to how essential their trips are seen to be, for example, emergency vehicles pay less than tourists.

Applying Theoretical Ideas

Theoretically acceptable policy objectives The rules from the direct- and indirect-effect strategies were sufficient to derive a universally acceptable policy objective, with respect to the discourse of the limited number of respondents that were interviewed, for which to use road pricing. It was argued that the policy objective for urban road pricing should be solely to raise revenue for the provision of services that drivers need and for the alleviation of the environmental impact that drivers cause. Consequently it is acceptable to use road pricing to finance a range of measures: from roads to meet the needs of drivers; physical barriers to protect the milieu from the impact of driving; to public transport to both meet the transport needs of drivers and lessen the impact of vehicles on the environment.

Constraints on keeping to the theoretically acceptable policy objective Taking the example of using road pricing to finance a park and ride public transport service, an issue arises about how much the drivers who switch to using the park and ride service should pay in relation to those that continue to drive. If it is worth financing park and ride as a solution to drivers' needs and problems, it is in the interest of drivers that some of their number switch to using the service. However, who should use park and ride should not be based on who is willing to pay more to drive, as this contravenes the second rule of the direct-effect strategy. It is acceptable, though, that everyone that needs the park and ride service, either as a user or as a driver who gets benefits from people switching to park and ride, should share the cost of the service, to concur with the third rule from the indirect-effect strategy. Therefore, drivers in similar vehicles with similar essentiality of trip purpose (to take account of differences resulting from suggestions from the contribution strategy) should pay the same road pricing rate, regardless of whether they continue to drive or switch to park and ride. If the charge was a flat fee the amount would be the same but if it was calculated according to distance travelled or journey time the amount would only be the same if the distance travelled or time taken were comparable between driving and park and ride.

Equal charges between drivers and public transport users, though, is only warranted when neither group would be better off being independent of each other. For example, if the park and ride service and necessary measures to protect the environment from its impact can be provided at a lower cost independent of receiving money from people that continue to drive, then there can be no prerogative to pay more than necessary by paying the same amount as people who continue to drive. Similarly, drivers might be better off by not investing in public transport alternatives but in, perhaps, technological improvements or barriers to protect the environment. Full twists, turns, nuances and challenges to the argument for applying the grounded theory are dealt with in Chapter 8 (pp. 159–66) and Chapter 11 (pp. 216–191).

Using the revenue to finance transport-related measures also puts a constraint on a government to account for existing taxes that motorists pay, as many respondents thought that a proportion of this taxation should be spent on transport and that they should not have to pay a road pricing charge as well. Any government will have to make clear that revenue from road user charges will be spent on measures that are needed for which there is no money available from existing taxation. Thus road pricing provides finance that is additional to current sources of revenue, such as fuel taxes and vehicle excise duty. Or a government will have to reduce existing motoring taxes by the amount it expects to raise from road pricing. It is also possible to argue that urban road pricing is a fairer way of distributing the cost of transport-related measures amongst drivers than current levies, because it reflects the amount of road use in urban areas.

Varying the amount that different groups of road users contribute — Some drivers will be in vehicles that contribute a greater or lesser amount than the average vehicle to the need for measures, e.g. buses, heavy goods vehicles, low-emission cars, motorcycles. Those groups that can be considered independently of other groups (i.e. those groups not receiving subsidy from other groups and thus required to pay the same charge rate to be theoretically acceptable — such as park and ride users in the previous example) should pay more or pay less in proportion to their greater or lesser contribution to the need for investment. However, if the implication of a group paying their contribution to measures separately from other groups results in all groups paying more, it is in that group's interest to accept the lower standard charge. The latter situation might arise when the cost of operating a system of different charge levels costs more than the savings gained.

Other drivers will be part of a user group whose trip is seen as more essential than others, for example, trips by emergency and utility vehicles and by disabled people, where essentiality refers to having priority to use the road over other groups. If the costs of measures needed for driving in urban areas would be less with just essential users on the roads then they could acceptably claim entitlement to a lower charge. However, if they get economy of scale savings from more users on the roads then there is not a theoretically acceptable case for paying less, because they would have to pay more if the less essential drivers were not using the roads. The full argument is given in Chapter 11 (pp. 216–191).

Also, this argument does not contradict the argument about equivalent charges between drivers and public transport users (assuming part of the road pricing revenue subsidises public transport) because it is not about one group getting benefit from some of their members switching to another mode. e.g. Assume a scenario where low emission vehicles pay a lower rate and the road pricing revenue is used to finance a park and ride service, although drivers that do not find park and ride convenient can still continue to drive. When the drivers of low emission vehicles approach the charged area they will have to pay a road pricing fee at the reduced rate. They then have the choice about which measure to use, whether to continue to drive or to use the park and ride service.

Differentiating the level of charge by area and time The theoretically acceptable rules cannot, of course, predict the area of operation of road pricing or the time that the charge is levied. However, the above style of argument can be used to decide when the charge level should be differentiated by area and when by time. Some areas and time-bands will need more expensive measures to be implemented and so it is fair, according to the grounded theory rules, that the drivers in these areas or driving at these times should contribute more. It is only worth doing so, though, if the added cost of operating a more sophisticated and fairer charging system results in users paying less.

Charging structures The grounded theory rules were also used to decide between the charging structures, which could be cordon-, distance- or time-based. Time-based options were rejected as likely to be unacceptable because the amount that people paid could rise above the cost of the measures, due to delays that were not attributable to the drivers paying the charge. Cordon charging and distance charging will be more acceptable because the amount that drivers pay can be more effectively linked to the cost of measures. The choice between cordon and distance pricing, though, will depend on which transport measures road pricing revenue is used to fund.

Further Research

Testing and Adapting the Grounded Theory

The application of the grounded theory to decide on policy objective and design options for road pricing makes some suggestions that are inconsistent with other research that has considered the acceptability of urban road pricing. The most notable difference is over the recommendation that park and ride users and people that continue to drive should pay the same rate of charge (assuming that park and ride is funded by road pricing revenue and that one is comparing groups of similar users).

Other research, described in Chapter 11, has argued that drivers that switch to park and ride should pay less than their counterparts that continue to drive. However, such arguments involve making other assumptions in addition to the grounded theory rules of acceptability. Consequently, these arguments do not refute the grounded theory recommendations, which should be applied completely independently of other arguments to avoid compromising the theoretical ideas to researchers' prejudices.

However, the grounded theory is a fledgling theory, and it still needs testing and adaptation. Before applying the ideas in practice it would be desirable to check the plausibility of the grounded theory by more rigorous testing. In this research, the theory was developed from responses of a sample chosen according to theoretical sampling guidelines. A more rigorous test would be to choose a larger sample, and have it be representative of the population as a whole, using statistical sampling techniques. The testing of the theoretical ideas might refute the theory or raise ideas that could be incorporated into the theory. It could also give information about the spread of use of the strategies, indicating the popularity of certain types of arguments.

Applying the Theory to Other Practical Problems

The grounded theoretical ideas can also be used to stimulate new theoretical work in other areas, where acceptability is an issue. Obvious examples would be in other areas of transport planning where there is overlap in the subject matter. A more interesting and wider area, as mentioned in Chapter 11, would be in the application of economic rules to policy decisions. The recommendations that are made for design of a road pricing scheme, from a welfare economics perspective, differ from the grounded theory approach. The grounded theory could be used to establish which economic arguments can be seen as universally acceptable to a sample and how they might be adapted, such as by the suggestion to use money raised from charging to cover the cost of externalities to minimise the effects that caused those externalities. If such research is done it will help planners and politicians decide how far economic ideas should be followed.

Using the Theory to Help Academic Understanding of the Social World

If the grounded theory is not applied in a practical manner, yet is proved to be plausible, it can still be used in an academic sphere to understand why universally acceptable options might not have been taken by policy makers.

Habermas (1984) argues that societies have historically created systems that are unfair. However, this is paradoxical, he thinks, because inherent in the language in which people construct their arguments are principles about fairness. Therefore, he argues, in order to construct social systems, such as the state or capitalism, the fairness principles in language (that he calls communicative action) must have been corrupted. This distortion in language occurs for reasons such as loss of meaning, withdrawal of legitimisation, confusion, anomie (lack of ethical standards) and alienation. Rasmussen (1990) argues that Habermas' theory is not plausible, though, because it cannot be shown that there is a communicative action that is inherently fair.

This research on the development of the grounded theory of acceptability of road pricing has gone some way to show that it is possible to derive principles in language – even if they are not the same as Habermas'. Therefore, not dissimilar to some recommendations by Scambler (1996), the idea of Habermas, to understand the world by looking for how principles in language are violated, can be rescued.

Consequently it would be possible to critically examine the development of road pricing schemes. When it can be shown that the design options are contrary to the grounded theory principles (such as not having equal charge rates between people that continue to drive and those that switch to park and ride), the reasons for the differences can be discovered and in doing so one learns more about how the world, and language in particular, works. This might be because of the tendency for social systems to average out opinions instead of trying to incorporate all opinions into a decision, as mentioned in Chapter 11. For example, if the design option is based on averaging out people's values of time, such a system cannot incorporate an opinion of a person who believes that their time should not be valued in money terms. Of course, there are likely to be many other ways of distorting communicative principles waiting to be discovered, and also the chance that some are not distortions but universally acceptable principles in their own right.

Where the Suggestions for Further Research are Leading

This research project has been an unashamed attempt to redefine the decision-making process in transport planning. The central tenet is that decisions that have been seen as the preserve of politics need not be so. The very objectives of transport policy (and perhaps other public policy areas) can be derived from principles of language, and if followed there is no need to vote on which course of action to pursue. The role of the politician becomes that of overseer of government and not policy-maker.

Thomas More envisions politicians in this way in his work *Utopia*. Of course, utopia means no place and as such implies the idea of decisions not being political is unrealistic and unachievable. While theorists may be forced to agree that it is unimaginable that the entire range of governmental activities can be established from a few universal principles derived from a restricted sample of discourse; they do not have to concede it is impossible to achieve it in some subsets of government. The grounded theory research in this thesis has shown that in a bounded policy area a theory grounded in relevant arguments can discover principles that can be used to decide between some design scenarios. The principles cover rights and responsibilities and in the course a philosophy emerges that suggests it is clear when people should be free to pursue their individual activities and when they should take on responsibility for ensuring their activities do not interfere with the lifestyles of other people.

This should not mean that policy proposals and solutions to problems are the sole preserve of a plebiscite, out of whose discourse it is argued principles should emerge, and that a government should take no role in putting forward and carrying out transport measures. To some degree, people in government might always be more concerned than the average member of a plebiscite with creating and applying practical measures to solve problems. However, even if potential solutions derive from government, the principles under which the acceptability and legitimacy of these proposals should be assessed should come from arguments exhibited in the discourse of the plebiscite.

Postscript

Overview

Since the research project described in this book was completed in 1999, the UK has seen exciting developments in urban road pricing policy. At the time of publication, London is expected to introduce the country's first full scheme, and the legal foundations for local authorities elsewhere to use the policy measure have been laid. These developments have increased the relevance and urgency of critically examining public and political acceptability issues. Such research would be able to draw on recent evidence from London's experience in order to expose acceptable and unacceptable practices. It would have many practical benefits for London, in terms of suggesting how the scheme can acceptably evolve, and for other potential charging authorities, which could learn from London's experience.

This postscript undertakes a simple analysis of some of the evidence from London, using the sociological method for investigating acceptability explained in this book. It establishes the relevance of the grounded theory of acceptability for interpreting acceptability issues in London and notes additional arguments that were not used in the Cambridge and Edinburgh case studies. Lessons from London are then drawn based on a theoretical interpretation of the evidence. However, a full analysis, which would be a research project in itself, would be needed to rigorously establish the plausibility of the recommendations. This would involve further grounded analysis, theory development and testing, and a thorough investigation of possible alternative interpretations. The simple analysis should properly be viewed as further demonstrating the value of this sociological research method, illustrating its possibilities and throwing new ideas into the ring.

Urban Road Pricing Developments in the UK

Background

In recent years, the UK has undergone a process of devolution and continued local government reorganisation. Throughout this process, the government has remained committed to the potential of road pricing outlined in the Transport White Paper (DETR, 1998), discussed in Chapter 11.

In 1999, an Assembly was set up in Wales and a parliament in Scotland, which have the necessary jurisdiction to establish laws to allow road pricing schemes in their respective principalities. In London, a Greater London Authority was established in 2000, which is headed by an elected mayor, to form a second tier of government over existing London authorities, such as the boroughs and the police. Specific legislation was passed to allow the GLA to introduce road pricing. Other local authorities throughout Britain are considering electing mayors, and some have already done so. Recent transport legislation now allows all English local authorities scope to create road pricing schemes.

London Congestion Charging

Legislation for London was passed ahead of elsewhere in the UK, because of the necessity to devolve power to the GLA prior to its election in 2000. In order to introduce road pricing, the GLA Bill (1999) requires that a charging authority, specified as Transport for London, submit a Scheme Order for approval by the mayor. In order for the mayor to confirm the Order, it should be compatible with the aims of the mayor's transport strategy and commit to spending the surplus revenue on local transport improvements for 10 years. The consent of the Secretary of State for Transport is only necessary if the charge will apply to a main trunk road.

This opportunity for introducing road pricing has been taken forward; the mayor has already confirmed the Scheme Order, which did not need the consent of the Secretary of State; and the scheme, called London congestion charging, is due to commence operating during the schools' half term week in February 2003. It is an area-based scheme that is similar in concept to that tested in the Greater London Council study in 1974, briefly described in Chapter 2. Its main policy objectives are to reduce congestion and to raise revenue for local transport improvements, particularly for public transport.

Under the scheme, drivers will face a £5 per day charge to drive in the part of central London bounded by the inner ring road, which includes the City of London and parts of the City of Westminster, Camden, Islington, Southwark and Lambeth. The charge will be levied between 7.00 a.m. and 6.30 p.m. on weekdays, excluding bank holidays, and will be enforced by an automatic number plate recognition system. When drivers pay the charge, possible at a wide range of outlets, their vehicle licence numbers are entered onto a register of authorised vehicles. A series of cameras positioned at entry points to the zone and within the zone, take images of the licence plates of passing vehicles. If a licence number is not found on the list of that day's authorised vehicles, fines similar in scale to parking fines will be issued. There is scope to avoid a fine if the charge is paid by 10.00 p.m. on the same day. Exemptions and discounts are available to a limited set of essential users and low impact vehicles including residents and disabled persons, and alternative fuel vehicles and motorcycles, respectively. Heavy goods vehicles pay the same rate as others to minimise the impacts on business and the economy.

UK Developments

Transport legislation for English local authorities, which refers to the policy as road user charging, adopts a similar process as set up in London. Authorities are able to submit Orders for introducing schemes, which then, in most cases, will need to be confirmed by the Secretary of State for Transport. There are similar constraints on using the policy to ensure that the measure is integrated with local transport plans and that there is a 10-year commitment to investing the revenue in local transport. Otherwise, local authorities have a relatively freehand in designing schemes to best suit their needs.

Interested local authorities have formed a Charging Development Partnership to help each other pioneer schemes. There are several ongoing studies, although none, at this stage, are committed to introduction because of, to a large degree, continuing public and political acceptability concerns. Amongst the most advanced could be considered Bristol City Council, which has road user charging as a key part of its local transport plan. Overall, though, implementation still seems a long way off, and concerns have been expressed that road pricing is in danger of grinding to a halt.

A Parliamentary Select Committee (2002) commented that, outside London, the implementation of the policy seemed to be stalled. It questioned the government's commitment to road pricing and whether it still considered it a key element in its transport strategy. It concluded that: 'The Department has turned its back on local charging schemes rather than provide the leadership required to implement one of the most crucial elements of the White Paper' (House of Commons, 2002, Part III).

Reasons for Differing Rates of Progress

It has been possible to take London congestion charging forward at a faster rate than road user charging elsewhere in the UK because of a combination of political and socioeconomic issues.

/or is nominally independent of the main political parties, which
om from following national party political guidance, which would
nore tentative approach, as witnessed in local authorities outside
Aost of these do not yet have the mayoral system and are dominated
by the main political parties.

Considering the introduction of road pricing was also part of the mayor's
ostensibly radical agenda prior to election. However, since he has been in
office, he has been thwarted in fulfilling several election pledges and his
radical reforming image can be viewed as hanging on the implementation
(and success) of congestion charging. Transport concerns are relatively high
amongst that the mayor has taken radical action as well as providing a much-
needed funding source for further improvements.

London also has certain characteristics that make it easier and less
controversial to introduce pricing than elsewhere in the UK. On balance,
far fewer Londoners rely on car travel in the central business district. Yet
the revenue from congestion charging will be spent on public transport
improvements used by a greater proportion of local people than elsewhere in
the UK. Therefore, on the whole, there is a greater number of people potentially
getting something for nothing. Also, central London is economically robust
and it should not, on the whole suffer, from the congestion charge. Elsewhere
in the UK, cities and towns have more fragile economies that compete with
neighbouring cities and towns. There are greater concerns that economies will
suffer if road pricing is introduced.

In addition, once London was committed to going ahead with the scheme,
it created an opportunity for local authorities to wait and see what happens in
terms of the impacts and electoral consequences.

A Simple Analysis of the Acceptability of London Congestion Charging

Evidence and Approach

During the design and development of London congestion charging there
have been many debates over its acceptability, which has produced a wealth
of evidence. There was extensive public consultation during 2001, prior to
the confirmation of the Scheme Order, which was followed by a failed legal
challenge in the High Court. There has also been extensive coverage of the
debates for and against the scheme in the media.

The evidence covers arguments from individuals and interest groups (as analysed in the research project described in this book) and also those from the perspectives of institutions, such as the GLA and TfL. It was not possible to analyse institutional arguments during the course of the research project as, in part, these had not been developed at the time. Therefore, London congestion charging presents a significant amount of new data that can be used to refine and test the theoretical ideas of acceptability, developed from the sociological method for studying acceptability descried in this book. This simple analysis further strengthens the case for this type of research by showing:

1 how the sociological method of discourse analysis can used to interpret this new evidence;
2 how the theoretical ideas can be refined to accommodate the new evidence;
3 the types of policy recommendations that could be derived for both London and elsewhere.

Individual and Interest Group Arguments

Specific evidence for the spread arguments from members of the public and interest groups have been taken from an internet forum (BBC *Talking Point*, 2002), media articles on road pricing (BBC, 2002) and the TfL report on consultation (2002). There appears to be good correlation between the types of arguments collected in the research project and those used during the course of the London planning process. There is one new argument, on the adequacy of consultation processes that does not fit easily with the grounded theory of acceptability, which points to an area in which the theory could be improved. This consultative argument closely links individual/group arguments to institutional positions – as it is through consultation that individuals/groups can influence policy and vice versa.

Influencing demand These are a sets of arguments based on the advantages and disadvantages of using charging to influence the amount of traffic so as to directly meet transport policy objectives such as congestion reduction, environmental improvement and economic growth.

Excerpt 13.1 (BBC *Talking Point*)

I don't care how much they charge as long as it gets rid of the ever-present queue of cars along Newgate to St Paul's. I nearly choke to death on all the car fumes along there every day, and wince every time I see a poor cyclist trying to squeeze through his/her cycle lane that a kindly driver has veered into because they can see a two inch gap 100 yards up the road!

Excerpt 13.2 (BBC *Talking Point*)

I live in a street in Tower Hamlets less than 200 metres from the boundary of the zone. The increased traffic passing my kids' primary school so as to avoid the charging zone is going to be really dangerous for my kids and the others at our school. The Highway is already one of London's most dangerous roads and traffic levels towards Tower Bridge are likely to soar.

In Excerpt 13.1 an individual clearly associates the benefits of road pricing with congestion reduction and environmental improvements, and to some extent with road safety for cyclists. Typically, individuals and groups will consider, as well, the fairness implications, as shown in Excerpt 3.2, in which an individual comments on the increased traffic near to the border. Both these types of argument are covered by the theoretical framework for acceptance. (See Chapter 7 for a full explanation.)

Excerpt 13.3 (BBC article)

Chief executive of London First, told BBC London: 'We think that the Mayor should get on with it. London is being strangled by its own success.'

Excerpt 13.4 (BBC *Talking Point*)

Theoretically, city tolls are probably the best way to clear the cities of automobiles. Unfortunately, there are still far too many firms, particularly in London, that will pay the charges for their employees, in the same way as they currently provide free parking in their office car parks.

Excerpt 13.5 (BBC *Talking Point*)

No one appears to have mentioned one particular sector of society who will be affected. The small business community ... Obviously we cannot run the business using public transport so we will have no choice but to give in and pay up. Ultimately the charges would have to be passed on and we would not be alone in doing this. The price of all goods and services will eventually rise.

In terms of affecting economic interests a number of issues are raised. Excerpt

13.3 indicates support for the scheme in order that the economy of London can continue to develop. However, Excerpt 13.4 puts a view that the success of London firms will itself undermine the effectiveness of the scheme to influence demand, as companies might absorb to charges. Meanwhile, Excerpt 13.5 raises concerns of the small businesses, with an inference that it is unfair. Again, the concepts used are covered by the theoretical ideas for acceptability and are similar in type to those above. They merely replace needs for congestion reduction and environmental protection by economic interests.

Excerpt 13.7 (BBC article)

> London Campaigns Co-ordinator for Friends of the Earth said: 'Traffic congestion in London is appalling. It's bad for business, bad for the environment and bad for health … However, congestion charging alone is not enough. The public must have a cost-effective and viable alternative to the car. London's public transport system must improve, and must improve quickly.

Excerpt 13.7 summarises the direct effects of congestion charging and brings in the idea of complementary measures, which can be used to alleviate adverse impacts and provide alternatives. In the development of the theory of acceptability, these types of arguments have been well-noted and illustrate the balance between using pricing to directly affecting demand to solve transport problems and using pricing to raise revenue to fund other measures that then solve transport problems.

Raising revenue These arguments cover issues of using road pricing to raise revenue, in which it is seen as indirectly meeting policy objectives by providing finance for other measures. In London, the arguments, more so that elsewhere in the UK, seem weighted to a presumption that any money will be invested in public transport improvements. In part, this is because it has been explicitly stated that the scheme was designed to raise finance for public transport and because public transport is widely seen as the only viable solution for such a densely populated city.

Excerpt 13.8 (BBC *Talking Point*)

> Since motorists already contribute to the road network via car tax, fuel duty and VAT, surely then they have paid enough and this is just an insult? No one in their right mind would use public transport as it is.

Excerpt 13.9 (BBC *Talking Point*)

> Rush hour travel on trains or tubes is already a claustrophobic nightmare. If this is really meant to get cars off the road, where are the ex-drivers meant to go? ... I would be very worried about dangerous overcrowding.

Excerpt 13.8 raises a typical concern, addressed by the theoretical framework, that motorists have already paid sufficient in other road-related taxes. Meanwhile, Excerpt 13.9 points to the issue of public transport not being a good enough alternative to cater for displaced trips, although not explicitly stated, even though investment would improve the system. TfL (2002) recognise that concern over the adequacy of public transport is a primary concern of individuals and interest groups. It describes other arguments on how far public transport should be improved ahead of the introduction of the charge. Although partially addressed by the theory of acceptability, it is recognised that there is scope to develop this issue on the acceptable extent of improvements prior to road pricing.

Contributions, discounts and exemptions These arguments reflect the contribution of a vehicle type to a problem and the essentiality of trip purpose. During the consultation phases of London congestion charging many challenges regarding fair contribution were made. Some argued for straight exemptions for those with no alternatives, such as disabled drivers (from outside Greater London), commercial delivery companies, NHS staff on emergencies and residents. Others argued for discounts or exemptions in order to maintain staffing levels, such as the NHS and voluntary sector workers. It was also argued that discounts/exemptions be extended to all alternative fuel vehicles that are less environmentally damaging and to smaller passenger service vehicles that still help to solve traffic problems. The arguments are all described by the theory of acceptability under its contribution strategy.

Consultation Individual members of the public and interest groups questioned the adequacy of the consultation process. They argued that the time was not long enough to consider the Scheme Order, and that the information was neither detailed enough nor accurate enough to give an informed response (TfL, 2002).

The consultation process, itself is not a topic that the grounded theory of acceptability has so far been developed to interpret. It does not negate the theory, but presents a chance to adapt it, and make it even more applicable to road pricing. It is likely that it provides a link between individual/group arguments and institutional practices, which a robust theory would be able to interpret.

Institutional Arguments

Evidence for institutional arguments is taken from objections raised by the City of Westminster Council (2002) in its High Court challenge to London Congestion Charging and from arguments in support made by the mayor (2002) and TfL (2002). Some of the arguments are adequately addressed by the ideas in the theory of acceptability. However, there are several new arguments, which cover decision-making and legal requirements and expand on the role of consultation. They require that the theoretical ideas be refined for fuller understanding.

Excerpt 13.10 (City of Westminster)

1   First, the necessary information is lacking. Westminster Council believes the mayor failed to obtain all the information he needed to satisfy himself that the scheme should be approved, or could not be improved.

2   Second, that the Scheme Order was made in breach of the requirement to obtain and consider an Environmental Impact Assessment. The City Council believes that the significant impact of the scheme on those who live, work and travel within and immediately outside the area covered by the scheme means that an environmental impact assessment was legally required.

3   Third, that the mayor's decision not to hold a public inquiry was unlawful. The City Council believes that the potential adverse impact on local people, particularly the residents immediately outside the proposed zone boundary, and businesses within the zone boundary is so great that they have a right to a fair and public hearing in the form of an inquiry.

4   Fourth, that the mayor failed to act lawfully in accordance with his obligations under the Human Rights Act 1998. The City Council believes that the mayor had a positive obligation to ensure that the rights of those affected by the scheme were safeguarded and that he has not discharged this obligation.

Excerpt 13.10 illustrates the four grounds on which the London Borough of the City of Westminster, in partnership with two residents from Kennington, challenged the legality of congestion charging. The first two points focus on the lack of information on the impacts of the scheme, and the second two points raise consultation issues.

TfL has done extensive traffic prediction and modelling work, drawing on experience going back to the first London road pricing studies. A large part of the case in support of congestion charging drew on this technical experience. In terms of the grounded theory of acceptability this uses arguments about the direct impact of road pricing, with one side claiming greater credibility than the other. However, there are other institutional arguments that are used as well, which essential to support traffic and environmental predictions.

Excerpt 13.11 (mayor's supporting statement)

> In a sense, with a scheme like this, there will never be a time when the information available is wholly complete, because the immediate effects may differ from the longer-term effects, since traffic patterns will adjust and re-adjust, and nothing is wholly predictable.

Excerpt 13.12 (TfL)

> There is not a requirement under national law for an environmental impact assessment to be undertaken for the proposed scheme. Nevertheless TfL consider that the scheme should be implemented in accordance with good environmental practice and that sufficient understanding of the environmental consequences be gained ...

In Excerpt 13.11, in a statement by the mayor, he clearly explains how decisions need to be made without perfect knowledge, which is ultimately unattainable. The theory of acceptability does not fully address the institutional context of making decisions without adequate knowledge of the impacts. There is scope to further understand how such decisions can be reached within an environment of partial knowledge. Meanwhile, in Excerpt 13.12, TfL explains that further predictions, such as environmental impact assessment are not legally required. It then says that recognised standards should be met and – although not shown – it goes on to argue that overall impacts will be beneficial and adverse in only isolated cases. By drawing on the legal requirements, it brings in a concept that is not explicitly dealt with by the theory of acceptability, which would be important to include. The issue that the overall impacts will be beneficial is, on the other hand, able to be interpreted by the theory as it stands. It is based on the common strategy of balancing the greater benefits against adverse impacts – utilitarianism against fairness.

It is this problematic fairness topic of balancing interests that led the City of Westminster to ask for a public inquiry and a judicial review under human rights legislation. To counter the arguments, TfL and the mayor drew heavily on the predictions and the net gains of the traffic, economic and environmental modelling work. However, other arguments are used that are theoretically more illuminating.

Excerpt 13.13

> To hold a public inquiry would reassure objectors, but would in some ways be merely the easy option of deferring a decision where positive and prompt action is called for (and expected by those very many Londoners who have repeatedly expressed support for congestion charging). I am advised by TfL that congestion which the proposed scheme would tackle is currently costing the equivalent of two million pounds per week. These are strong arguments against further delay.

Excerpt 13.14

> TfL considers that the Mayor is acting as a 'public authority' when considering the Mayor's decision on whether or not to confirm the Scheme Order and whether or not to hold a public inquiry ... Conceivably, therefore, the Mayor's decision might need to comply with Article 6 of the Convention – the right to a fair trial. However, this right only arises where the decision of a public authority determines 'civil rights and obligations'. The grounds on which a public inquiry has been suggested – the relevance of the proposed scheme, its functioning, its potential impacts and the nature and scope of the exemptions from charges – involve matters of transport planning and political judgement which can be properly decided by the Mayor.

Excerpt 13.13 argues that decisions cannot wait as traffic related problems mount. This reflects a temporal pressure on institutions to take action. It was explained in the previous section that the political reputation of the mayor and his chances for re-election, in part, depend on being able to implement congestion charging and it being a success. Not only does it have to be implemented during his term in office, but there has to be time for voters to get used to it and for the scheme to start showing benefits. A public inquiry would considerably cut down the chances of implementation during his first term. Of course, the City of Westminster's actions can be viewed as taking advantage of these temporal pressures and the call for a public inquiry as a delaying tactic. If Westminster had been successful, it would have undermined the chances of the mayor being re-elected and, possibly, the incoming mayor would be against congestion charging.

Excerpt 13.14 gives the opinion of TfL with respect to the legal claim that human rights are not protected. The full range of legal arguments used in the case has not been analysed, which would undoubtedly give a more complex picture. In essence, though, TfL says that congestion charging is not a matter of 'civil rights and obligations' but of 'transport planning and political judgment', which can be decided by the mayor. This sets up a dichotomy between civil rights that everyone can comment on and transport planning of which TfL is, in relation to road pricing in London, expert. By shifting the ground to transport planning they can be seen as turning the argument back to the claims of their predictions. The tactic is not addressed by the theory of acceptability as it stands.

Theoretical Implications

Clearly, the above review of the spread of arguments used for London congestion charging points to areas in which the grounded theory of acceptability can be refined. If this is done then any recommendations derived from the theory, see next subsection, will be more plausible. It can be expected that the theory would need to be refined because it was developed from case studies in Cambridge and Edinburgh, which are geographically very different to London. Also there has been more discussion in a range of fora that has also included institutions as well as members of the public and interest groups.

Overall, the grounded theory of acceptability covers many of the arguments used in London: more so for individuals/groups than for institutions. It does omit appropriate consideration of:

1   the extent of improvements necessary before a scheme is introduced;
2   consultative practices;
3   decision-making constraints (time pressures and imperfect predictions)
4   legal practices.

It is interesting to note that these are all practical implementation issues that could not be adequately addressed during the book's research project, which had to be based on hypothetical scenarios. By expanding the theory of acceptability to include these issues, the controversial theoretical recommendations will be better balanced by practical concerns of, in part, government.

Given a refinement in the theory, there are two ways in which its recommendations can develop:

1   the recommendations as they stand (see Chapter 12) remain valid but new recommendations are added to show acceptable methods of putting them into practice;
2   the expanded theory changes the set of recommendation summarised in Chapter 12.

For the purpose of illustrating the types of recommendations that could be made, it is assumed that (1) will hold, as (2) is an impossible scenario for which to make predictions. Also, (1) is an attractive hypothesis in that it reflects that individual/group opinions win over institutional constraints. And the institutions can be seen as delivering schemes considered acceptable to the electorate and not themselves. On the other hand, (2) presumes that institutional needs might dominate over those of individuals and groups.

Recommendations based on Theoretical Interpretation

Based on the assumption that the theoretical recommendations so far made in this book hold but need to be supplemented by practical implementation guidance based on London congestion charging, two distinct sets of recommendations can be made: one for London and the other for elsewhere in the UK. In London, recommendations focus on how the scheme can be developed, opposed to the implementation issues, which largely appear to have been resolved (although not necessarily acceptably). Outside London, the theoretical recommendations for design summarised in Chapter 12 are considered to hold, but need to be complemented by the practical lessons of implementation.

London The theoretical ideas of the grounded theory of acceptability can help to decide which policy objectives to continue to use congestion charging to meet, the future contribution of different groups of road user, the potential for extending the charged area and time, and differentiating the amount of the charge paid by area and time.

1   The theoretical ideas, in their present state of development, would suggest that congestion charging adopts the sole policy objective of raising revenue. The revenue should be used for the provision of services that drivers need and for the alleviation of the environmental impact that drivers cause. TfL should adopt practices to show how revenue is being spent in accordance with this theoretical recommendation for acceptability. This goes further

than the statutory requirement to spend revenue on local transport for 10 years, which does not fully hold the charging authority accountable to spending the revenue on traffic-related projects directly linked to the needs and impacts of the drivers that pay the charge.

2   The approach to contributions, exemptions and discounts, which reflect essentiality of trip purpose and contribution to problems, concur with the broad theoretical ideas as they stand at present. As the scheme evolves and more knowledge is gained, it is recommended that options of varying the amount of charge by group is explored, which might improve fairness. The fair amount should be related to the contribution to the need for revenue expenditure.

3   It is recommended that the charged area be extended, where it can be established that revenue is being spent on measures needed by drivers outside the central area or to protect others from the impact of drivers outside the central zone. As revenue appears set to be spent throughout London under the current scheme design, there will be a theoretically acceptable case for extending the charged area. Note that it might be that investment is needed for central London but that outside areas get a benefit (for example, increasing bus capacity is required due to problems in central London but not outer London, added bus capacity will improve transport in outer areas). In this case, it could be argued that the charged area need not be extended.

4   There is a weaker argument, in terms of the theoretical ideas, for extending the time of operation. Most of the measures appear to be needed for problems during the busy daytime periods during the week, when the charging is in operation. The existing infrastructure, largely, caters for the needs of drivers and the problems drivers cause at other times.

5   Charges could be differentiated by road user groups, area and time ((2), (3) and (4) above). It should be remembered that it is only worth having charging differentials if the added cost of operating a more sophisticated (and potentially fairer) charging system results in groups of users paying less. It might be that the technology of a differential charging system makes it financially impractical.

6   The final theoretical recommendation is the most controversial, and insists that the most acceptable system is one in which drivers pay the same amount as public transport users, if road pricing revenue is used to support public transport. (The full argument is presented in the book.) As this is the case in London, there is a strong theoretical argument for linking congestion charging to the travel card system for public transport within

the central zone. Such a suggestion is, theoretically the most transparent way of ensuring that drivers are not forced off the road because of low income and that revenue is spent on improving the whole transport system, whether a person prefers to travel by car or public transport. There would be no presumption being made by the charging authority on how people should travel and choice remains in the hands of the individual.

Elsewhere in the UK Similar recommendations on acceptable policy objectives and design options for potential schemes elsewhere in the UK (as outlined above and in Chapter 12) would hold if the theory of acceptability, in its current state of development, is applied. However, it has been realised that the theory would need to be expanded to adequately and acceptably navigate around institutional constraints, if any of the recommendations were to move from the theoretical to the practical realm. Any suggestions on implementing road pricing would, of course, be applicable in situations where road pricing schemes are not based on the theoretical design recommendations. Although in need of refinement and further testing, the simple analysis of London Congestion Charging indicates that acceptable implementation would involve an adequate programme of improvements prior to implementation, predictive plausibility, practical decision-making, good consultative practice and legal mastery.

1   Investing in improvements prior to implementation has been recognised as important for increasing acceptability in the Norwegian tolling schemes, described in Chapter 2. In London, prior to the scheme, significant investment has been made in bus services and traffic management to deal with the re-routing of journeys to the periphery of the charged area. Most local authorities that are considering road pricing will already be following this advice. But it is an important element in being able to demonstrate that unnecessarily adverse impacts have been considered in consultation, public inquiries and even legal challenges.

2   To a large degree, TfL and the mayor have been able to implement road pricing because they won the argument on the plausibility of their predictions. This gave them a strong position in consultation and in the High Court challenge, in which they, in part, turned the argument onto the quality of their models, which they knew to be superior to the quality of opposition predictions. For the first local authorities implementing schemes, it is going to be essential that they win predictive arguments as TfL did for the mayor. As more local authorities implement schemes,

it is likely that the predictive modelling challenges will be easier and less important. On the approach to winning the predictive arguments by TfL, there are questions over the acceptability of its practices involving a culture of secrecy. It can be seen as controlling the flow of information to members of the public for them to make independent interpretations. It could reasonably be hoped that local authorities will be more open in sharing information, which might well have very positive outcomes on satisfaction with consultation.

3   It should be realised that predictive modelling only goes so far and that decisions need to be based on incomplete evidence. In legal terms, it appears that local authorities will be given leeway, and do not have to gain consensus opinions on the impacts. This raises a question of what is an acceptable accuracy on which to base decisions. Ultimately this will depend on the amount of resources available, such as time, money and staff skills. For example, it has been seen in the London evidence that predictive accuracy has been traded off against time constraints. It appears acceptable institutional practice to make such trade offs, which will be useful for local authorities when making cases for implementation.

4   Until road user charging becomes mundane, successful consultation is going to be key. Public inquiries, as an official form of consultation should not be ruled out *a priori,* but, as in London, balanced against time pressures. The important aspect of consultation appears to be to show that people have been listened to and that the scheme evolved in response. There are conflicting views on how far TfL and the mayor have achieved this. It is recommended that the consultation process is transparent and that it is clearly explained how views are incorporated into decisions.

5   By following the above recommendations and ensuring statutory duties are followed, any legal arguments should be won based on current understanding of acceptability of governmental decisions. However, there are principles of payment and scheme design that arguably do reflect rights and obligations that have not been argued in London. In future, legal challenges could be made based on such issues. The challenge in London focused on environmental effects rather than the principle, which is still, in the author's opinion, open to interpretation.

Conclusion

This postscript has outlined recent urban road pricing policy developments in the UK. It described the anticipated scheme in London and the slow progress being made elsewhere in the UK, which is in part waiting for the outcomes of the London experience.

A simple analysis of the acceptability of the London congestion charging process is undertaken which demonstrates the applicability of the sociological method for studying acceptability developed in this book. The analysis raises ideas for refining the theory of acceptability to increase the plausibility of its recommendations.

By way of illustration, likely suggestions that a fully developed theory of acceptability would be able to make are given. For London, these focus on the evolution of the design of the scheme. Elsewhere in the UK, the suggestions focus on the implementation issues.

It is stressed that the research work needs to enter a new stage of development and testing. If this is undertaken, the recommendations will be more plausible. It will also provide further evidence on the practicality of using such a sociological approach. At least in the field of transport, it is considered essential to carry out this work because the method offers a new way of approaching and overcoming the problems the profession faces in implementing much-needed and controversial solutions.

Bibliography

Banister, D. (1994), *Transport Planning*, E&FN Spon, London.

BBC LONDON (2002), The Argument for Congestion Charging, www.bbc.co.uk/london/features/environment.shtml.

BBC News *Talking Point* (2002), 'Are Congestion Charges the Answer to Gridlock?', <http://news.bbc/co.uk/hi/talking_point/1431849.stm>.

Begg, D. (1998), 'Gaining Public Acceptance for Urban Congestion Charging, Chartered Institute of Transport Conference: Urban Congestion Charging – Has its Time Come?', The Waterfront Conference Company, UK.

Bell, M.G.H. (1997), 'Comment on Talvitie's Paper' [see below], *Transportation*, **24**(1), pp. 33–4.

Benson, D. and Hughes, J. (1983), *The Perspective of Ethnomethodology*, Longman, Harlow.

Blaikie, N. (1993), *Approaches to Social Enquiry*, Polity Press, Cambridge.

Blumer, H. (1969), *Symbolic Interactionism: Perspectives and Method*, Prentice Hall, New Jersey.

Borins, S.F. (1988), 'Electronic Road Pricing: An Idea whose Time may never Come', *Transportation Research-A*, **22**(1) pp. 37–44.

Button, G. (1991), *Ethnomethodology and the Human Sciences*, Cambridge University Press, Cambridge.

Button, K.J. (1993), *Transport Economics*, 2nd edn, Edward Elgar, Aldershot.

Catling, I. and Harbord, B.J. (1985), 'Electronic Road Pricing in Hong Kong 2. The Technology', *Traffic Engineering and Control*, **26**(12), pp. 608–15.

City of Westminster (2002), 'Congestion Charging Update for Area Forums', 15 May, www.westminster.gov.uk.

Clark, D.J., Blythe, P.T., Thorpe, N. and Rourke, A. (1994), 'Automatic Debiting and Electronic Payment for Transport – the Adept Project. 3. Congestion Metering: The Cambridge Trial', *Traffic Engineering and Control*, **35**, pp. 256–63.

Coase, R.H. (1960), 'The Problem of Social Cost', *The Journal of Law and Economics*, **3**, pp. 1–44.

Connell, J. and Lowe, A, (1996), 'Grounded Theory: Using its Methodology to Uncover Marketing Management Processes', in *Research Methodologies for the New Marketing*, Proceedings of ESOMAR/ESOMAC Conference, Latimer, UK.

Craib, I. (1992), *Modern Social Theory: From Parsons to Habermas*, 2nd edn, Harvester Wheatsheaf, London.

Dawson, J. (1998), 'The Government's Road Pricing Adventure, Chartered Institute of Transport Conference: Urban Congestion Charging – Has its Time Come?', The Waterfront Conference Company, UK.

Dawson, J.A.L. and Brown, F.N. (1985), 'Electronic Road Pricing in Hong Kong 1. A Fair Way to Go?', *Traffic Engineering and Control*, **26**(11), pp. 522–9.

Decorla-Souza, P. and Kane, A.R. (1992), 'Peak Period Tolls: Precepts and Prospects', *Transportation*, **19**(4), pp. 293–311.

Department for Environment, Transport and the Regions (1998), *A New Deal for Transport: Better for Everyone (The Government's White Paper on the Future of Transport)*, Cm 3959, HMSO, London.

Department of Transport (1993), *Paying for Better Motorways: Issues for discussion*, HMSO, London.

Department of Transport (1995), *The Government's Response to the Third Report 1994–95 of the Transport Select Committee: Urban Road Pricing*, Cm 3019, HMSO, London.

Dunn, W.N. and Swierczek, F.W. (1977), 'Planned Organizational Change: Toward Grounded Theory', *The Journal of Applied Behavioral Science*, **13**(2), pp. 135–57.

Forester, J. (1989), *Planning in the Face of Power*, University of California Press, London.

Fox, S. (1990), 'Becoming an Ethnomethodology User: Learning a perspective in the field', in Burgess, R.G. (ed.), *Studies in Qualitative Methodology, Volume 2*, JAI Press, London.

Garfinkel, H. (1984), *Studies in Ethnomethodology*, Polity Press, Cambridge.

Gartrell, C. and Gartrell, J. (1996), 'Positivism in Sociological Practice 1967–1990', *The Canadian Review of Sociology and Anthropology*, **33**(2), pp. 143–58.

Giddens, A. (1984), *The Constitution of Society*, Polity Press, Oxford.

Giuliano, G. (1992), 'An Assessment of the Political Acceptability of Congestion Pricing', *Transportation*, **19**(4), pp. 335–58.

Glaser, B. (1978), *Theoretical Sensitivity: Advances in the methodology of grounded theory*, Sociology Press, California.

Glaser, B. (1992), *Basics of Grounded Theory Analysis*, Sociology Press, California.

Glaser, B. and Strauss, A. (1967), *The Discovery of Grounded Theory*, Aldine, Chicago.

Gomez-Ibanez, J.A. and Small, K.A. (1994), *Road Pricing for Congestion Management: A survey of international practice*, National Academy Press, Washington DC.

Goodwin, P.B. (1989), 'The Rule of Three', *Traffic Engineering and Control*, **30**(10).

Greater London Authority (2002), Statement by the Mayor concerning his Decision to Confirm the Central London Congestion Charging Scheme Order with Modifications, <www.london.gov.uk/approot/mayor/congest/index.jsp>.

Grieco, M. and Jones, P. (1994), 'A Change in the Policy Climate? Current European Perspectives on Road Pricing', *Urban Studies*, **31**(9), pp. 1517–32.

Habermas, J. (1984), *The Theory of Communicative Action Volume 1: Reason and the rationalisation of society*, Polity Press, Oxford.

Hammersley, M. (1993), *Social Research: Philosophy, politics and practice*, Sage, London.

Hammersley, M. and Atkinson, P. (1995), *Ethnography: Principles in practice*, 2nd edn, Routledge, London.

The Harris Research Centre (1991), *A Road User Charge – Londoners' Views*, National Economic Development Office, the London Planning Advisory Committee.

Holland, E.P. and Watson, P.L. (1978), 'Traffic Restraint in Singapore', *Traffic Engineering and Control*, **19**(1), pp. 14–22.

Holland, T.P. and Kilpatrick, A.C. (1991), 'Ethical Issues in Social Work: Towards a grounded theory of professional ethics', *Social Work*, **36**(2), pp. 138–44.

House of Commons (2002), *Transport, Local Government and the Regions – Eighth Report*, House of Commons, Publications on the Internet, <www.publications.parliament.uk/pa/cm200102/cmselect/cmtlgr/558/55802.htm>.

Ison, S. (1996), 'Pricing Road Space: Back to the future? The Cambridge Experience', *Transport Reviews*, **16**(2), pp. 109–26.

Jones, P. (1991), 'Gaining Public Support for Road Pricing through a Package Approach', *Traffic Engineering and Control*, **32**(4), pp. 104–96.

Jones, P. (1995), 'Urban Congestion Charging', in House of Commons (Transport Committee), *Urban Road Pricing Volume II: Minutes of Evidence*, HMSO, London.

Jones, P. (1998), 'Urban Congestion Charging: The Key Issues and Overview of Past Congestion Charging Schemes, Chartered Institute of Transport Conference: Urban Congestion Charging – Has its Time Come?', The Waterfront Conference Company, UK.

Jones, P. and Hervik, A. (1992), 'Restraining Car Traffic in European Cities: An emerging role for road pricing', *Transportation Research-A*, **31**(9), pp. 133–45.

Knight, F.H. (1924), 'Some Fallacies in the Interpretation of Social Cost', *Quarterly Journal of Economics*, **38**, pp. 582–606.

Kroes, E.P. and Sheldon, R.J. (1988), 'Stated Preference Methods: An introduction', *Journal of Transport Economics and Policy*, **12**(1), pp. 11–26.

Langmyhr, T. (1995), 'Planning for Road Pricing: A Multi-Rationality Approach', *Scandinavian Housing and Planning Research*, **12**, pp. 73–91.

Langmyhr, T. (1997), 'Managing Equity: The case of road pricing', *Transport Policy*, **4**(1), pp. 25–39.

Larsen, O.I. (1988), 'The Toll Ring in Bergen, Norway – the first year of operation', *Traffic Engineering and Control*, **29**(4), pp. 216–22.

Lester, M. and Hadden, S.C. (1980), 'Ethnomethodology and Grounded Theory Methodology: An integration of perspective and method', *Urban Life*, **9**(1), pp. 3–33.

Lewis, N.C. (1993), *Road Pricing: Theory and Practice*, Thomas Telford, London.

Lindblom, C. (1959), 'The Science of "Muddling Through"', *Public Administration Review*, **19**(2), pp. 79–88.

Locke, K. (1996), 'Rewriting the Discovery of Grounded Theory After 25 Years?', *Journal of Management Inquiry*, **5**(3), pp. 239–45.

Marshall, A. (1890), *Principles of Economics*, Macmillan, London.

Mason, J. (1996), *Qualitative Researching*, Sage, London.

May, A.D. (1975), 'Supplementary Licencing: An Evaluation', *Traffic Engineering and Control*, **16**, pp. 162–7.

May, A.D. (1992), 'Road Pricing: An international perspective', *Transportation*, 19, pp. 313–33.

May, A.D. (1997), in O'Flaherty (ed.), *Transport Planning and Traffic Engineering*, Arnold, London.

May, A.D. and Gardner, K.E. (1991), 'Transport Policy in London for 2001: The case for an integrated approach', *Transportation*, **16**, pp. 257–77.

McGlynn, R.F. and Roberts, J. (1977), 'The Impact of Traffic Policies in Singapore 3. Attitudes to Traffic Policies in Singapore', *Traffic Engineering and Control*, **18**(7), pp. 357–61.

Meland, S. (1995), 'Generalised and Advanced Urban Debiting Innovations: The Gaudi Project 3. The Trondheim Toll Ring', *Traffic Engineering and Control*, **36**(3), pp. 150–55.

Ministry of Transport (1964), *Road Pricing: The Economic and Technical Possibilities (The Smeed Report)*, HMSO, London.

The MVA Consultancy (1991), 'Joint Environmental Transportation and Environmental Study: Final Report', presented to Lothian Regional Council, The Scottish Office, Environment Department and Edinburgh District Council.

The MVA Consultancy(1995), *The London Congestion Charging Research Programme. Final Report. Volume 1: Text*, HMSO, London.

Nellthorp, J. (1994), 'A Model of Demand Suppression and Demand Diversion – under UK Motorway Tolling', MA dissertation, Institute for Transport Studies, University of Leeds (unpublished).

Newbery, D.M. (1995), *Reforming Road Taxation*, The Automobile Association, UK.

Ove Arup and Partners (1997), *Avon Traffic Restraint Study – Stage 2 Final Report*, Bristol City Council.

Parkin, M., Powell, P. and Matthews, K. (1997), *Economics*, 3rd edn, Addison Wesley Longman, Harlow.

Pearce, D.W. (1993), *Economic Values and the Natural World*, Centre for Social Economic Research on the Global Environment and Earthscan, London.

Pearce, D.W. and Nash, C.A. (1981), *The Social Appraisal of Projects: A text in cost-benefit analysis*, Macmillan, Basingstoke.

Pigou, A.C. (1920), *Wealth and Welfare*, Macmillan, London.

Polak, J. and Meland, S. (1994), 'An Assessment of the Effects of the Trondheim Toll Ring on Travel Behaviour and the Environment', First World Congress on Applications of Transport Telematics and Intelligent Vehicle Highway Systems, Palais des Congrès, Paris.

Poole, R.W. Jr (1992), 'Introducing Congestion Pricing on a New Toll Road', *Transportation*, **19**, pp. 383–96.

Rasmussen, D.M. (1990), *Reading Habermas*, Basil Blackwell, Oxford.

Richards, M. (1998), 'The Challenges of Administering Congestion Charging, Chartered Institute of Transport Conference: Urban Congestion Charging – Has its Time Come?', The Waterfront Conference Company, UK.

Richards, M. and Gilliam, C. (1996), 'The London Congestion Charging Research Programme: 6. The Findings', *Traffic Engineering and Control*, **37**(7/8), pp. 436–41.

Riley, R. (1996), 'Revealing Socially Constructed Knowledge through Quasi-Structured Interviews and Grounded Theory Analysis', *Journal of Travel and Tourism Marketing*, **5**(1), pp. 21–40.

Roberts, J, (1977), 'The Impacts of Traffic Policies in Singapore: 1. Pedestrian Activity and Accidents, Noise and Air Pollution', *Traffic Engineering and Control*, **18**, pp. 152–7.

Sacks, H., in Jefferson, G (ed.) (1992), *Lectures on Conversation Volumes 1 and 2*, Blackwell, Oxford.

Sager, T, (1994), *Communicative Planning Theory*, Avebury, Aldershot.

Scambler, G. (1996), 'The Project of Modernity and the Parameters for a Critical Sociology: An argument with illustrations from medical sociology', *Sociology*, **30**(3), pp. 567–81.

Schutz, A. (1972), *Phenomenological Sociology: Issues and Applications*, John Wiley, New York.

Seale, K. (1993), 'Attitudes of Politicians in London to Road Pricing', Seminar F, 21st Summer Annual Meeting, PTRC.

Sharrock, W. and Anderson, B. (1986), *The Ethnomethodologists*, Ellis Horwood, Chichester.

Sheldon, R., Scott, M. and Jones, P. (1993), 'London Congestion Charging: Exploratory Social Research among London Residents', Seminar F, 21st Summer Annual Meeting, PTRC.

The Shorter Oxford Dictionary (1993), Oxford University Press.

Simon, H.A. (1967), *Models of Man*, John Wiley and Sons, New York.

Small, K.A. (1992), 'Using the Revenues from Congestion Pricing', *Transportation*, 19, pp. 359–81.

Smith, M.J., May, A.D., Wisten, M.B., Milne, D.S., Van Vliet, D. and Ghali, M.O. (1994), 'A Comparison of the Network Effects of Four Road-User Charging Systems', *Traffic Engineering and Control*, **5**, pp. 311–15.

Smith, J. (1998), 'Case-Study: Leicester Environmental Road Tolling Scheme, Chartered Institute of Transport Conference: Urban Congestion Charging – Has its Time Come?', The Waterfront Conference Company, UK.

Stern, P.N. (1994), 'Eroding Grounded Theory', in Morse, J.M (ed.)., *Critical Issues in Qualitative Research Methods*, Sage, London.

Strauss, A. and Corbin, J. (1990), *Basics of Qualitative Research: Grounded Theory Procedures and Techniques*, Sage, London.

Talvitie, A (1997), 'Things Planners Believe In and Things they Deny', *Transportation*, **24**(1), pp. 1–31.

Transport for London (2002), 'The Greater London (Central Zone) Congestion Charging Order: Report to the Mayor', <www.tfl.gov.uk/tfl/cc_report_mayor.shtml>.

Transportation Research Board (1994) *Curbing Gridlock: Peak Period Fees to Relieve Traffic Congestion*, Volume 1, National Academy Press, Washington.

Turner, B. (1981), 'Some Practical Aspects of Qualitative Data Analysis: One Way of Organising the Cognitive Processes Associated with the Generation of Grounded Theory', *Quality and Quantity*, **15**, pp. 225–47.

Tyson, W. (1998), 'What Powers do Local Authorities and PTEs Require, Chartered Institute of Transport Conference: Urban Congestion Charging – Has its Time Come?', The Waterfront Conference Company, UK.

Useem, M. (1990), Book Review of *Planning in the Face of Power* by Forester [see above], *Administrative Science Quarterly*, **35**, pp. 565–8.

Vela, D.G. (1996), 'The Role of Religion/Spirituality in Building Strong Families: Respondent's Perceptions. A Qualitative Grounded Theory', PhD thesis, University of Nebraska.

Vickrey, W. (1955), 'Pricing in Transportation and Public Utilities: Some Implications of Marginal Cost Pricing for Public Utilities', *American Economic Review*, Supplement 1955–56 – Papers and Proceedings, pp. 605–620.

Willman, P. (1982), *Fairness, Collective Bargaining, and Incomes Policy*, Clarendon Press, Oxford.

Wilson, P.W. (1988), 'Welfare Effects of Congestion Pricing in Singapore', *Transportation*, **15**, pp. 191–210.

W.S. Atkins Planning Consultants (1994), Cambridgeshire County Council – Stated Preference Project.

Index